THE FENRIS WOLF

Issue no. 9

Edited by
Vanessa Sinclair & Carl Abrahamsson

TRAPART *books*

The Fenris Wolf, issue no 9
Edited by Vanessa Sinclair & Carl Abrahamsson

Trapart Books, 2022

Paperback ISBN 978-91-986920-6-8
Hardback ISBN 978-91-986920-7-5
E-book ISBN 978-91-986920-8-2

Copyright © 2017/2022 The individual authors, unless otherwise stated
Front cover painting: *Venus Castina* © 2017 Val Denham
Back cover painting: *Miss Maud Fealy as Hekate* © 2017 Ken Henson

Trapart Books
P.O. Box 15
SE-598 21 Vimmerby
Sweden

info@trapart.net
www.trapart.net
www.psychartcult.org
www.patreon.com/vanessa23carl

THE FENRIS WOLF, ISSUE NO 9

CONTENTS

Editors' Introduction:
Looking back at the crossroads

In 1953, psychoanalyst and anthropologist George Devereux published a collection of works from various psychoanalysts entitled *Psychoanalysis and the Occult*, which explored the intersection between the practice of psychoanalysis and occult phenomena, including contributions from Freud himself on 'Premonitions and Chance', 'Psychoanalysis and Telepathy', and 'The Occult Significance of Dreams'. Additionally, Freud's paper 'Notes on the Unconscious' was published in the journal of the Society for Psychical Research in 1912. Since that time, however, the majority of psychoanalysts willing to traverse occult terrain have worked within a Jungian framework, as the topic itself was central to the split between Freud and Jung, with the former insisting the burgeoning field of psychoanalysis be scientific and not spiritualist. However, Freud maintained an interest in occult phenomena longer than many of his followers would like to believe, and it is time to explore this aspect of his work further.

Until now, the intersection of psychoanalysis and the occult has perhaps been most richly explored through the arts. Most well known are the Surrealists, who espoused Freud's theories, and who were fascinated by the unconscious, dreams, synchronicity, automatic writing and chance encounters. These themes and methods are also featured in the work of the Symbolists, Futurists, Dadaists, Fluxists and Actionists, as well as in the work of avant-garde artists of our day.

With all of this in mind, an idea grew inside us to create a cross-disciplinary, intellectual interface that would not only shine the light on similarities and differences, but also heal the unnecessary divide that in so many ways bars development and progress. This idea gradually expanded into the conference *Psychoanalysis, Art & the Occult*, which was held in London on May 5-8, 2016, and organised by us (Vanessa Sinclair of das Unbehagen and Carl Abrahamsson of The Institute of Comparative Magico-anthropology).

The purpose of this conference was to bring together a diverse group of psychoanalysts, occultists and artists to share their views on human subjectivity and culture. Through an investigation of the unique modes and methodologies utilized by each individual practitioner, we believe it's possible to explore human experience via the convergence of domains that rarely speak to one another yet often work in similar and complementary ways. And that's more or less exactly what happened during these three highly inspirational days in London.

The conference space (the Candid Arts Centre) exhibited relevant art, with works by Natan Alexander, Jhonn Balance, Vanessa Sinclair, Jesse Bransford, Genesis Breyer P-Orridge, Val Denham, Ken Henson, Derek Elmore, Steingrímur Eyfjörð, Katelan Foisy, Billy Jacobs, Malcolm McNeill & William S. Burroughs, Roberto Migliussi, Juan Sebastian Montoya, Annette Rawlings, Charlotte Rodgers, K Lenore Siner, Austin Osman Spare, and Fredrik Söderberg. Besides this exhibition and the actual talks (with ensuing discussions), we also arranged for musical performances, film screenings, sales of books from pioneering publishers, and even a final ritual facilitated by Langston Kahn and Khi Armand, with the expressed desire to heal and overcome the interdisciplinary divide. Needless to say, most participants were overwhelmed, enthusiastic, inspired and eventually exhausted!

This issue of *The Fenris Wolf* collects most of the papers and talks from the conference, including additional ones from the different panels' moderators. It presents a colourful bouquet of wisdoms, experiences, perspectives, traditions and attitudes that we believe is the first of its kind (but surely not the last).

It's interesting to see how people from the different disciplines felt challenged to enter, to varying degrees, into new fields of information. Occultists took on psychoanalysis, and analysts, occultism. One of the greatest rewards of the conference was this audacious attitude of looking at new things and new areas in the company of savants; the overall bouquet benefiting from this speculative bravery.

The inspiration and insights from the conference linger on in those who attended, and in those who have since heard and read about it. It is our sincere hope that this issue of *The Fenris Wolf* will carry on in that experimental Promethean spirit we all conjured up together at this literally analytic, creative and magical crossroads in time and space.

We would like to extend our thanks to everyone who participated as speakers, artists, booksellers and attendees; with special thanks to Andrew Lahman, James Birch, Malcolm McNeill, Andrew M McKenzie, Gail Denham, Danny Loker, Oli Novadieks, Jeanne Delvin, Caleigh Fisher, Sheer Zed, Jordan Osserman, and Claus Laufenburg & Xavier Laradji of Timeless Editions.

An editorial note: As the texts in this issue stem from various minds from various cultures, there are obviously some stylistic inconsistencies. We have chosen to keep these, including possible "magical" language quirks and experiments, in the name of heterogeneous and creative integrity. However, for any spelling or typographical errors, pure and simple, we assume full responsibility.

Vanessa Sinclair & Carl Abrahamsson

New York & Stockholm, Vernal Equinox 2017

Invocation:
Homage to the spirits of the land/London

Katelan Foisy

We stand on this land with thick roots/ Roots that vine out over two thousand years and dig deep into the sound of bogs and gravel sprinkled islands/ Here the Romans created a trading post called Londinium/ Here the cry of Boudica's revolt temporarily tore it apart/ This was the first great fire of London and the beginnings of the golden age of trade/ From Nero to Constantine II, the once golden empire began to wane with attacks across the land/ Here lies land that by mid fifth century was abandoned and almost forgotten/ But ports will always be ports of entry.

Saxons moved in to Lundenwic lured by the Thames/ It became seven separate Kingdoms/ Within the inner workings of power, great wealth came to the land and along with that, Viking attacks/ Alfred of Wessex moved them out, but after his death they attacked once more/ The Danish Cnut unified the lands, and after his death it was placed in the hands of the Saxons' Edward the Confessor.

It was here Westminster Abbey was founded/ King Harold was his successor, but William the Conqueror took the throne/ And the Tower of London was built by the newly defeated English/ The Tower would have a long tale to tell, one of two princes imprisoned and disappeared/ And during the Tudor years its cells claimed the bloodiest years/ From the destruction of fire came the birth of London Bridge/ Thirty-three years later, the twenty gothic arches, chapel, and shops gave little room for passersby/ Once again, the fires from Southwalk consumed/ Three thousand died trying to escape it/ The ports of entry of the magic Thames can both consume and deliver.

But with fire comes ice, and the bridge's freezing and expanding collapsed five arches/ Queen Elizabeth was blamed/ The people gave to it small digs, "London Bridge is falling down, my fair lady"/ To mock or oppose the monarchy was unwise, as William Wallace soon learned/ As a Scottish freedom fighter with his tar soaked head displayed on the spikes above the stone gatehouse/ Jack Cade, Thomas More, Guy Fawkes and Oliver Cromwell shared the same fate.

The Guilds became norm by the twelfth century, and with that the Liveries/ The roots then and the roots now/ The Liveries look after the city's heritage and with that the only secular stone structure still standing in the city/ It survived both the Great Fire of London and the Blitz and held the treason trials of Lady Jane

Grey/ Sir Thomas Gresham opened the floor for the Royal Exchange, providing retail and very briefly financial exchange/ Mondays were made for mass hangings during the Reformation/ Many breathed their last breath at Tyburn Tree/ It took up to twenty-four bodies at a time/ The underbelly of London absorbed at the root/ At first it was elm and then manmade/ As the bodies were cut from the trees crowds gathered, as their parts were thought to cure disease/ Entertainment came in various forms.

The roots brought James Burbage to build the first theater/ Others followed, including Lord Chamberlain's company of players building the Globe/ Shakespeare, a shareholder, became its prize ticket/ But the violent underbelly would not let go/ Bear bating and bull bating saw bloody ends to chained animals, a popular Tudor pastime/ The brothels of Suffolk and the geese entertained many a gentleman as the sun departed for the evening.

Running water came by way of Hugh Myddleton/ The roots of architecture and art whisper the names of Christopher Wren, during the Stuart period, and Inigo Jones, a traveler introducing the influence of Rome and the Italian Renaissance to Britain/ While architecture grew so did the plague, Samuel Pepys' diaries would explain/ The plague pits grew roots, too, and even now it's rumored the Picadilly line swoops around to avoid them/ And one year after the plague, fire hit yet again/ With almost 80,000 people without homes, London rebuilt itself yet again.

Coffee houses became the rage, promoting productivity/ And from coffee, London Stock Exchange/ Auction houses Sotheby's and Christie's formed/ And once the coffee craze waned, the Gentleman's club began/ Fashion took hold on Rotten Row, and the age of the Dandy began/ The roots of exchange had their underbelly, too, as private medicine took root and the trade of human bodies was not only accepted but demanded/ This was the invasion of the body snatchers/ Sitting vigil at graves to protect those they loved/ And with the Anatomy Act, the disappearances and theft were ended.

And with one underbelly removed, another took form in Gin/ Meant to bring tax and revenue, it made the streets mad until the Gin Act was passed/ Pleasure gardens took over and brought music and refinery, the first legs of amusement parks today/ John Nash began to rebuild Henry VIII's hunting grounds, and his plans for the city went underway but never fully came to fruition/ All Soul's Church is the only Nash still standing/ Cholera swept through the city as Victorian cleanliness was questioned/ Dr. John Snow found the cause through a popular water pump and thus the sewer system began.

Expanding trade brought new docks/ London was becoming a larger port of entry/ Workers were employed but soon went on strike/ The roots of the working man and fair pay had begun/ William Cuffay and the Chartist movement, the first mass political movement of the British working class/ Mary Prince presented her anti-slavery petition to Parliament/ As servants of the people, Metropolitan Police set the pattern for policing that is still followed today/ Technology blossomed as the railway was set forth/ The poor were evicted to make way for new lines and travel and marked the end of old coaching inns.

Our dear Charles Dickens looked for work at age twelve, after his father was sent to debtors' jail/ The streets became the homes of the people he put to pages/ He became a champion of truth as he outed the ways prisons and mental institutes acted the same, treating the poor as animals and not as human beings/ The Great Exhibition began with Prince Albert's consent, and Henry Cole and Sir Robert Peel, and earned the nickname the Crystal Palace/ 100,000 exhibits from around the world, a pendulum that hung from the roof/ Once again fires burned and took down that Palace.

The East End brought on another darkness when the poor were considered less than lowest/ It became "The Abyss" which gave way to the darker days of Jack the Ripper/ But humor formed with Cockney Rhyming Slang, which covered the dodgy dealings/ It was a secret language of its own/ The 'Africa Times and Orient Review' was the first political journal produced by and for Black people ever published in Britain with words by Marcus Garvey/ And London saw its first Black Mayor John Richards, Archer of Battersea/ Fire swept through again in 1917, through a TNT factory in Silvertown/ With seventy-three dead and many homeless, the rumors of Germany began although the reality was quite mundane/ Poorly treated workers and the site had not been maintained.

With the death of Queen Victoria came joie de vivre/ Edward VII brought luxury and the arts, accessibility was high as the underground system and the omnibuses emerged/ Picadilly brought the Ritz, and for those who couldn't afford it, tea houses/ The moving pictures along with theater gave new energy to a city thriving in the face of war/ 1938 brought Sigmund Freud, father of psychoanalysis, escaping the Nazis/ He died in exile the next year/ The Blitz of WWII destroying the city just as the Great Fire had three hundred years before.

And once again London rose from the ashes/ As London rebuilt the Empire, Windrush arrived at Tilbury; brought the first of waves of African and Asian immigrants/ And with this the National Health Service and London Transport were created to help London recover/ Still in despair, London welcomed the Olympics, and for the first time they were broadcast on BBC/ Britain finished with twenty medals, three of which were gold/ The Festival of London brought joy back to the land one hundred years after the Great Exhibition/ 3D domes allowed for a glimpse into the future with large TVs, and for many it was the first time they had seen one/ And with this they saw the birth of air travel and airports/ In the wake of the Notting Hill riots in 1958, Amy Ashwood Garvey co-founded the Association for the Advancement of Coloured People/ London became the "Swinging City" in the 60s and the capital of cool/ Music and fashion were hot, and rebellion against former generations persisted/ But every star dims and with that came unemployment.

There are patterns that emerge in roots/ Some overlap and some create their own path/ From the sounds and the song of bogs to those gravel sprinkled islands, we stand here on this land among the ghosts of the past walking in the ancestors' paths/ We gather here today on what would be Sigmund Freud's 160th birthday and the last city he stepped foot in, creating our own roots, entwined with those who came before us.

Art As Alchemy[1]

Sharron Kraus

I am interested in the relationship between suffering and art. As an artist I draw heavily on dark themes and dark states of mind. Yet what I think of as the stereotype of the Tortured Artist has never seemed an accurate image for the relationship between my art and life; for the way I feel about my own work. In this paper I'll explore and contrast the idea of the Tortured Artist with that of the Artist as Alchemist. The Tortured Artist image is a pervasive one and there are plenty of artists who seem to fit this stereotype. Must artists suffer for their art, though? And must their suffering be ongoing or can it be transcended, transformed? The idea of art as alchemy, as a way of transmuting the 'base materials' of sadness, loss, depression and darkness into something golden, is a more optimistic and inspiring model of creativity, and one that gives us a way of understanding why art is so important to us.

What role does suffering play in creativity? I'll start by looking at some ways of thinking about the relationship between them.

1. Inseparability:
suffering is both necessary and sufficient for creativity

The Tortured Artist stereotype seems to be based on two ideas: the idea that great suffering makes great artists, and the idea that without great suffering it's impossible to be a great artist. We look at an artist like Billie Holiday and imagine that she's the singer she is because of how much she suffered, that her singing is so strongly affecting because it expresses real heartbreak and deep despair. We may assume that the depth of her suffering is intrinsic to her singing, and that if her suffering were to end, her inspiration would dry up. I want to question both of these assumptions. An artist's suffering clearly feeds into their art, but the way it does so isn't as straightforward as this.

If we assume that a suffering artist's suffering is what makes her the artist she is, isn't that to diminish the importance of talent, intelligence, determination, hard work and craft? If we imagine that anyone who went through what Billie Holiday went through would sing as sublimely as her, how do we explain the rarity of such singers? There are thousands of women who've lived lives not dissimilar to the life

---

1 This paper grew out of correspondence with Nick Medford on the relationship between creativity and darkness and I am grateful to him for stimulating discussion.

Billie Holiday led, and most of them have died leaving no trace. What made Billie Holiday unique was not her suffering – it was what she did with it.

Suffering is not sufficient for creativity, then, but perhaps it's necessary? Perhaps tortured artists are the only true artists? Perhaps suffering or madness are the prices that must be paid for true inspiration? This seems to be something that's widely assumed, that we're eager to accept, and artists like Holiday, Janis Joplin, Sylvia Plath, Syd Barrett are romantic, tragic figures. But even though there are many artists who fit this tragic stereotype – living lives of extreme suffering – this can't be the only model for creativity. There are artists who stand as clear counter-examples – Kate Bush is one who springs to mind: she seems to have had an idyllic childhood, been part of a close-knit, happy family, and yet is one of the most unique and inspired songwriters alive. This seems to suggest that though suffering may be an important component of creativity, it's just one of many possible components. Also, even if suffering is necessary in some sense, ongoing, unrelenting suffering doesn't seem to be.

An aside: why do we expect or want our artists to suffer? We don't expect the same from people who excel in other fields, sportsmen and women, for example. The fact that some footballers suffer more than others is not taken to be an indicator of their ability on the pitch, so why is the suffering of artists often seen to be a measure of their creative genius? What is it about art that seems to require this?

2. MOTIVATION: SUFFERING IS WHAT MOTIVATES US TO CREATE.

It might be thought that it's only when we're suffering that we're driven to create, and conversely the idea of creating when we're happy might seem a nonsense: "If you're happy, why would you bother creating?", someone might ask.

The idea that it's only when they're unhappy that artists only create is a depressing one. If it were true it would seem to trap artists in a prison of perpetual suffering, risking losing their inspiration if ever they found happiness. It's only if we're in the grip of the Tortured Artist image of creativity that this kind of link between suffering and creative impetus seems right, though. If that's not how we're thinking of creativity; if instead we're thinking of it as a process of exploration and discovery, motivated in part by curiosity, or a response to the world around us, or a way of communicating ideas, creating seems just as likely to be something we do when we're happy as when we're sad. If anything, the times that are our most difficult, painful and low ones are often the times when we're least creative. Great suffering is debilitating and paralysing, and even those artists who seem to most embody the Tortured Artist stereotype will struggle to create when life becomes most unendurable. People whose lives are a daily grind, who struggle just to survive, who have no time to rest, no time to reflect, do not become artists. Even if art draws on suffering, it tends to only be made once the suffering abates.

There's a sense in which suffering is at least part of what motivates us to create; suffering in the broader sense. Death waits for all of us, and every love brings with it the inevitability of loss. The world around us can seem cruel, or, worse, indifferent. This is the context in which we work, and it does seem that suffering in this existential sense is part of what motivates us to create, albeit unconsciously.

Against this backdrop of the suffering that is the human condition, though, the things that motivate us to create seem a mix of positive and negative, with suffering being just part of the picture. Creating, like gardening or baking, loving or socialising, is something we're just as likely to do when we're happy as when we're sad. For an artist, creating is a part of everyday life, something done through thick and thin, and also, like these other activities, it's something that contributes to our happiness and wellbeing.

3. GERMINATION:

DARK TIMES ARE NECESSARY IN ORDER FOR IDEAS TO GERMINATE.

Even if our darkest times are not necessarily our most creative, perhaps it's true that only by experiencing dark times can we go on to create. Perhaps the dark times are a gestation period; perhaps they are as necessary for creativity as germination is for flowering. The writer Alan Garner believes this to be the case with his own writing. He writes about a bleak low that had him sitting silent and motionless for two years. A year after he snapped out of this state, he started work on his most challenging book and was full of energy, firing on all cylinders. He sees the two states as being essentially related and thinks that he needed a period of semi-hibernation to recharge his batteries and ready him for the creative burst that followed. He calls the low state 'a necessary though unpleasant part of a positive and creative process.'[2]

The experience Garner describes is a longer, more crippling gestation period than most of us experience and than any of us would want. Understanding his breakdown as a gestation period for the rewarding creative project that followed is a way of making sense of it, giving it meaning and purpose. I'd question its being necessary, though: Garner's insistence on this seems post hoc to me and all we can really say is that one state preceded the other, not that the one brought about or was necessary for the other. An alternative reading of what happened to Garner, one I find more plausible, is that his illness was something beyond his control, that served no purpose, but that he went on to contextualise and put to good use. I don't believe that in general suffering happens for a reason – that idea seems too teleological for me. I believe that we suffer, and that we struggle to make sense of our suffering; attempt to take something of value from it. That we can do this with suffering seems an important and wonderful thing: we take something dark and meaningless and make something beautiful and meaningful out of it. I'll be returning to this idea.

It does seem likely that periods of doing nothing are important to creativity. Planting seeds in the subconscious and leaving them to germinate seems a part

---

2 Alan Garner, 'Fierce Fires & Shramming Cold' in *The Voice That Thunders* (The Harvill Press 1997), 212.

of the creative process, and this horticultural imagery, of planting seeds, tending them, and having the patience to allow them to shoot in their own time, seems a good metaphor. If we think of the creative process in this way, the darkness necessary for germination need not be the darkness of suffering; it may be the darkness of sleep, of temporary forgetting, of meditation or ritual work, or just a period of time during which the spotlight of our conscious attention is turned off.

4. Subject matter: sadness/suffering/darkness are good copy; they're what the most profound art is about.

Suffering, tragedy, violence, madness, etc. do feature highly in great art, but so too do things like love, hope, courage, kindness and joy. Whatever ingredients go into the pot, whether we succeed in our creating depends on what we do with them, not just on them being there. A catalogue of suffering doesn't automatically make for great art any more than a shopping list of exotic ingredients guarantees a tasty meal; we must combine our ingredients skillfully. An artist must take suffering and make something with it, do the actual creating. Suffering, along with anything else that goes into the pot, has to be transformed.

It's worth stopping at this point to reflect on the role art plays in our lives. Why do we value art? Why do artists make art? Jeanette Winterson is eloquent on this subject. She talks about art as the thing that stands between us and the abyss, saying 'the tragic paradigm of human life is lack, loss, finality, a primitive doomsaying that has not been repealed by technology or medical science. The arts stand in the way of this doomsaying.'[3] and 'Art shows us how to be more than we are. It is heightened, grand, an act of effrontery. It is a challenge to the confines of the spirit... art is a daily rebellion against the state of living death routinely called real life.'[4] Art is our way of resisting the tragedy of human existence; of turning tragedy into ecstasy. Winterson talks about the 'original role of the artist as visionary'[5], and about art as healer, saying 'I know of no pain that art cannot assuage'[6].

That art can release us from the prison of suffering is a large part of why we value it and why we continue to make it. That art enables us to make sense of suffering, death and struggle, enables us to relieve our pain and that of others is a wonderful thing. That we can take suffering (as well as the other things we experience), put it into the alchemical vessel and transmute it into gold is the magic of creating.

5. Art as alchemy: suffering is base matter that an artist transmutes into something precious.

Though suffering and the darker side of life are important to creativity, then, as artists we're not forced into lives of suffering – creativity can rescue us from suffering.

3 Jeanette Winterson, *Art Objects: Essays on Ecstasy and Effrontery* (Vintage 1996), 19.
4 Winterson, 93-94.
5 Winterson, 133.
6 Winterson, 156.

Whatever we suffer, and however important suffering is to our art, as artists we can take our suffering and shape and transform it. This shaping and transforming is essential to art and as artists we have access to tools and techniques that enable us to take in suffering and darkness and create meaning, beauty, and joy.

What is the transformation process? How does art work this alchemical magic?

Before addressing this question, let me say that if art truly transforms suffering in this way then art is magic, and artists are magicians. Alan Moore has made this point: 'I believe that magic is art and that art, whether that be writing, music, sculpture, or any other form, is literally magic. Art is, like magic, the science of manipulating symbols, words or images, to achieve changes in consciousness. The very language of magic seems to be talking as much about writing or art as it is about supernatural events.'[7]

There seem to be two main ways that art transforms suffering: firstly, by reframing or recontextualising it, and secondly, by radically transforming it. The first is relatively straightforward and the second is where the real alchemy lies.

Sometimes we create by taking an experience and presenting it in a way that imbues it with meaning. Something we experience can be shown to parallel the experiences of countless other people, to take on a universal or even mythic quality; or it can be seen as part of a bigger picture, a dark but necessary part of a beautiful whole. How this is done depends on the skills of the artist. When a novelist decides what aspects of a scenario to put in and what to leave out, whether to make a narrative linear or non-linear, what aspects of the characters to show us and how and when to do so, she does all of these things in a way that frames or presents the story to us in a certain way. In doing so, she works her magic; showing us beauty, form and pattern where we'd otherwise fail to see any; creating links or resonances where previously there were none; taking disparate elements and connecting and harmonising them.

Sometimes in creating, a greater alchemy is necessary. Our starting points – experiences, emotions, ideas and aims – undergo a radical transformation and what emerges as the finished work bears no more resemblance to them than a butterfly bears to the caterpillar that went into the chrysalis it came out of. (And this analogy is apt: caterpillars don't *grow* into butterflies – the transition that takes place in the chrysalis involves an intermediary state of complete breakdown into a formless 'caterpillar soup' which the cells that grow into wings, antennae, etc. feed on.)

I think it's helpful to think of the space in which creating takes place as an alchemical vessel, a hermetically sealed space free from outside interference. What happens within it is governed by its own own (aesthetic) rules and is not an extension of ourselves, a place for our egos to run wild or our insecurities or repressed desires to be pandered to, for desires for things such as money, recognition and success to dictate how we work. It's not even a therapeutic space – what we do there shouldn't be governed by our desire to be healed.[8] When any of these external pres-

---

7 Dez Vylenz dir., *The Mindscape of Alan Moore* (Shadowsnake Films 2008).
8 The way art heals may seem paradoxical: healing may occur but only if healing is not what we aim

sures manage to exert themselves within the space, they warp the creative process. We must put ourselves in service to the creative process, putting aside these other things whilst we work. We should be vigilant at keeping them out, notice when they try to smuggle themselves in, as they'll inevitably do.

We must let the work go beyond what initially motivated us. The relationship between artist and artwork is like the relationship between parent and child in this respect. To succeed at parenting we must have our children's best interests at heart and act to serve their needs, not cling to them or use them to serve our interests. It's the same with our creative work. If our work serves as a receptacle for our fantasies and unfulfilled wishes, if it serves to bolster our self-esteem, boost our egos, we'll fail as artists. Though our experiences inform the work, we must grant the work independence, allow it to cut its ties with them, to develop according to its own rules, forgetting them, leaving them behind like a boat cut adrift on a wide sea floats far from the shore. We must relinquish control and allow the work to lead us.

We inhabit the symbolic realm of the work and work and rework within it, manipulating symbols according to its own rules; these rules, like the rules of a game, allowing some moves and not others. We don't impose things from outside – we don't project our shit onto the work, we don't allow considerations such as whether our audience or our critics will like it to constrain or direct the work. Whatever experiences inspired us to start on this work are now forgotten as we focus on the medium and the symbols we're using; words, sounds, melodies and rhythms, for example. We edit and tweak, changing words that don't scan, finding rhymes where appropriate, change chords and rhythms to create mood, shuffle components around if a new shape or direction starts to emerge. The work will only have integrity if it's formed in this way, without bowing to external concerns.

The process will at times be chaotic, formless and confusing, and we won't know how long it will take or what will emerge at the end. Sometimes it'll feel like we're achieving nothing and at other times there'll be exhilarating breakthroughs and a sense of things falling into place. We'll need to trust the process and follow where it leads us. If we do so, in the end we'll emerge with something precious.

And what we emerge with, as well as being something that works on its own terms – as a work of art – will possess magical healing powers. Once we've finished our work, we see that the patterns and shapes we've created within it mirror patterns and shapes in our lives, and in the world. The work becomes a mirror that reflects and reveals truths. If we've given it the freedom to develop and grow on its own terms, to go beyond the limits we would otherwise have imposed upon it, it'll be capable of reflecting deep truths. (If we don't give it this freedom, it will only reflect the superficial.)

At the end of the process, when we bring these treasures home, we find that the pain or suffering that engendered the work has been transformed.

---

for. The structure of this apparent paradox is shared by a number of other situations. To reap the benefits of love, for example, we must forget about reaping benefits and must instead be motivated by concern for the beloved. We must forget ourselves and focus on others instead.

The Seven Layers of the Vodou Soul

Demetrius Lacroix

Vodou is also known as *Sevie Genin*; this means to serve Genin or Africa, as well as the mythologized place Africa became in the memory of the enslaved Haitian community. To serve the spirits and ancestors brought a sense of belonging as well as a way to check into the spiritual and ancestral world they were forced to leave behind. To return to the point of origin and then come back to the present, fulfilled and refreshed, is the pursuit of Vodou and most, if not all, Diaspora traditions.

In Haitian Vodou, as well as other African Diaspora religions, the power of possession is still seen as a blessing and honor. Surrender as a state of mind is the key to understanding some of the more nuanced and subtle ritual aspects of Diaspora traditions. Ritual possession is the moment when the immortal meets the mortal, and the divine comes to earth to join the body of the participant to open the way to Voice, memory and communal understanding. The Vodouizan enters the ritual, not to just talk to "Gods", but to become the "Gods". This viewpoint and perspective is often seen as frightening and evil, as it has been painted by the perceptions of others, in particular the Catholic and Protestant churches and the secular world.

In the early days of the Catholic church, possession was seen as one of the holy sacraments; that the world of good and evil had made your corporeal body the battle field; where one who survived could have access to the divine and to the ones who died by untreated trauma, would later become candidates of canonization. While not all possession is beneficial, as in the case of the Haitian Zombie, the general outlook is positive and invited.

To understand Haitian Vodou and the power of spirit possession, one should understand the levels and layers of the soul

The first, primary level is called *Corps Cadavre*. This is the literal body; the portion that interacts with everything on the physical level. This refers to the physical meat and matter.

The second layer, the *N'ame*, the spirit of the flesh, is the portion of the soul that reflects the physical health. This is a second layer that can be visually perceived; where one can see if one is afflicted by spells or malefica, or natural illness. This is also the layer that can be developed and altered by spiritual contact; it is the *N'ame* that is altered the most by spirit possession, as this layer determines how your corpse cadavre will "settle".

The next layer *Z'etoile/Z'etwal* – the star of destiny – is the line of destiny that one is born into, and the luck one will have throughout ones life. In some ways, this is the most important level. The *Z'etwal* also deals with spiritual obligations, "the calling" to priesthood, or the ability to perform feats of power. In reverse, it can be used to blame conditions for one's life.

The least perceived levels are the *Gros bon Ange* and the *Ti Bon Ange*. *Ti bon Ange*, or the little good angel, is the layer that is the personality; the part of the soul that reflects your character. It is the *Ti bon Ange* that is "pushed" out of the way during a Vodou Possession. The *Gros bon Ange* is the part of the soul that animates the body, that moves all functions; it is the actual spark of life.

The layers of the soul have a symbiotic relationship; if one is out of balance, all will be out of balance. When they are out of alignment it can cause chaos and uncertainty to exist, bad luck, disease, even death.

The moments during the beginnings of a possession are often called "Crisis" where your physical body (*corpse cadavre*) must let go of the *Ti bon Ange*; this can be seen in the acts of uncontrollable dancing, shaking, and vocal phenomena. The losing of the *Ti bon Ange* is creating a momentary state where one is bereft of one's own identity and another identity fills its space. The drums and song are the instructions to the spirit and the key to successful possession. The transformation of the possessed person's face, voice and mannerisms all become that of the spirit they are calling to. The final features are perhaps the most impressive; it is now when the spirit is seated in the person that now the embodiment of collective memory of the spirit can be heard, and the community reunited. This is the positive and invited form of ritual possession.

The final layers are more nuanced and in many ways act accordingly to the others, they are *Chamin*, the road, and the *Met Tet*. The *Chamin* is the road that you were born to follow, the *Z'etwal* is the guide down this road. The belief in Vodou follows the idea that before birth you choose the destiny you will live, and so you are placed on the road by your own choices, knowing that if you can resist the things that would otherwise lead you astray, you will reach a place that is perfect for your being. Your guide down this road, aside from the *Z'etwal*, is the *Met Tet* or master of the head; this is the Lwa or Spirit that guides you down the road. Spirits are attracted to people for a few reasons; sometimes it is that the human and the spirit have similar dispositions, or that the human lacks certain qualities that are required for them to live a better life. The *Met Tet* is also the main spirit that usually comes to possess an individual.

When the layers of the soul are outside of their homeostasis, spiritual and physical ailments arise. Possession without cause can be a sign that something could be wrong with an individual; it could be as simple as a lack of control over self or the spirits, or something far more serious like a situation. Aside from possession, physical/mental ailments also are indicative to spiritual turmoil. All interactions with any layer of the soul will have physical repercussions, beneficial or otherwise. The power of a curse, an unfulfilled promise, or an interaction with a person or place can sometimes be all it takes to knock the layers of the soul out of balance. Most situations can be corrected or assisted with some spiritual intervention. Most often for very serious issues, Initiation into Vodou is often a recommendation for a cure, but so could be a prescribed spiritual bath or ritual service.

On the far end, the most extreme end of spiritual sickness is Zombification. This process has been engineered and mastered by *Bokors* or sorcerers and the secret societies of *Haiti Zobop, San pwel, Bizango*, etc. This ritual unwellness is often a community response to destructive and dangerous persons. Zombification is one way the Haitians can police themselves and see some level of justice served if no other way seems possible. This combination of ritual techniques and application of ritually prepared neurotoxins allows for a state to bring all levels of the soul out of balance, in particular the *Ti bon Ange* to be displaced from the body and controlled by the Bokor, and to change the course the *Z'etwal* of your destiny is taking you. This is accomplished by the previous rituals and by using personal effects and biological materials to anchor the spirit into another vessel. It should be noted that there is great distinction between the zombie of the walking and rotting dead of fiction and fantasy and the living person, living in between the border of life and death, doomed to this position by their actions or as the selected fate of the individual by a shadow council. This person – the *Zombie* – is now just the corpse cadaver and the *Gros bon Ange*; destiny, stable health, and personality are stripped from the individual. Often the affected are forced into pressed labor, which, when examining this from an historical perspective, is the ultimate form of loss of identity; eternal spiritual slavery and the loss of roots and familial connection. The loss of one's roots to the Haitian culture essentially dooms the person to wander and not live a good life. The ritual of zombification holds more dangers (for both parties) than overdosing on poison or having your mind broken by spirits and ritual. The power of perpetual loss of self is just the beginning of the list. The zombified are rarely if ever recovered from this state; death is their only known reprieve, at least from the native beliefs and speculations of the Western world.

The key point to all the layers of the soul is that even if they are unseen layers, they still affect the person physically. The soul in the western world exists in limbo. Understand the situation you exist within in nature, and you come to better understand yourself. Knowing the layers of the soul exist is just the first step of many, as we as a nontraditional society should strive to re-understand; the spiritual body as the host that supports physical life.

Haitian history and spirituality, science and culture are inseparable. To better understand Vodou, and the people who are woven into the fabric, the individual can see how perhaps the limited perspective of the modern atheistic of the psychoanalytic community at large dismisses many things in the world of spirituality, especially ecstatic experiences, as pathological. Our culture has removed our agency to communicate and understand ourselves in a natural way; as whole people who are members of nature who have cut themselves off from the source of life. The world of the unseen within reason has the ability to help unfold mysteries and issues that are still unclear to us today and can serve to help people who otherwise feel the loss of what it is to be connected to the source of life, wellness and well being.

SUBLIME FRAGMENTS: THE ART OF JOHN BALANCE

Graham Duff

John Balance (born Geoffrey Laurence Burton, 1962) is best known as vocalist and lyricist with the British experimental group Coil. Whilst many musicians and groups describe themselves as experimental, paradoxically they will often end up utilising a signature style. However, John Balance and co-creator Peter Christopherson were genuinely relentless experimentalists.

Interestingly, in relation to Coil's recordings, Balance was fond of saying "We made the studio sacred, then we blasphemed." That is to say, they created a restriction and then deliberately rebelled against it.

From 1982, until Balance's untimely death in 2004, Coil repeatedly switched and flipped their modes of expression. Their sound world encompassed synth pop, atonal noise, delicate string arrangements, acid house club tracks, dronescapes, film sound-tracks, ritual music, sequencer driven kosmische, industrial cacophony and beyond into the truly uncatagorisable. Seldom was a group so unrestricted in the scope of its endeavours.

Yet, whilst the sonic elements of their work changed and evolved, Coil's lyrical con-cerns remained fairly constant. A cosmology of interests including but not limited to hedonism viewed as an heroic pursuit, the price of existence being eternal struggle, respect for the power of elemental forces, the bestial often being indistinguishable from the celestial, an honouring of the magickal, the occult and the arcane, a fascination with altered states, with death itself often viewed as the ultimate altered state.

Throughout Coil's existence, Balance was also privately, yet prolifically producing a vast body of visual artworks. In these artworks, he applied the same open ended experimental approach which characterised Coil's musical output.

This is evidenced by both the range of styles and the variety of media he employed to manifest his work. He switched freely between coloured pencil drawings, collages, watercolours, purely abstract paintings, cartoons, grotesque caricatures, surrealistic landscapes and so on.

Until 2014 – when the first edition of the Balance monograph *Bright Lights And Cats With No Mouths* was published by Timeless Editions – very few people were even aware of the existence of his paintings and drawings. And it's clear that Balance himself didn't regard his artworks as worthy of much, if any, serious consideration. His pictures were never destined to be exhibited. In fact, they were never intended to be seen by anyone, except perhaps very close friends. They were kept in private notebooks and drawing pads or tucked away in green box files.

Therefore, because of the secretive nature of the work's creation, much of what I have to say is opinion and speculation. With the exception of the materials used and the dates they were created, there are very few facts about John Balance's artworks. And even the dates of many of the pieces are unknown.

One possible reason for Balance's ability to leap from style to style, medium to medium, is the very private nature of his visual creativity. A visual artist's signature style is often their selling point. Therefore many visual artists think long and hard before changing direction. But, as there was absolutely no public conception of Balance as a visual artist, he was free to do whatever he wished. His central desire seems to have been to experiment.

But of course, by definition, not all experiments come off. Not everything Balance touched turned to gold. And I feel sure there are pieces included in the monograph which he would have felt awkward about exposing to the public.

There are numerous occasions where his vision exceeded his technical abilities. Often he would experiment with mind altering drugs and draw or paint whilst under their influence. Sometimes this would produce startling results. But, it's probably not too presumptuous to suggest that there were occasions when Balance's technical abilities were curbed by his chemically altered state of mind. Without doubt, there are works included in the monograph which could easily be dismissed as stoned doodles. But equally there are other pieces which could just as easily be dubbed stoned masterworks.

A good number of the pieces are in biro or magic marker. Tools which are used relatively rarely by fine artists. Perhaps Balance was reaching for whatever tool was handy in the moment of inspiration. If so, we can read this as him rising to a challenge. Taking these most unsophisticated of tools and creating something of visual significance.

Or, we can flip it around and read it as yet another part of a – perhaps unconscious – strategy to distance his artworks from serious consideration. By using biros and felt tips, is he saying 'This isn't fine art. These are just domestic daubs'?

Whatever the reason for Balance's use of these tools, there's one definite knock on effect. Unlike graphite or pigment, biros and magic markers cannot be removed or reworked. What lands on the page stays on the page. There is space for elaboration, but not for erasure. This shows Balance's commitment to the automatic process.

As one might expect, throughout the work, there are strong, recurring themes; death, daemons, dogs, hybrid beasts, unknown gods, spirit worlds, oneiric visions, the sun and the moon. Personal obsessions with universal resonance. Another key element of Balance's artworks is eroticism and the manifestation of sexual energy.

Again, this should come as no surprise. Even a cursory glance at the song titles and lyrics which Balance created for Coil, quickly reveal a fascination with erotic desire, sexual energy and sensual overload. Coil were, after all, dedicated explorers of the altered state. And sexual excitation and orgasm are amongst life's greatest altered states.

'Horse' (1988, see colour section, page 33), is a drawing on paper in ink and coloured crayons. The creature stands upright on its hind legs. All around, nature is wild and untamed in a technicolor ecstasy. The red horse stares out at us with a soft and charming eye. But there's no doubt that our attention is being directed to the nipples and especially the weighty penis. This is sexuality seen as a form of savage yet noble splendour. Also, the nipples, navel and penis seem to form a human face – perhaps reminding us that man is just another animal with sexual urges.

In the drawing 'Penis Dog' (date unknown, colour section, page 34), sexual energy is shown to be an animalistic need. The objects in the bottom right hand corner could be penis plants, reminding us that sexual urges are part of nature. Or conversely, they could be penis aliens, suggesting that sexual energy is inherently otherworldly. And as such in conflict with the construct of the cosy domestic world of the home.

'Portrait of a Sexual Demon' is an ink and coloured pencil drawing on paper from 1988. The demon is depicted as a grotesque clown, its own penis partially erect, dripping and somehow apologetic. Meanwhile, nearby two disembodied hands masturbate a two headed penis which sprays gobs of sperm in both directions. This feels like a depiction of someone who recognises they are at the beck and call of their own rapacious sexual appetites. At the mercy of the Sexual Demon.

And yet, elsewhere, Balance treats sexuality and desire in a far more playful and humorous manner. Drawings such as 'Dinosaur Dick', 'Happy Pee-Ness' (colour section, page 35), 'Nazi Nob-enders' and 'Mythologically Strange Female Sees Burning Vision of Pork Sword' have a daft cartoon like quality. These drawings are not so much erotic as they are camp. That is to say they exhibit some of camp's key attributes, namely ostentatious display, exaggeration and impertinence. Again, this could easily be construed as Balance attempting to throw us off the scent. By infusing his work with crude and camp elements could he be saying "Don't pay too much attention to this. It's all a bit silly."?

Yet clearly camp, crudity and sexual innuendo are far from incompatible with high art. In fact, these very elements play a part in the most revolutionary of art. The work of Marcel Duchamp is heavily weighted towards camp, crudery and sexual innuendo. Be it the deployment of a urinal as an artwork, the reproduction of the Mona Lisa baring the coded message "She Is Hot In The Ass", or his final work, the peep show diorama 'Étant Donnés', in which we witness a naked woman sprawled on the ground, legs spread.

And of course the soundworld of Coil also displays a rich throbbing vein of camp. Examples include the elaborate and ornate cover version of the theme tune to the 1970s sit-com 'Are You Being Served?', and the naming of a suite of aggressive noise pieces 'Tunnel of Goats' – a quote from the TV sitcom *Father Ted*.

In fact, the influence of comedy on Balance cannot be underestimated. A phrase which comes up on numerous occasions in Balance's writings and lyrics – including the 'Coil Manifesto' – is the description of Coil as 'decadent and symmetrical'. A phrase rich with Blakean portent. It is, in fact, a quote from a 1988 TV comedy sketch by the British comedy duo French and Saunders, wherein Dawn French, in the role of an art critic, says "As long as it's decadent and symmetrical I call it art."

Perhaps this doesn't quite fit the popular image of Balance as the wild eyed Surrealistic visionary. But this camp, comic playfulness is very much a cornerstone of both Coil's music and Balance's visual art.[1]

As previously stated, the majority of Balance's works were created via automatic drawing or painting. This is a technique most readily associated with Surrealism and was pioneered by the French Surrealist André Masson. It's a way of removing rational control and allowing the image to flow directly from the psyche onto the page. What the Surrealist leader André Breton referred to as "pure psychic automatism".

Balance was a huge fan of several Surrealist artists and had a number of their works in his personal collection. And it's easy to view his own work through the prism of Surrealism. And yet, whilst Balance is clearly plugging into the energy of Surrealism, and embracing its privileging of chance and accident and its mining of the subconscious, he appears to be doing it largely on his own terms.

Many contemporary artists who engage with Surrealist tropes end up mining seams which were exhausted several decades ago, adopting the most familiar visual signifiers of Surrealism; bowler hats, eyeballs, figures dressed in the fashions of the 20s and 30s, ladders leading up to clouds, sub-Dalinian landscapes and so on. But I believe such artists make the crucial error of believing Surrealism to be a specific visual style, as opposed to an attitude or state of mind. Consequently, their work comes across as what might be termed visual karaoke; out of tune renditions of classic forms.

If we look at the works of the first and second wave of Surrealist artists – Salvador Dali, Max Ernst, André Masson, Leonor Fini, Hans Bellmer etc. – we can see there is hardly any crossover in terms of imagery. Because each artist followed their own personal obsessions, and produced imagery born of those individual obsessions. One cannot simple adopt imagery born of another's obsession and expect one's own work to resonate with the same power. No more than the putting on of a head chef's hat will enable one to produce a gourmet meal. And yet, Balance himself was not above utilising the stylistic devices of other artists. And one of the clearest examples of this is the artist Brion Gysin.

Gysin was one of the key figures of the Beat Generation. Yet, unlike fellow beats – Jack Kerouac, William S. Burroughs and Allen Ginsberg – Brion Gysin never made the cross over into wider public consciousness. However, he could very easily claim to have had a comparable cultural impact.

He was an accomplished novelist and poet who pioneered the permutation

---

1 With this in mind, I toyed with giving this essay a far less reverent title. Options included 'John Balance, The Magic Marker' and 'Experimental Bent'. But for the longest time, my favourite title was 'Pork Sword & Sorcery'.

poem. He also created, or, if you prefer, discovered the cut-up technique – a form of word based collage, whereby pre-existing texts are spliced together. Gysin showed the method to his friend and former lover William S. Burroughs, who went on to employ the cut-up in the creation of a sequence of novels including *The Soft Machine* and *Nova Express*. Although clearly the cut-up has ramifications far beyond the world of literature.

Gysin also created the dream machine, a stroboscopic device which pulsates at a frequency which alters the brain's electrical oscillations, thereby causing hallucinations. He saw certain musics as having potent hallucinogenic or magical applications. He was interested in cultural disobedience and believed that the artist is an eternal outsider. And, he was openly queer at a time when such honesty could easily lead to serious con-sequences. For all these reasons, Gysin was an obvious touchstone for Balance and Christopherson.

But the aspect of Gysin's oeuvre which concerns us here, is his visual artwork. He was a highly accomplished painter and collagist who exhibited internationally. He had studied Japanese and Arabic and his work had long felt the influence of calligraphy. But Gysin claimed that his true fascination with the form came in 1956, in Morocco.

Gysin had opened a restaurant in Tangier by the name of *1001 Nights*. Yet, he was obviously unpopular with the locals, as one day, he found a small pouch lodged behind one of the restaurant walls. Upon opening the pouch, Gsyin discovered it was in fact a curse. Inside were an amulet, seeds, pebbles, shards from a broken mirror, small balls of hair matted with blood, a cut-out silhouette of Gysin himself and, crucially, a square of paper with a spell written both in lines right to left and up an down, thus forming a grid. The grid of words read "Make Master Brahim leave this house, as smoke leaves the fire, never to return."

Sure enough, a little while later, the restaurant folded and Gysin was out with just the shirt on his back. But the grid of words had make a deep impression on his artistic sensibilities. The grid would become the mainstay of Gysin's visual artworks. Whilst text – or frequently a visual form which appeared to be calligraphy – would also come to play a prominent role in his paintings and collages.

The fact that he was inspired by a curse – and a successful one at that – is deeply significant. It shows that for Gysin, art and magic would come to occupy the same space. Similarly, he refused to make a clear distinction between word and image.

Gysin himself described the grid as "the bright jungle gym of mathematics; an exercise for controlling matter and knowing space".[2] And interestingly, what we see in Gysin's work, is the tension between the formal certainty of the grid and the swirling calligraphic chaos which he weaves around it. Gysin seems to see the grid not as a limiting form, but something to struggle against and overcome. And there are obvious echoes of this approach in Balance's statement: "We made the studio sacred, then we blasphemed."

In visual terms, we can clearly see Gysin's influence in several of Balance's art-

2 Brion Gysin, "Cut-Ups: A Project For Disastrous Success," in Weiss, *Back in No Time* 125-132.

works. In a number of pieces, Balance combines calligraphic forms in grid formations. Although Balance's word grids have a looser and more lyrical tone than Gysin's, they too appear to be spells or incantations. Balance's handwriting asserts his individuality, the repetition of the words affirms their power, whilst the grid symbolically locks in their meaning. Yet, if these are spells or incantations, then we cannot know what their pur-pose or intention was. These are private spells, and that is a major part of their power.

In some of Balance's calligraphic pieces, the words are clear. In others, the text has been more densely woven together. Words are being seen not just in terms of immediate meaning. Rather they are being viewed in terms of shape and pattern. The letters become deliberately entangled on the surface of the paper, woven end to end, so that individual meanings are subsumed by magickal intent.

A coloured pencil drawing from 1988 entitled 'Prayer' (colour section, page 36) is possibly his finest calligraphic grid work. Both its title and its form tell us this is an image with spiritual or magickal intent. Here, we can see Balance is operating away from the direct influence of Gysin. With its restricted colour pallet, it has real delicacy, fluidity and grace. But one of the most significant aspects of 'Prayer', is that here, Balance has dispensed with recognisable language altogether. The pencil marks are as much like musical notation as they are text. With 'Prayer', Balance is invoking magick via a language that is entirely his own.

Another work which uses calligraphic forms in a manner distinct from Gysin is 'Noise or Signal (Disabled Landscape With Language #1)', a watercolour and felt-tip pen piece from 1994 (colour section, page 37). Here, as the title suggests, Balance is taking language into a direct engagement with the natural world. The language becomes a component of the landscape itself. The hillside is literally formed from densely written words in red ink. But what is especially interesting, is that Balance describes this as a 'Disabled Landscape'. I think what he's suggesting, is that language itself can actually act as a barrier to understanding. That by introducing language into the landscape, we are disabling nature and preventing it from being understood on its own terms. The label is not the thing. The de-scription is not the thing.

The other artist who inevitably arises when we discuss the artwork of John Balance, is of course the British artist and occultist Austin Osman Spare.

Spare was born in 1886 and occupies a unique position in the history of British art. Much modern day discussion of Spare centres on his outsider status and focusses on the archetypical image of the penniless, eccentric artist starving in a garret. Whilst his reputation as an occult magician pushes him further out into the margins of society.

But it should also be remembered that Spare had started out on a very conventional and conservative route. He was the son of a policeman, he studied at the Royal College of Art, he was an official war artist and, at least initially, he exhibited at fashionable London galleries.

Yet he would go on to develop a highly personalised and detailed system of magickal beliefs. He also employed automatic drawing – a technique he developed contemporaneously to, but completely separately from the surrealists. He believed that his hand was being guided by spirits or elemental forces. He also pioneered siderealism – a visual experimentation with a logarithmic form of anamorphic projection, creating what might crudely be described as images with a slanted approach.

Balance and Christopherson were avid collectors of Spare's artworks and writings. I asked Balance's close friend and fellow Coil member Ossian Brown how many of Spare's artworks Balance and Christopherson owned. He estimated it to be around 90 individual pieces, plus an entire bound sketch book containing all the original drawings for Spare's *Book of Ugly Ecstasy*. So it's fairly safe to say that the imagery of Spare was an important and constant presence in Balance's home life.

With this in mind, it's obviously tempting to look for traces of Spare's style in the work of Balance. But, in truth, there is little to be found. Spare was a painter of great technical skill and a draughtsman par excellence. Whilst Balance's approach is best described as intuitive or perhaps primitivist. And yet, we can still see examples of Spare's cosmology of interests in Balance's art. In his depiction of worlds populated by daemons and elementals, in his embracing of the grotesque, in the belief that sometimes the artist's hand is guided by spirits and of course in his employment of automatic drawing.

Although, the visual influence of Spare may be slight, Balance's relationship with Spare went well beyond the imagistic. In an interview with *Fortean Times Magazine* in 2001, Balance said: "I have a very intimate relationship with Spare. He's my mentor. I communicate with him through his pictures and often ask his advice, as an ancestor. A lot of his beliefs were shamanic and to do with ancestor worship. I don't have a very close connection with my ancestors, my real family, other than my mother's parents, so I talk to Spare for advice. I think he still exists, in his art and in the aether. He's around as a helper."

He then jokingly goes on to say:

"Sounds a bit flaky doesn't it, maybe I should couch it in cyber terms!"

It's certainly easy to imagine Balance communing with the Spare pictures in his collection and seeking answers. Be they questions to do with personal issues or creative decisions.

Balance and Christopherson had a life long interest in the magickal, the arcane and the occult. But they were far from purists. Their interests included paganism, discordianism, Thelema and so on. But rather than embrace any one specific doctrine or practice, they cherry picked the elements which were personally inspiring to them. And sometimes, they would simply take the spirit of an idea or practice.

And of course art itself can be seen as a magickal or alchemical act. The transmutation of base materials such as pigment, paper, clay and canvas into items of visual, spiritual and indeed monetary value. Yet for Balance, there was no question of him selling his works to others.

There are numerous possible reasons for Balance not pushing his artworks out into the public arena. Perhaps it was because he saw them as objects of purely personal magickal significance. A private matter. As, indeed, most magickal acts are. But the most obvious reason is probably Balance's lack of confidence in his work's intrinsic artistic value. I asked Ossian Brown about Balance's opinion of his own work. He said, "He loved painting and drawing but he wasn't greatly confident and was quite dismissive of his pictures technically." Indeed, in an early letter to Val Denham, Balance described his own art as "rubbish."

And of course we cannot underestimate what it must have been like living and working with a visual artist of the scope and stature of Peter Christopherson. Aside from being a musician, Christopherson was a photographer, a graphic designer and a film, video and commercial director. He was one of three partners in the world famous Hipgnosis design team. And as such was responsible for some of the most iconic album sleeves of the 1970s and 1980s, including work for Led Zeppelin, Peter Gabriel and Pink Floyd. Many of Christopherson's images for others became both iconic and truly ubiquitous. For, whilst a relatively small portion of the populace will ever visit an art gallery, album sleeve art is potentially seen by millions.

In the shadow of Christopherson's sophisticated and polished work, it's quite possible to see how Balance – sitting at home or on tour, filling notebooks with images in ball-point and magic marker – could easily begin to dismiss his own work as mere sketches and doodles, of little consequence or purpose.

I may seem to be overstating Balance's reticence to have his visual artworks put out there for consideration. But consider this: by most group's standards, Coil's discography is enormous; scores of albums, live releases, singles, EPs, CDRs, plus albums and EPs released under various aliases. And yet, with the exception of a handful of limited run CDRs, none of them has a sleeve featuring artwork by Balance. Which seems a genuine shame, as there are numerous drawings and paintings which would have made marvellous Coil cover artwork.

So, in conclusion, although it's obvious that Balance himself placed very little value on his artwork, the fact that he was continually producing a vast body of visuals with no aim other than experimenting and exploring modes of expression, may well be his art's greatest strength. Because, in the end, the unguarded nature of the work's creation means these images provide a direct line to the subconscious of a truly visionary artist.

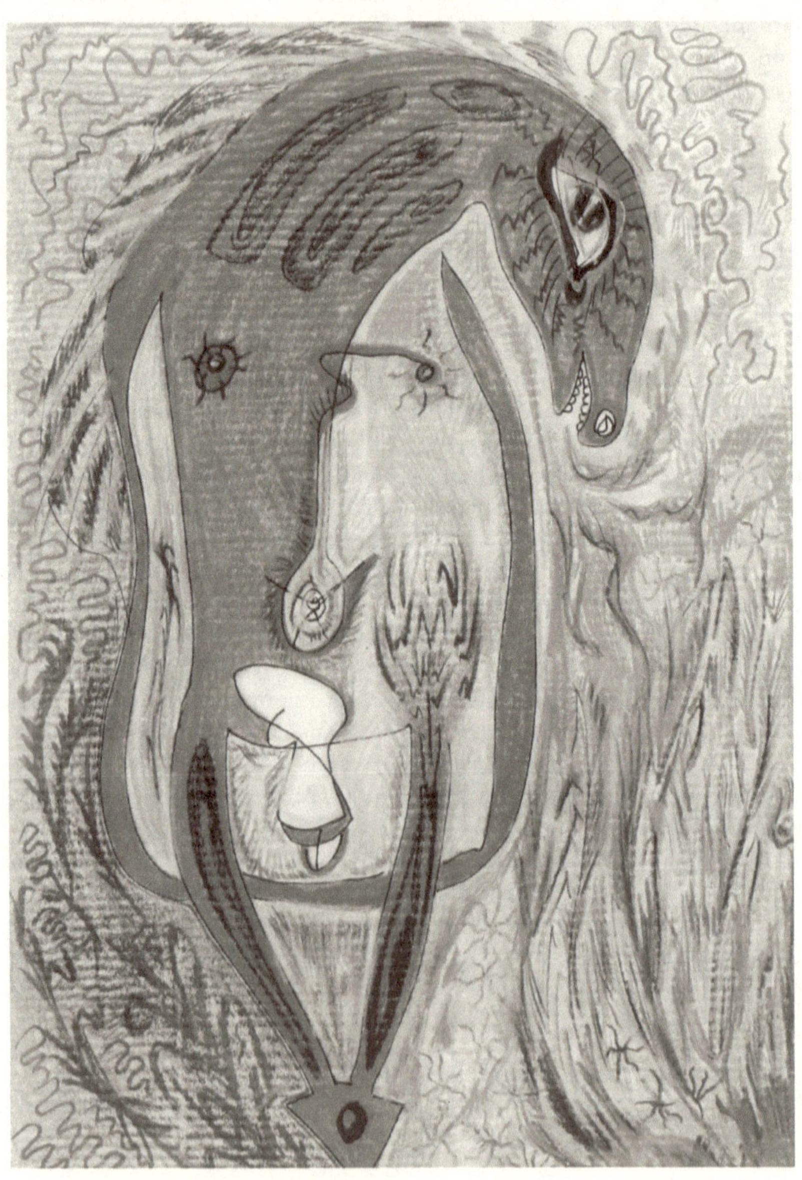

John Balance, *Horse* (1988)

John Balance, *Penis Dog*

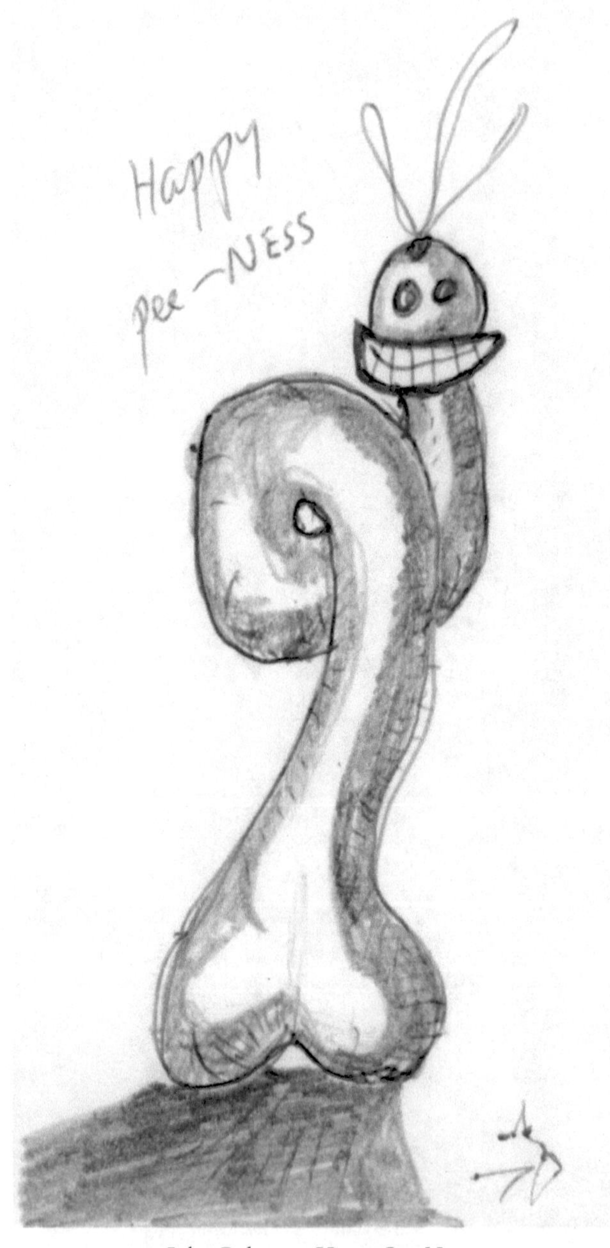

John Balance, *Happy Pee-Ness*

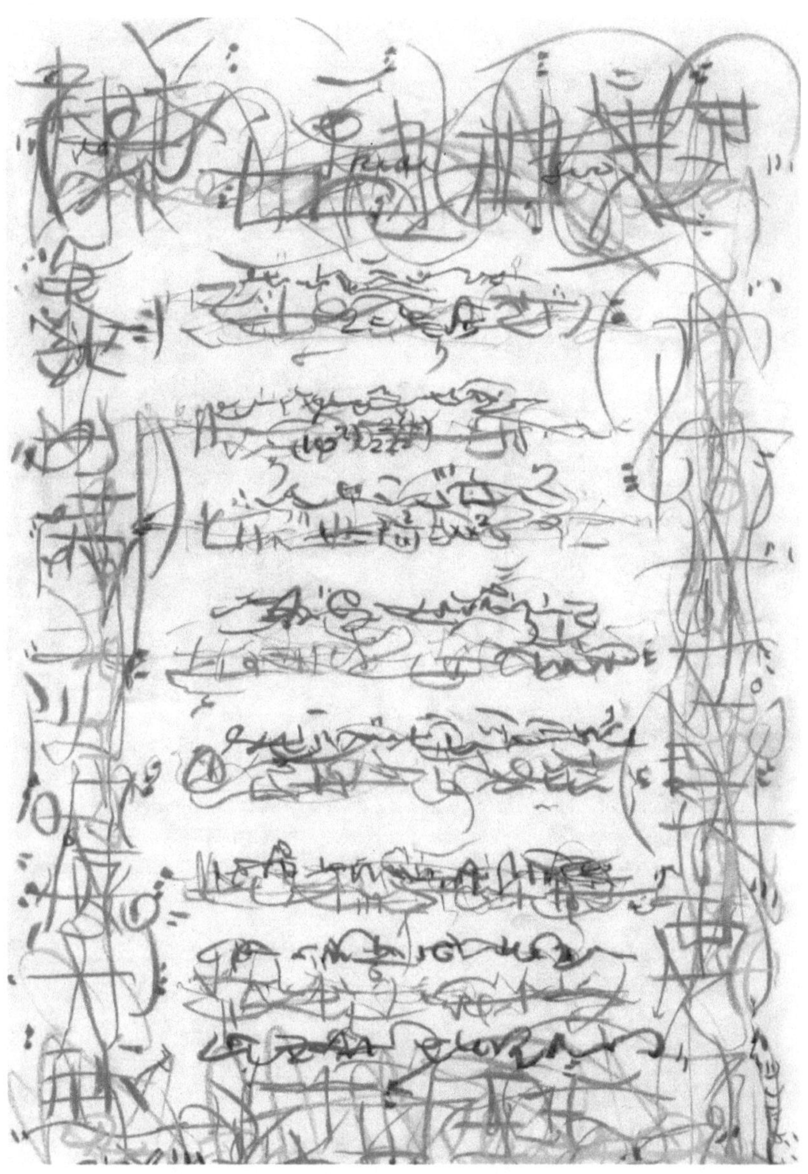

John Balance, *Prayer* (1988)

John Balance, *Noise or Signal (Disabled Landscape With Language #1)* (1994)

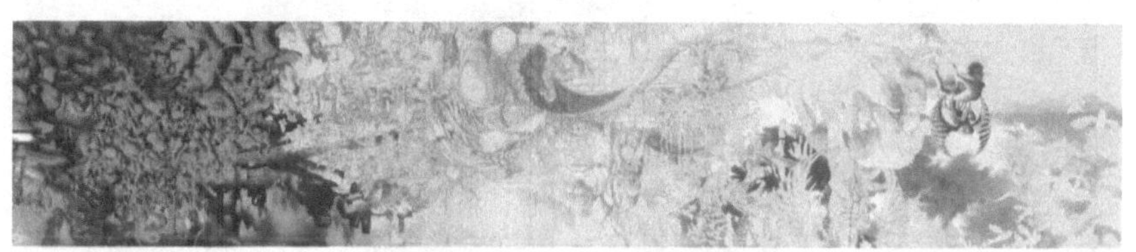

Malcolm McNeill, *End of Days*
(Exhibited at the Psychoanalysis, Art & The Occult Conference, London, 2016)

Ken Henson, *Miss Maude Fealy as Hekate* (2016)

The American Occult Revival In My Work

Ken Henson (Platonic One)

As a melting pot, American occultism is influenced by traditions the world over, and especially the various cultures of Europe. We see the influence of the Irish, the Germans, the French, the Swedes, and the Italians, to name a few. Currently, our most direct influence comes from England. Perhaps this is because it is the immediate culture that gave birth to America. Though America rebelled against England, American culture continues to be more similar with English society than any other culture. Perhaps for this reason, we rarely draw distinctions between an English and American occultism. Similarities include a shared zeal for Hermetism, and the profound influence of Eliphas Levi. In fact, discussion of the 19th century Occult Revival tends to center around England and particularly members of The Golden Dawn. Though American occultists were reading the works of English occultists, such as A. E. Waite, in terms of theory and practice, American occultism was more influenced by the Germans. Yet, despite the similarities, there are indeed key philosophical differences. At its heart, American occultism is less systematic and ceremonial than The Golden Dawn, because the American spirit is the Rebel Spirit, which requires being resourceful and breeds innovation.

One way the 19th Century Occult Revival in England and America differed was the professions of the key figures in these two locations: the English scene was comprised largely of artists of various stripe, while it was medical practitioners and chemists who would take up the occult in America, and particularly the American Midwest. In this particularly historical instance, art is the expression of the culture, while 19th century science saw a boom in technological innovation.

I live in Cincinnati Ohio, a German settlement, where the influence of German Renaissance alchemy and magic are dominant, along with a strong dose of Swedish influence (Swedenborgianism.) Homeopathy and Eclecticism, two competing brands of natural medicine, were dominant strains of practice in The Queen City. As a German city, Paracelsus' magic and medicine triumphs over all. It's unclear if the anti-establishmentarian character of Paracelsus' magical philosophy informed the disdain for ceremony found in American occultism, or whether America's Rebel Spirit attracted her to Paracelsus (insert chicken/egg paradox here.) Regardless, the critical philosophical difference between English and American occultism in the 19th century can be located in Paracelsus' writings:

> The exercise of true magic does not require any ceremonies or conjurations, or the making of circles or signs; it requires neither benedictions nor maledictions in words, neither verbal blessings nor curses; it only requires a strong faith in the omnipotent power of all good, that can accomplish everything if it acts through a human mind who is in harmony with it, and without which nothing useful can be accomplished. True magic power consists in true faith, but true faith rests in knowledge, and without knowledge there can be no faith. If I know that divine wisdom can accomplish a certain thing, I have the true faith; but if I merely believe that a thing might be possible, or if I attempt to persuade myself that I believe in its possibility, such a belief is no knowledge, and confers no faith. No one can have a true faith in a thing which is not true, because such a "faith" would be merely a belief or opinion based upon ignorance of the truth. (Hartmann, Franz, *Paracelsus*, pg. 114, 1887, George Redway, London)

Mesmerism in part finds its way to our culture through Samuel Hahnemann, the founder of Homeopathy, which was itself influenced by Paracelsus' ideas on magnetism, and would play a role in the rising fervor for Spiritualism (contact with spirits of the dead), which grew from rural New York, and Spiritism (contact with other spirits, such as angels and elementals). This trance-magic impulse can also be seen in the works of Jacob Boehme, another German who influenced my lineage, and Swedenborgianism, which had a strong grip on our community, though for the sake of brevity, I will not go into detail here.

The painting that accompanies this article is titled "Miss Maude Fealy as Hekate". Gallery-wrapped with sides gilded in silver, this painting, like many of my works, doubles as an altar, as I burn candles and place offerings to Hekate on top of the panels of the painting. I am working with Hekate because she is not only the goddess of magic, but also the goddess of medicine, and it is the fusion of magic and medicine, with a pagan impulse, that defines my lineage. And just as we should be careful not to distinguish too much between Paracelsus' magic and medicine, we should keep the same in mind when considering Hekate. My forefathers studied Booerhave, and so were aware that Zosimus and Plato believed that chemistry was taught by demons to women for sexual favors.

Miss Maude Fealy, the model I cast in the role of Hekate, was a stage and silent film actor. My choice to work with the dead is that it not only gives a face to the goddess I am working with; it also sets up the opportunity to work with two particular spiritual forms: 1. The dead (Spiritualism), and 2. A goddess (Hekate).

Embedded in John Uri Lloyd's great American occult novel Etidorhpa (Aphrodite backwards) is a passage titled "The Alchemistic Letter" which discusses several alchemists and magicians, highlighting the important lessons they left for us. Among those mentioned are Gueppo Francisco, for his treatise about "Elementary Spirits". Paracelsus was the first to pen a treatise on elementary spirits: the fiery salamander, the airy sylph, the watery undine, and the earthy pigmy. Summoning the elemental spirits was one of the basic activities of the Hermetic Brotherhood of Luxor, the homeopath's magical order of choice. Other 19th century magical groups such as the Golden Dawn also worked with elementals, but focused more on angels from the Judeo-Christian tradition. Perhaps the pioneer spirit imparted to the American Occult Revival the reverence for Greek and Roman nature deities, such as Aphrodite, Diana, and the nymphs. A statue to the nymph Egeria was dedicated to Cincinnati's Spring Grove Cemetery in 1850, and there is a Temple of Love (temple to Aphrodite) located a short walk from Lloyd's home.

A side-note that should be interesting to the reader who is interested in the theme of Psychoanalysis, Art and the Occult which permeates this issue of *The Fenris Wolf*, Justinus Kerner, the Spiritualist who inspired Rorschach's ink blot method, was a Swedish homeopathic physician who used inkblots to scry spirits. The significance of Kerner's influence on this aspect of psychoanalytical method is under-investigated, and deserves more attention, as it highlights one specific way that a spiritual concept became replaced by a psychological concept, supplanting the spirit world with the idea of the unconscious. This impulse to cloak or merge spiritual concepts with the language and paradigm of the growing materialist science can also be seen in the writings of my forefather Jirah Dewey Buck, a leading homeopath who founded the Cincinnati chapter and first American Section of the Theosophical Society. Buck, who would become integral to the development of the New Age, was the very embodiment of Paracelsus himself.

Apologia:

My apologies to you for not being able to approach the subject at hand without addressing the current political climate. Admittedly, I fear that the title and body of this essay will create concern that I am swept up in the present American patriotism which is associated with the fascist Alt Right. Nothing could be further from the truth. I don't want to "Make America Great Again." America has always been great, and shows no sign of slowing down. I submit Her innovation as my evidence. We don't need to make America great again, rather, we need to carve the horrors out of America; the horrors of capitalism, such as greed, ignorance, sexism, racism, corporation governance, and yes, blind nationalism. I am not proud to be an American because I was born in this land. I am proud to be an American because I have always identified with the Rebel Spirit, which sets up shop in every heart that is truly American. Though I am proud of the spiritual current of my people, I am not proud of my country's current regime or its bigoted principles. To value stagnation and homogeneity is not rebellious, leading to liberty, and therefore patently not American. One day, when spirit conquers greed, the real America, the American Spirit, will shine untarnished by this current moral plague. So Mote It Be.

WAS FREUD AFRAID OF THE OCCULT?

Gary Lachman

Was Freud afraid of the occult? That the father of psychoanalysis took a no-nonsense, scientific approach to the mysteries of the human mind is a common view, and it suggests that while Freud dismissed the occult as a load of superstitious rubbish, he wasn't particularly afraid of it. Yet an episode in his relationship with his erstwhile successor Carl Jung may suggest otherwise. We can call it "the curious incident of the poltergeist in Freud's bookcase."

During a visit to Vienna in 1909, Jung had a conversation with Freud about the new study of parapsychology. Freud dismissed the whole subject as nonsense, something Jung, who had had ample experience of it, could not accept. As the conversation grew heated, Jung, who wanted to keep relations with Freud cordial, found it difficult to hold back his feelings. After all, he had been chosen by Freud to inherit his throne, and he had great respect, even love for his mentor. But Jung also had his own genius and ambitions and found it difficult to toe the party line. Now, as he looked at Freud he felt his diaphragm glow, as if it was becoming red-hot. Suddenly a loud bang exploded in Freud's bookcase, and both men jumped up, afraid it would fall on them. Jung said to Freud "There, that is an example of a so-called catalytic exteriorisation phenomenon," Jung's long-winded circumlocution for a poltergeist or "noisy spirit." Freud retorted "Bosh!" Jung shook his head and predicted that another bang would soon follow. When it did, Freud looked at Jung "aghast," and from that moment on was mistrustful of him. Jung said the way Freud looked at him it was "as if I had done something against him."

Not long after this, again in Vienna, Jung again visited Freud, and he later recalled a peculiar conversation they had, during which Freud asked Jung to promise that he would never abandon the sexual theory of the origin of neurosis. Freud told Jung that they must make "a dogma of it, an unshakeable bulwark." Jung said that Freud spoke in the tones in which a father would ask his son to promise that he would go to church every Sunday. When Jung asked Freud why they had to affirm the sexual theory so vigorously, and against what they had to make it a bulwark, Freud replied "against the black tide of mud of occultism." By this time Jung knew that he could never assert the sexual theory with the same finality as Freud did. He already had reservations about it but had kept them to himself. This request to collaborate with him on erecting a dogma was a sign that these reservations would soon have to come out. As we know, they did.

Jung had grown up with the occult. As his autobiography *Memories, Dreams,*

Reflections shows, his family was steeped in it. His mother, grandmother, and other relatives attended séances regularly. Jung himself attended many, drawing from them the material for his doctoral dissertation *On the Psychology and Pathology of So-Called Occult Phenomena.* Jung's mother spoke in voices and his cousin frequently "channelled" departed relatives. Jung himself experienced a period of "split personality," in which as an adolescent he would find his psyche being taken over by what he called Personality No. 2, an austere masterful older gentleman of the eighteenth century.

Throughout much of his career Jung played his occult cards close to his chest and minimised his public appreciation of it. It was only in his last decades that he came out of the occult closet, as it were, and spoke openly about astrology, alchemy, spirits, synchronicity, and other occult or mystical subjects now associated with him. Yet those who knew him also knew that occult phenomena happened around him. Visitors to his hideaway at Bollingen remarked that when Jung was deep in thought, the pots and pans would rattle, and at his home in Küsnacht, the furniture and woodwork would creak, evidence of what one guest called his "exteriorized libido." There is every reason to believe that when Jung tells us his diaphragm got red-hot, with the inference that it then somehow caused the bang in Freud's bookcase, he is telling the truth.

Freud at least thought so. At the time of the poltergeist in his bookcase, Freud admitted to being strangely moved by the experience and there is reason to believe that he felt that Jung had somehow made it happen. This was perhaps why he looked at Jung "aghast" and took the "catalytic exteriorization phenomenon" personally. Yet after Jung returned to Switzerland, Freud soon reverted to type. He quickly reduced Jung's "exteriorized libido" to simple imagination. In a letter to Jung, Freud explained that "the phenomenon was soon deprived of all significance for me" and his "readiness to believe vanished along with *the spell of your personal presence* [my italics]." While Jung was there, the sceptical, hard-nosed Freud was somehow moved enough to accept that Jung could have been right. But with Jung gone, Freud snapped out of it, and got to work explaining the incident in purely rational terms.

Freud's emotional investment in Jung as his chosen successor may have accounted for the mistrust he began to feel toward Jung after the incident. It may also explain why Freud asked Jung to, in effect, take a loyalty oath. But was there more than this? Did Freud mistrust Jung because he recognized that he somehow possessed the kinds of powers that Freud so easily dismissed? Without his presence, Jung's "mana" faded, and Freud could easily convince himself that nothing had happened. But with Jung around this was not so easy.

Jung replied to Freud's letter, apologizing for his "spookery," yet at the same time he affirmed it as an expression of what he called a "special complex" associated with the "prospective tendencies in man;" he spoke about this in a way that seems to presage his later ideas about synchronicity, or "meaningful coincidence." Jung also told Freud that his "spookery" helped him get rid of a father complex he had toward Freud. He then goes on to talk about the "objective effect of the prospective tendency," by which he means its ability to arrange events in the outside world. If for "objective effect of the prospective tendency" we read "the mind" – which in plain English is what Jung means – we are talking about something occult indeed. Jung is saying that somehow, the human mind can arrange events in the outside world. Next to precognition, this has to be one of the strangest of all occult phenomena.

Freud himself had an experience of this. And it was precisely about this that he felt the strongest resistance.

Freud had an upbringing very different from Jung's and his attitude toward the supernatural was also very different. Although, as mentioned, Jung was circumspect about his occult interests throughout much of his career, he finally did speak openly about it, and in his last decades he became a very vocal advocate of various occult ideas. More than anyone else Jung, I think, is responsible for the widespread popular acceptance of occult, mystical, and paranormal ideas that has been with us since the 1960s. Jung even agreed with the hippies about the coming age of Aquarius, and the Beatles were his fans, as they were Aleister Crowley's.

Freud was never so forthright about his own occult interests, which he certainly had, all public dismissal of it notwithstanding. Even more than Jung, Freud kept the few occult interests he had very much to himself and shared them only with a small band of followers. He allowed himself only a few, very muted and unsatisfying expressions of his fascination with the "black tide of mud" that he wanted his crown prince to help him keep at bay.

Freud's writing on occultism make up a few papers and some remarks scattered here and there in other works. The best known of these writings is "Psychoanalysis and Telepathy." This paper was not published in Freud's lifetime – although the material did appear in some other places – and was first read at an informal gathering of Freud's closest followers in the Harz mountains in August 1921. Freud's other papers on the occult include "Dreams and Telepathy" (1922), "The Occult Significance of Dreams" (1925), and "Dreams and Occultism" (1937).

"Psychoanalysis and Telepathy" was originally supposed to report on three cases, but Freud told his select audience that in classic Freudian style his resistance to talking about the occult made him leave behind the material for one case – the most interesting one, in fact, which we will get to further on. So he was forced to work with other material. The paper begins with a note of paranoia. "We are not destined, so it seems," Freud told the faithful few, "to devote ourselves quietly to the extension of our science." Here Freud is referring to recent attacks on him by the apostates Jung and Adler. But they are not the only threat. It has come to Freud's attention of late that an association between psychoanalysis and occultism is being made in some quarters. He would rather not speak about this but it was no longer possible to avoid it.

There are, he admits, some superficial similarities between psychoanalysis and occultism. Yet while he recognizes that a study of occultism may be unavoidable – if only to clarify its differences from psychoanalysis – it can also have a damaging effect. Psychoanalysis should avoid being tarred with occultism's brush, and in order to do this Freud tells the faithful that he has even had to decline several offers to write for various magazines and journals specialising in the occult.

Freud then refers to Einstein's theory of relativity and the discovery of radium, remarking darkly that these developments in some way undermine "the objective trustworthiness of science." What Freud means is that these new developments were undermining the kind of science that Freud was comfortable with, namely the nineteenth century mechanistic kind which Einstein, radium, and quantum physics had by this time already made obsolete. Freud seems to be hinting that in some way, occultism is in league with Einstein and Madame Curie in a plot to overthrow the kind of cause and effect universe in which he felt at home.

Freud recognized that in the popular mind, psychoanalysis and occultism shared a certain opprobrium from conventional ways of thinking, and that both can be seen as aiming to widen and broaden this in the face of fierce resistance. They could in this sense be seen as fellow travellers. Yet while this is true there is an absolute fundamental difference between the two. Occultists, Freud says, place much trust in faith – although which occultists he had in mind and how they would respond to this remark we don't know. However, psychoanalysis, Freud continues, is motivated by "an extreme distrust of the power of human wishes and the temptation of the pleasure principle." Here we can say that Freud is advocating a "hermeneutic of suspicion" well in advance of the philosopher Paul Ricoeur's coining of that phrase. And indeed Freud is one the modern thinkers, along with Marx and Nietzsche, on whom Ricoeur based the idea.

Unlike faith-besotted occultists, analysts, Freud told his own faithful, are fundamentally "incorrigible mechanists and materialists." They study the occult so to "finally exclude the wishes of mankind from material reality." If they attended to occult phenomena, rather than ignoring or denying them, it "would mean surrendering the impartiality, lack of prejudice and prepossessions" that make up their "analytical armour."

Even worse, if they attend to occult phenomena, analysts would soon see they actually did happen. Psychoanalysis would then be involved in a practice that proved the reality of the occult. We must take note here. Freud is saying to his closest confederates that occult phenomena are real. They do occur. But knowing this, psychoanalysis must not in any way assist in this truth being revealed. It must even ignore what it knows to be true and do its best to *maintain the opposite*. It must do this because if occult phenomena were revealed to be true, this would have a damaging effect on the populace. It would, in effect, make them weak-minded – something, we should note, that some critics of psychoanalysis accused it of doing itself.

For Freud, admitting the reality of occult phenomena would "extend belief in whatever explanation and to those easiest and most to their [the public's] taste." If we accept that telepathy or clairvoyance are true, what's next? Angels and devils? Relativity and radium are already breaking windows in Newton's universe. Do we really want to break more? No, we must remain steadfast, and form a bulwark of nineteenth century rationalism. Occultism is bad because it panders to our credulity. It is "joyfully acclaimed by all the credulity lying ready to hand since the infancy of the human race and the childhood of the individual." As far as Freud is concerned, credulity is something to avoid. But if occultism is true, as Freud suggests, how can it be credulous to believe in it?

But never mind such quibbles. They pale in comparison to the threat waiting in the wings, namely the "fearful collapse of critical thought, of determinist standards and of mechanistic science," that would result if the truth about the occult were to be told. For Freud, accepting the reality of the occult would mean the end of the world as he knew it, and he was not giving up without a fight.

In many ways Freud's fear in the face of the occult is similar to the reaction to it of other severe rationalists, such as the neo-Marxist philosopher Theodore Adorno and, oddly enough, the horror fiction writer H. P. Lovecraft. Freud would agree with Adorno's characterization of occultism as the "metaphysics of dunces" and that its embrace signalled a "flight from reason" in the historian of the occult James Webb's famous phrase. It marked a regression in critical thinking and kept the populace happy with astral bread and circuses. Although he was the author of several classic horror tales, many of which employ various occult devices, H. P. Lovecraft maintained a ferocious materialist view of the world, denying in fact the metaphysical terrors that he created in fiction. Like Freud he believed that too much knowledge about the occult can be a bad thing, as the protagonists of many of his tales discover to their woe. As his letters show, Lovecraft preferred Adler to Freud, but he agreed with him that too much knowledge is dangerous and knowledge of the occult is the most dangerous of all. They both would agree with T. S. Eliot's dour dictum that "humankind cannot bear too much reality."

Yet while Freud warned against a public affirmation of the occult, in private he hit a different note, saying his interest, though genuine, was "personal," like his cigars and his Jewishness, and had nothing to do with psychoanalysis. It was a kind of hobby. This double think clearly indicates a profound ambivalence, one he feared and sought to resolve through sheer force of dogma. We can see this ambivalence in his writings. As his daughter Anna remarked, "the subject fascinated, as well as repelled him." His biographer Ernst Jones said that Freud enjoyed telling stories of strange coincidences and mysterious voices, and that these things had a hold on him. Freud once even "propitiated the gods" by sacrificing one of his cherished antiques, when his daughter Malthide was ill. If Freud's own "credulity" was enough for him to make an offering to supernatural powers in order to secure his daughter's health, we must agree that between his public and private relation to the occult there was a profound dissonance, even more than in the case of Jung.

This ambivalence can be found in Freud's other occult writings. In "Dreams and Telepathy," Freud tells us that we will not learn anything about telepathy in the paper, not even whether he believes in it or not. He had, in fact, no opinion on it, one way or another, which might suggest to an unsympathetic reader that he should not have bothered to write it. Yet in 1925, a few years after announcing his diffidence toward telepathy in this paper, Freud and Anna conducted "informal" telepathic experiments. According to Peter Gay, another biographer of Freud, their exact nature is unknown but they had something to do with hunting for mushrooms. Yet, even after this Freud advised Sandor Ferenczi not to read a paper on these experiments to an upcoming psychoanalytical congress.

Freud, it seems, could not let the occult go, but neither could he embrace it seriously, in the way that Jung did. He did a neurotic two step with it, indulging his interest, but then declaring that it was fundamentally unimportant and not necessary for psychoanalysis. Unlike Freud, Jung brought the occult into his work, or rather, his work grew out of it. Where Freud wanted to plug a hole in the psyche's dam, so that the muddy tide of the occult would not leak through, Jung not only pulled his finger out, he positively knocked down the dyke. The Oedipal agon doesn't get more serious than this.

"Dreams and Telepathy" was read to another gathering of a select few. In it Freud relates two cases of fortune telling – precognition – which did not come true. He tells us his attitude toward the cases is "unenthusiastic and ambivalent," and that he is "disagreeably affected" by them. He relates the cases "under the pressure of the greatest resistance." And he concludes that "nothing can be done against such clear resistance." What was Freud resisting?

I think he was resisting synchronicity. This becomes clear, I think, if we look at the case Freud left out of his paper on "Psychoanalysis and Telepathy," given to his inner circle in the Harz Mountains, having conveniently left his notes about it behind. In psychoanalysis, resistance is a sign that the patient is unwilling to talk about something. Why was Freud unwilling to talk about this case?

It concerned a patient Freud was seeing during a fallow period following the First World War. Freud had agreed to see Herr P., but only on a limited basis, and it was clear to Herr P. that Freud was not that interested in him and that once Freud's practice picked up again, he would terminate the analysis. Herr P., we can assume, was not happy with this arrangement, but Freud would not budge and Herr P. was forced to accept what he could get. One day, just before Herr P.'s session, Freud received a message that his British disciple David Forsyth had arrived in Vienna and was eager to catch up. Freud would have seen him immediately, had it not been for Herr P. But he couldn't cancel his appointment, and so he told Forsyth that he would see him when Herr P. had left.

At Herr P.'s next session, suddenly out of the blue he started to tell Freud about a woman he knew who used to call him "Herr Vorsicht." *Vorsicht* in German means caution or, as it is in English, "foresight." Freud was struck by the coincidence of his patient telling him that he was once called Herr Vorsicht, or "Mr. Foresight," when Freud was happy to have renewed his contact with his own Mr. Forsyth. The similarity in sound of "foresight" and Forsyth seemed remarkable, as was the fact that Herr P. had never mentioned his strange nickname before, and had done so only after Freud's own Mr. Forsyth had turned up. Herr P., of course, did not know of Freud's British student and the coincidence of Freud's student arriving and his patient claiming to, in effect, have the same name as him, was, to say the least remarkable. We can say that Herr Vorsicht displayed a strange foresight about Mr. Forsyth.

Freud believed that Herr P. had somehow intuited that Freud was happy about Forsyth's arrival, which marked the end of the fallow time following the war and the return of his foreign students, and was impatient with having to continue treating him. Herr P. already knew that he was, in Freud's eyes, really only "second best," and in order to secure Freud's attention, he transformed himself into his own Mr. Forsyth, in effect saying to Freud, "Don't neglect me. I am a Forsyth too." Strangely, Herr P. had earlier introduced Freud to the work of the novelist John Galsworthy, specifically the novels of his *Forsyte Saga*.

In Jung's case, this would have counted as a classic example of synchronicity, that is, the "acausal connecting principle" at work in "meaningful coincidence," accounts of which can be found in many places in Jung's work. Freud too believed that something more than coincidence was at work in this case, but he preferred to rationalize this as an effect of the transference going on between himself and the unfortunate Herr. P. Freud indulges in some word juggling, but in the end he accepted that some kind of "thought transference" between himself and Herr P. must have taken place. But Freud was so troubled by this that he terminated the analysis shortly after Herr P.'s "Forsyth" episode – no doubt something that Herr Vorsicht himself must have foreseen.

That Freud mislaid the notes for this story suggests, as Freud said himself, a profound resistance to it. Its subsequent history adds to this. The original notes were missing for some time. In 1933 a definitive text was finally put together, but it would not be published until 1941, two years after Freud's death. The original copy of this version also went missing until 2010. That Freud mislaid material for what seems a remarkable case, and then for the text of the talk to also go missing for decades, suggests that something very powerful was at work here, *repressing* what for Freud must have been a very uncomfortable thought. I suggest that the poltergeist in Freud's bookcase, revealed or introduced by his one-time heir apparent Carl Jung, so shook the revered master that for the rest of his life, he was always a little frightened of the occult.

REFERENCES

–⚬– Theodore Adorno, "Theses Against Occultism" http://www.autodidactproject.org/other/adornocc.html
–⚬– Sigmund Freud, *Collected Works Vol. XVIII* (London: Hogarth Press, 1975)
–⚬– Peter Gay, *Freud: A Life For Our Time* (London: Little Books, 2006)
–⚬– Marsha Aileen Hewitt, *Freud on Religion* (New York: Routledge, 2014)

—⁓— Carl Jung, *Memories, Dreams, Reflections* (London: Flamingo Paperbacks, 1989)
—⁓— Gary Lachman, *Jung the Mystic* (New York: Tarcher/Penguin, 2010)
—⁓— H. P. Lovecraft, *Selected Letters I* (Sauk City, WI: Arkham House, 1965)

Fly the Light

Peter Grey

The occult is traditionally seen by its practitioners as an art of shadows, their calling, casting, conversation and compulsion. From figures on the cave wall, to goetic ritual and necromantic enquiry, the shade has been our constant companion. Yet our companions have been anathematised, and so too have those of us who continue to traffic with them (in that descriptor I include psychoanalysts). I will argue that the shadow itself is being entirely excised in late capitalist culture, and to make the counter assertion that it is in casting shadows and the practice of the occult arts that we are most complete. Occultists have consistently developed strategies to negotiate the unseen worlds, but these have a consistent physiological basis that has been steadily eroded by the mono-culture and neglected by modern practitioners.

Jung writes, 'One does not become enlightened by imagining figures of light, but by making the darkness conscious. The latter procedure, however is disagreeable, and therefore not popular.' (CG Jung, *Alchemical Studies* 265–266). Such an unpopular procedure is the hallmark of the eldritch realms of both psychoanalysis and the occult. The shadow is the unconscious, the devil with whom we must engage in conjunction. It is what we fear and despise both in ourselves and as a culture. So we share common ground. But magic is wary of psychoanalysis, and with good reason. One does not have to be Foucault to realise that psychoanalysis can be seen as part of the continuum of control mechanisms of state, church, school, factory, hospital and prison; a device for producing and replicating compliant and well adjusted workers. In a witchcraft context, it is a descendant of the inquisition relying on the testimony of women in particular to articulate its script.

Our 'cure' includes the performative and ritual aspect that psychoanalysis for the most part lacks, and we are, for the most part, both literate traditions with our jargons and procedures, and our preoccupation with making the darkness visible. We have in fact more points of agreement than either side have acknowledged, our shadows have been dancing together, even if psychoanalysis once sought to exorcise us in search of credibility. We could in fact be described as the shadow of psychoanalysis. Indeed, James Hillman wrote in 1976, 'Some people in desperation have turned to witchcraft, magic and occultism, to drugs and madness, anything to rekindle imagination and find a world ensouled, [...] But these reactions are not enough. What is needed is a revisioning, a fundamental shift of perspective out of that soulless predicament we call modern consciousness.' I see no fundamental reason why our living ensouled magical world, for which we have a tradition and battery of techniques, is not the very answer that Hillman sought, though I am mindful that much of occultism remains as reactive, immature and ill-starred as the culture which cradles it. Psychoanalysis, like Prospero, must ultimately accept Caliban, and Shakespeare gives the simple ritual formula required: 'This thing of darkness I acknowledge mine.'

If we are looking for a statement of intent in shadow work, then this is the one to employ, and perhaps a worthy statement of intent for this conference.

Jung writes, 'Everyone carries a shadow, and the less it is embodied in the individual's conscious life, the blacker and denser it is.' (CG Jung, 1940 *CW* 11: para 131) It appears as a rupture, a criminality, a mark of the primitive and less ideal man, an idea that is contiguous with Kristeva's semiotic, which '… contains childish or primitive qualities which would … vitalise and embellish human existence, but convention forbids!' I observe here that the dense shadow of the occult is finding ever darker expression. There is a tendency to fall in thrall to the rejected aspect and transfer our loyalty to it. Our goal is not to be subsumed by the shadow, but to be able to employ it at our bidding. As Jung observed, 'A man who is possessed by his shadow is always standing in his own light and falling into his own traps.'

Ours then is a difficult task, the navigation of threshold states in the pursuit of power. I purposefully do not say knowledge, or self-realisation which may occur as side effects, but power which is the aim of our practice. The site of that enquiry is to be located in the body, which is ever partaking at the threshold of life and death, constructed of a patina of shadow and light.

THE BODY OF SURFACES

Michael Maier in *Atalanta Fugiens*, his alchemical emblem book, states in Epigraph 45, 'The Sun and its shadow complete the work.' It is a quote taken in turn from Aureus, and the even more shadowy Hermes Trismegistus who advises 'extract from the ray its shadow.' Jung too describes the shadow as the necessary component of a three-dimensional body. It is an observation drawn from lived physical experience which opens up the possibility of a revived occult practice.

The human body is a gnomon, the shadow placing us in time and space. By reading the shadow we know both who and where we are in relation to the light. The shadow revolves with the cosmic dance. The body is not a standing stone, but articulates a range of contrasting meanings, of stories and deceptions. It is a dynamic form which the practitioner must learn to manipulate, or is manipulated by.

The shadow is one way that we can communicate with the subtle intelligences in a dynamic exchange. However, my contention is that in the digital age the shadow has been excised, and deliberately so.

The seeming aim of late capitalist culture is to produce what I call the body of surfaces. By which I mean the virtual body, that by definition, can cast no shadow.

It is untethered from the relationship with light and shade that the body affords and that the heavens enact. In alchemical terms it partakes of no natural processes, meaning that it is entirely inert. Nor is such a body entitled to a shadow in the panopticon of the modern world where it is lit from every direction.

We are becoming a screen for images projected onto us and our increasingly barren environment; there is simply no shadow play possible in the digital sensorium. The old TOPY proverb states, 'our enemies are flat,' but so too are we and our supposed 'friends.' Our dreams are constructed for us by algorithms and become indistinguishable from our ever diminished waking state that is fractured into compliance by our addiction to the demands and small rewards of the simulacra. Subtlety is lost in blank text, the banality of gifs and crass emoticons: the shadows have been swiped away.

Therefore, the first paradoxical action in approaching the shadow is to recognise the body, a problem that neither Jung nor Freud faced. The body itself has become the shadow, and it has both waned and bloated. As a society we are skinny fat, presenting a form to the digital world that looks ideal but which is on the other side of the screen, diseased, depressed, degenerate and poverty stricken.

We witness the loss of the body, and this reflects the changing shape of capitalism, with robotisation set to permanently destroy many jobs not just driving, manual and factory work but the professions too. This erasure of the body is achieved in a destruction of differences that accomplish the triumph of the mono-culture. It is a step towards our bio-obsolescence as production units or sources of value. The body is already surplus to requirements, unless you desire to utilise its occult or creative powers. Magic and analysis may soon be the only tasks that computing cannot perform!

Much of our social life is relegated to the artificial world, which undeniably enables connection, but never consummation, for which we require shadows and flesh and place. This will be the next revolution, as presaged politically by Occupy and the Nuit debout and magically in the witchcraft revival. The most radical use of the internet is as a way to coordinate the movement of bodies into physical space. (This conference is a further demonstration of that possibility). We categorically do not need more information, we need context, and that context is the three-dimensional body as explored through the shadow arts.

Above all, the occult requires a renewed physical practice, of the restorative movement patterns, and an attention to diet and the breath; psyche. These are now largely the province of the high resonance narcissists of the New Age and the immortalist corporate high achievers. There has been an almost total loss of physical culture in the occult and in broader paganism. Witchcraft, it must be remembered, was once identical to anathematised forms of dance whether La Volta, the Sarabande or more rustic revels. Shadows are by their nature not fixed, but flicker and dance.

I state categorically that the realm of the flesh is the realm of the shadow. In a Christian sense, matter is an illusory form that clothes the Holy Spirit. That has an exact parallel in digital culture where the body is a 'meatsack' and the digital identity is where truth is to be sought. Mine then is a strictly Satanic conception, a return to the body and a return to the world as the site of being. Such a view of occult anatomy does not launch straight into a collection of spheres or paths, belts, wheels and sheaths but asks that we begin with the body itself in relation to place.

The occult has failed in seeking after a magical body, the shadow which it has not been able to relate to the physical body which casts it. Such a fundamental error is magnified by digital culture, a status game played without any requirement to demonstrate proofs by a dislocated populace whose starting point is an alienation from the corporeal. A questioning of reality and the necessary introspection that typifies an occult awakening all too often involves a rejection of physical culture and the world. I repeat, the body is the site of power. I am not suggesting that such an occult body needs to conform to a Greek ideal – often initiation is the result of sickness, often occult power is exhibited by the deeply hurt – but it can best be expressed if we put movement in our lives and practice, and if we become adept at navigating the boundary states.

One could propose that ritual is accomplished by dance, sound and sign making; all attributes and extensions of the dynamic body that with intent and training can project further into shadow as 'occult power.' The mimetic dance with the chiral symmetry of the cast shadow is pivotal to this. These are perhaps our oldest forms of ritual.

Shadow play, strategies and ritual

How then can sorcerers, whose art is precisely that of the shadow, work with this most ephemeral and enduring of forms? What strategies and ritual responses are to be employed in order to destroy the tyranny of the body of surfaces? We must, as Jung describes, repossess the shadow as the necessary component of a three-dimensional body.

Though I have talked about the body as shadow, the shadow in turn reveals the body, and the intent concealed within the form. We often consider the aura of an individual, but the shadow also speaks. Witchcraft can be employed as an art of drawing the shadow out of something, of revealing that which is being concealed from a client by themselves, or that which is being deliberately kept from us. In traditional witchcraft the shadow is vulnerable to injury and death, so if our shadows have been abducted, we must find them again, along with secrecy, agency and discretion. In working with the demonised forms of sexuality, the drives and the demons, we allow the shadow to manifest and to grow longer darker and more solid. The more antinomian forms of the occult that I mentioned at the start of my talk can therefore be considered as a vital coagulation.

Furthermore, the shadow can provide a counter magic or lay a curse upon the prevailing doctrine. The living shadow can disrupt the hierarchy (or ratio) of the senses. Rather than meditating on the candle we can meditate on the shadow, rather than adoring the sun or moon, we can turn our attention to what they cast; we can thus engage in a series of deliberate inversions that take our existing ritual modalities and make them three dimensional. We can transform the way we are in the world and be conscious and present practitioners of magic. There is almost never a need to add novel methods to occult practice, but rather to discover the depths in that which we already do. Even the finest line of shadow promises to open a breach through which magic will pour.

Marshall McLuhan recognised that, 'Sense ratios change when any one sense or bodily or mental function is externalised in technological form.' If digital media has, as I argue, fundamentally disrupted the sensorium, then I posit the shadow as the corrective. The shadow disrupts proportion: it is as plastic as Alice; it is, to pun in the manner of McLuhan, ir-*ratio*-nal. It magnifies and projects our power, out of proportion to our apparent size; this is an essential element in any strategy of asymmetric conflict. I suggest that the irrational disruption of witchcraft, and the radical decentralisation of the rhizomatic coven is a way of rediscovering our totality and escaping the sensory isolation wrought by the digital. Such forces of irrationality can be dangerous or healing. I say choose your poison, that of the spreading of shadows, or the cowled compliance of an oculus rift headset.

We do not need to accept Marc Prensky's concept of 'Digital Natives,' and consign voices of technological dissent to the box marked 'luddite,' or the even worse crimes in our culture: out of fashion and old. Instead we recognise that it is precisely the youth who are being betrayed, and that we as nomads, whether we are wanderers or have been displaced, must use our *techne* to abscond from the enclosed digital commons and gather instead upon the heath. A community of living shadows.

A magician knows that when you are being shown something – the function of the body of surfaces – it is because something else is being concealed. A trick, a prestige, from *praestringere* – to blunt the sight or mind. What is being concealed is the ultimate illusion, the removal of the world itself and its living systems. Thus we need to be adept at finding the shadow, realising where it is being hidden from sight. We are not only practitioners of magic, we are victims of it; that is, until we have stitched the discomforting shadows back onto our world. As a result, we cannot consider the dark web as the shadow of the internet, as it functions in the same way, namely as a marketplace that annuls the body. If we want to consider a shadow of the internet, it is to be found in the industrial architecture of servers and machines built and maintained with devastating environmental costs.

We live in quite the opposite to an era of *apocalypsis*, of revealing; we live in a redacted media culture peopled by reflections and opposed by solitary martyrs. More information will not save us from it; context and the body in action will. Mine is a corporeal witchcraft. It is the shadow's fluidity, its refusal to adhere to the form, to cross boundaries, that brings our attention to the occulted nature of being and what it means to be human. Ultimately I propose creating a libidinal breach, as the shadow is the realm of the erotic, and eros triumphs over thanatos. The calligraphic shadow is liberated when the written word is performed, the shadows reveal to us that we exist in relation to a cosmic dance in a realm more pliable than rational approaches can ever admit. We do not fly the light, as our detractors contend, but are truly creatures of light and darkness.

Proclaim Present Time Over

Val Denham

'Proclaim present time over.' I stole the title from William Burroughs' short piece in a paperback book called *The Award Avant-Garde Reader* (1965, ed. Gil Orlovitz, Maynard & Miles). I don't feel too much guilt about stealing such a great title because Uncle Bill stole it from Brion Gysin, who in turn probably stole it from me in the future.

Now please do bear with me. Some of what I am about to say will not immediately make sense, but keep listening and I'll explain soon why I've written like this at the beginning of my piece.

So what does 'Proclaim present time over' mean? Well, I'm not certain, but for me it means to continually state, "This moment is NOW." To awake from the dream for a second and realise that one is dreaming. We are all dreaming all the time, not just in sleep, but even when awake. We cannot keep continual awareness of the present because it moves too fast. Time as part of the fourth dimension of space-time is travelling at one hundred and eighty six thousand miles per hour or the speed of light. We are hurtling very fast towards our death. The instant we grasp the notion of 'this is now' it is gone, over, already in the past. So we cope with this enigma of speeding time by dreaming 24 hours a day. I'm not here; neither are you. We are atoms, molecules, each one the size of a cathedral held in place by electrons flying around protons and neutrons at the speed of light. Stardust from the Big Bang. Art does not exist – it is merely God dreaming – Proto-Deist Poetry embalmed in sub-atomic structures as divine alchemical recordings – inanimate objects lost in time and space. Does a chair think? Can a table love? Does the carpet feel sad?

Perhaps consciousness could be a form of DNA circuit board inherent in the unknown soul of art? The richest soul implantations that ask is art alive? Art does not exist.

Cassette recordings lying dormant as soul maps in paintings that only communicate when viewed in the past or the future – there is no present. The Universe itself is so eager to be known. The evolution of the species since the Big Bang that one day will ask questions – such as what is the Universe? Why are we here?

Dark energy exploding out from the singularity of the Big Bang as gravitationally suspended invisible spider webs hold and pull the Universe into order.

Consciousness is an energy that must remain in the Universe until the Big Crunch.

Dark consciousness as a constant energy. Dark love and dark hate. "May the force be with you" may not be as silly as we imagined.

Nothing is stationary because all atoms are forever dancing. Perhaps inanimate objects retain a memory. Art is haunted. Art has a soul.

In these rational atheist times of logic and science, why do we need to demolish houses where murders have taken place? Is it buried deep within the human psyche that stones, bricks, furniture, wallpaper can record negative energy and become toxic or somehow tainted with memory?

If you own a painting then you own a fraction of the artist. It has got a bit of the artist's essence inside its atomic structure. The artist is aware when work attains a soul. It becomes conscious at a sub atomic level, and possibly on a Universal level. Serotonin paths and connections reflect the dark matter and dark energy of the Universe. Everything is birth and death – yin and yang. Our Universe was born from the death of the previous Universe, when that previous Universe was crushed into a singularity, an impossible situation made by the dark energy in the previous Universe collecting together so many black holes that it formed the ultimate black hole of a Big Crunch. The result of that Big Crunch was that matter was squashed into no space at all and was then spewed out in reverse at the other side of the black hole, and that, well that was our Big Bang. So the Universe as we know it is only the recent one, to us anyway.

So why have I told you all this? And why have I told you it in this strange manner? I have done so because this is the information hidden deep within my subconscious. My brain told me all this stuff one night as I was washing up. I wrote it up just afterwards, letting go and letting the thoughts tumble unedited out of my head. So that part of this talk represents subconscious writing or subconscious thinking.

Dreams make us creative. We dream when we are awake; this is particularly true of creatives. Everyone is aware of dreams being wish fulfillment, so to create art, poetry, stories, paintings, film, plays and music etc. it is necessary to dream awake. We all balance our fore-conscious and our subconscious every day; we need our intuition to guide us. Every audience for every medium also brings their subconscious to bear too. For example, with every novel and radio play each member of the audience uses their own dreaming to create the pictures that close the circle between the artist and themselves. This is important; art is interactive.

In certain individuals, particularly creatives, the balance is in favour of the subconscious, the predominant mechanism of new forms of reason. An example might be me mixing a certain colour accurately with hardly any thought – my subconscious manifesting as intuition born of long experience. It allows me to know how to mix any given colour I need. The information is innate. Likewise a painting or work of art is wish fulfillment, even if when we think back to the Renaissance for example, it is the patron or commissioner's wish that is being fulfilled by the artist and his workshop. The wish fulfillment in regards to the paintings I make goes something like this. Born of my subconscious I see the completed painting in my mind and I wish that it existed. I make it so by using my analytical fore-conscious in combination with my natural artistic subconscious reasoning.

I believe that sometimes my subconscious mind can remind me in my dreams to create future artworks that I am unaware of as yet. Here is a good example.

First though here is the memory on which it is based. I briefly met a book shop owner in 2004 in Cartmel, Cumbria, when I was on my honeymoon. He was very memorable as he was an eccentric, ancient, like a huge Churchill and he was just entering the eighteenth year of an engagement to his lady love. He was sat at his desk near the front of his shop and was working his way through several sandwiches. I rummaged around the books for ages. We got chatting to the owner and he said to my wife and me, "Look at this, I can't even sell this because it's not Politically Correct."

It was a little book called *The Story of Little Black Sambo.*

"You can have it," he said. Its front cover was missing and I use it as a tea mat by my bedside nowadays. Anyway that's the bit that really did happen.

Now, for the actual dream, which I can still remember quite clearly. I had this dream in 2010. I was in a chaotic bric-a-brac shop and the proprietor of it was the book shop owner that we had met in Cartmel. In the dream I examine the vases in his second hand junk shop, but don't see anything spectacular, and then my eyes were drawn to the only CD album in the shop because of its simple red, yellow and black cover. I picked it up and it had a joyous looking cover, with an anachronistic kind of Art Deco woman's profile on it; her hair was blown by a breeze, her face was bright yellow and the background was red. There was one word written in her hair, 'MAD'. I was intrigued to know who did the album of songs, so I flipped it over and was surprised to find that the artist was myself, Val Denham. I was so excited to find a whole album of songs that I'd written that I didn't know existed. I asked the huge proprietor the price.

"It's fifty pounds" he said.

"Why is it so expensive?" I wanted to know.

"Because the cover is hand-painted and there are only 23 copies" he replied. Having insufficient funds, I waited in my dream until the proprietor had his back to me and I then I put the CD under my coat and stole it as I wanted it so much. I couldn't wait to hear it, but I woke up at this point and I was so disappointed that I hadn't heard a single note of this mysterious album.

Now, I'm going to stop recounting the dream there, as I'm sure you know where this is going. I made that CD exactly as I dreamt about it, right down to it being an edition of 23 with painted covers. It took several months to make, but they all went in one week. Incidentally one of the tracks is called *Hey Sigmund Freud* and another is called *Black Hole.*

In 2006 I was asked to paint an image for the cover of Black Sun Productions' double CD album *The Impossibility of Silence.* I asked the boys what they had in mind. Their response was, "It's up to you Val; you'll come up with something good."

So I slept on it and I had a dream that the cover was of giant boys of different colours reclining in the hills of Yorkshire. I have a track on the album called *Yorkshire Hills.* The giant boys were naked with figs in place of their heads. The Sun was eclipsed by a black spider like star. I painted this image more or less exactly as I saw it in my dream. Now my dream is locked in time on that cover as long as a copy of it exists.

Dreams can tell us so much; they can be psychic premonitions or mysterious divinations, remote internal supernatural visualizations of places and events that we have never even seen or experienced. One example of this dates from the late 1970s when I came to live in London so as to attend The Royal College of Art. It was Christmas 1979, and I went back to Leeds to visit my parents. My mother told me that she'd had a dream in which she had followed me into my art college. In her dream she was invisible and I was completely unaware of her presence. She followed a few yards behind me as I walked. She described the building at the back of a big museum, she described going through an arched doorway and up wide stone steps and up to a uniformed Scottish man who sat behind glass in a kiosk. She described how I signed in a big book there and how I made the Scottish man laugh with one of the different silly voices I greeted him with each day. She told me that I turned left through a door and then went right along a big long corridor which was painted all white, then up a narrow staircase to the top where a studio was with big skylight windows in its ceiling. She described the big long desk I used and the boy with glasses that I sat next to. I was astonished by her dream and the more I questioned her about it I discovered it was completely accurate. My Mother had never been to London at this point in her life. I told her that what she'd seen was accurate and her response was:

"I know," she said. "I just needed to see where you were".

A further example is when I was a child, I would sometimes experience nightmares, something which may be frequent in childhood as children try to work out how to deal with everyday fears. One such nightmare I had was so extreme that I have never forgotten it. In the dream I found that my parents had gone out somewhere leaving me alone in the house at night. I decided I should go to bed and I turned the light switch on at the bottom of the stairs, but the bulb was dead. There was very little light and the top of the stairs; it was very dark. I felt anxious and began to panic. To my horror, I saw a young boy, a teenager, walking down the stairs towards me. He moved slowly. He was all white. His face was white, but around his eyes were black corpse like smudges with his eyes unblinking. His hair was stuck out as if he was filled with electricity. His hair was white too and he was very thin indeed. I was afraid he was dead. He came very close to me and reached out his hand to touch me. At this point in the dream I awoke screaming and my parents ran into my bedroom to comfort me. It took a long time to calm me down after that particular nightmare as I was distraught. I thought on this dream for a long time afterwards.

Then, when I was nineteen the dream came true. One Friday night I had been out in Bradford with my friends from the Art College. We had been to our usual late night venue called "Macs", just down the road from the College. I was very wild in those days and I didn't even bother with taxis home, but simply ran from Bradford to my home in Leeds. I would run like the comic book character *The*

Flash, and when I did arrive home it would be so late that I was careful not to wake my parents, especially my Father, who I didn't get on with at that time. I would carefully unlock the door and creep upstairs to wash my face and get ready for bed. I didn't need to switch any lights on that particular night as there was a full moon which lit the bathroom and landing. I went to the sink in front of the bathroom window, there was a mirror hung from the frame. I looked up from where I'd bent over the sink to brush my teeth and caught sight of my reflection. I was absolutely horrified. The moonlight on my face made it appear white, my make-up had smudged blackly around my eyes, my blonde hair was stuck up in all directions from my run and also appeared white. I was very thin too at that age, anorexic actually. I realised that I, at 19, on this night, was the phantom from my childhood nightmare. I was my own ghost all along. I had simply seen the future me when I was a child. I went bed and I dreamt. I dreamt that I was walking slowly down the stairs of my childhood home and that at the bottom of the stairs was a very scared little boy with blond hair. I wanted to comfort him. I just wanted to hold his hand and tell him not to be frightened, that everything was fine as it was only a dream, but as I went to placate him, I awoke.

One final example of how dreams can bend time and space. Dreams are wish fulfillments. I continued to live in London when I graduated from the Royal College of Art and when I was coming towards the end of my rocky first marriage, which was around the time of the Millennium, I had a lovely dream about being back in Yorkshire. In that dream I was sat on a bench in summertime with the sparkly stars of reflected sunlight dancing on the calm water of Chellow Dene Reservoir in Bradford. I was sat holding hands with my first girlfriend Gail Shackleton. She'd been the first girlfriend I'd ever had when I was seventeen years old and we were at Bradford Art College together. I woke from the dream with an exquisite ethereal feeling of nostalgia for happier times. One day that scene also became reality. I did sit on that bench, it was summer, the sun was out and the water sparkled and I was holding hands with Gail once more. We've been together again for fifteen years this summer and married for twelve of those.

The two sides of reality, dreaming and being awake, the fore-conscious and the subconscious, age and youth, love and hate require balance, yin and yang and in my own case, male and female. In my dreams I am often, but by no means always, male. This doesn't disturb me in the least as I find it so interesting and I know that it is a psychological balancing mechanism that I need. I enjoy going to bed and the warm and cosy drift into sleep. The twilight where I'm neither awake nor asleep, but lie somewhere on the border of both states. It induces a drugged feeling; a great sense of comfort takes hold of me.

When I dream I am male I don't even look as I did when I presented as male. In my dreamscapes I am ultra-masculine, often bearded and with short hair. I flirt with attractive young women and often have sexual intercourse with them; I enjoy these dreams, and often find myself aroused. Strangely, if I fantasise during my waking hours then I am always a woman and imagine myself as subservient to a dominant man. When I dream I am female I dream I am younger than I am now; an attractive woman at the height of her desirability.

The other aspect of my psychological profile worth mentioning is that I have quite severe Obsessive Compulsive Disorder. One part of this is that I have extreme Koniophobia, which is the fear of dust. These problems manifest disturbingly often in my dreams with scenarios of plaster falling from walls, shit smeared on loo seats, wet carpets and layers of dust on surfaces that I have to clean. I dream of being at Art College often, even though it is thirty-four years since I was last in one. Often I dream it is the last day before I leave, so there is some sort psychological connection to this within me. Between Bradford and the Royal College I was a student for seven years, so perhaps leaving college was frightening to me as it meant I had to join the real world. Change makes me feel very insecure; I want everything to be the same forever, yet life is always about change.

Daily I am aware of fluctuations between my fore and my sub conscious. Another off-shoot of the O.C.D. is a very mild form of Tourette's syndrome. I get hooked on nonsensical phrases, words, odd noises and snatches of song and I am compelled to repeat them. It's very mild as it mostly takes place in the safety of our home. The interesting aspect of it is, for example, that I might start singing *Fly me to Moon* for no apparent reason as I wash up. I then make a game of it wondering why I sang that particular song, and there is always a reason. It's like join-the-dots. I may have seen a bee through the window, in search of pollen, a bee, a buzzy bee, Buzz Aldrin the second man on the Moon, so "Fly me to the Moon".

Every image I paint, every word I write, every song I compose has a very solid and logical foundation; it's just that I can't always see it. So what I do is trust myself. I trust that dialogue between my fore and sub conscious, between my sleep dreams and my awake dreams and I always follow my intuitions which are the instructions that my mind is giving me. If the reason for the particular set of instructions is unfathomable what does it matter? The unknowingness is like the mystery of the universe. What is magic other than undiscovered physics?

I have spoken mostly about artist creatives as that is my area of expertise. I do think though that what I've said applies across the whole of humanity. On the other side of my coin are the scientists, and I hope you see that without their dreamings, then many discoveries would never have been made. Scientists are logical creatives.

Finally, as it is the four hundredth anniversary year of Shakespeare's death I cannot resist quoting Prospero's most famous speech from *The Tempest*.

> Our revels now are ended. These our actors,
> As I foretold you, were all spirits, and
> Are melted into air, into thin air:
> And like the baseless fabric of this vision,
> The cloud-capp'd tow'rs, the gorgeous palaces,
> The solemn temples, the great globe itself,
> Yea, all which it inherit, shall dissolve,

And, like this insubstantial pageant faded,
Leave not a rack behind. We are such stuff
As dreams are made on; and our little life
Is rounded with a sleep.

– William Shakespeare, *The Tempest*, Act 4, scene 1, 148–158

REFERENCES

—∿— William S Burroughs
—∿— *Little Black Sambo*
—∿— *Mad*, CD album by Val Denham 2010
—∿— *The Impossibility of Silence*, by Black Sun's Productions 2006.
—∿— *The Flash*, DC Comics
—∿— *The Tempest*, by William Shakespeare

The Cut in Creation

Katelan Foisy & Vanessa Sinclair

So, to begin, we're going to pass around this oil. It's called the *Third Mind Blend* or *Third Mind Oil*. We are both practicing witches – we do things like create oils for the dead – and we decided to work on this oil from Brion Gysin's day of death to William S. Burroughs' day of death last year (2015). We each worked on our own oil separately and then, after Burroughs' day of death passed, we combined the two oils, creating the *Third Mind Blend*. The best thing to do is to use it on your third eye, a dab, but use it however you wish, or don't. It's up to you.

Also the other thing about our talks that is a little bit different than the other ones is if you have a question you are allowed to raise your hand and just say "Cut!" in the middle of our talk, and what that does is create a cut up of the talk itself, so each talk is unique to the audience.

But first, an invocation:

Operation rewrite... Maya... Maya... Illusion... Illusion. Do both seen while illustrate that precise confrontation to forget nothing and illustrate that Indeed, the final across thee world blow spiritual and physical come more creative and writers reason why the artistic world can't It's not sacred play with it – but we physical real challenge Of our universe I'll always be A word-man it's no calligraphy for closely. I'm quite sure someone I admire French prose. He's one of my favorites Thanks again. I look continues to unfold...

be the true self, her is situated in and matter, the by the passerby. Few know the clients become a master of your no fewer than a hundred it seems to work more where those who are structures us with Abraxas is "Why am I here? I am here because you are here... and let me quote to you young officers this phrase: 'No two minds ever come together without, thereby, creating a third, invisible, intangible force which may be likened to a third mind.' Who is the third person that walks beside you?"

sacrifice ourselves stop this cycle and anyway. Give me distant ancestors, active and concept of the state and co electro sexuality structures us with and breaking individual into history. The thrust is precipitated from manufactures for the sub- con This Another interest is that ov permutations and that transference tie relationships and then call me 3 years KEY IN DAY NIGHT changing her surroundings to it's no calligraphy for closely. I'm quite sure A spiral. A serpents Electricity and elementals. Atonal precedes the music lyrics I believe. When Cling to life our passioned flower representation of my spiritual and more why couldn't identity in a into which to become the moments, friends, cut up techniques. brought ab land of the the goal of perversion.

We live in a world of systems; of structure. We are raised to believe that this is inevitable, the natural order of things. Science proves it is so. But what happens when we start to question this order, dare to challenge it? And what would happen if we break it down, disassemble it, cut it up?

"The first step in re-creation is to cut the old lines that hold you right where you are sitting now," – William S. Burroughs, *The Third Mind* (1978).

The cut-up is aggregated in conventional life. It is in our speech, what we read, what we watch, how we watch it, and what we create. The cut is both physical and symbolic; a simple blink of an eye is a cut in itself: the cut between sight and darkness. The cut-up manifests itself through daily activities such as reading the newspaper – your eye is reading one article yet peripherally skimming the entire page. When reading or writing, you're bringing in other stimuli – you're bringing in sounds from the street, as well as sights, smells, and textures within the room. Memories and associations are brought up into your conscious awareness, and you integrate them with what you are doing now. This is time travel. You are not only bringing that memory up from the past into the present time, but also each and every time you have experienced that memory before. So, for example, if you're remembering something from 15 years ago, there is 15 years of remembering that memory and every single street corner you were on or situation you were in when you remembered it times before. These moments also provide opportunities where one can rewrite the memory, history, the narrative, altering it and thereby altering your waking reality as well.

The cut-up is integrated in the art of filmmaking, music, collage, dance, and every other art form. The cut-up is the act of living, each moment and memory a cut in time. The magic of the cut-up is that anyone can do it. You take a selection of writing, fold it in, cut it in four pieces or strips and pull at random. The act is a cut, and the coded messages will have special meaning to the cutter. The reader, however, will determine their own message from the cut-up.

Burroughs was adamant that we all need to be paying attention to what is around us all of the time. You might notice that you're reading about something and then will see something outside that reflects what you're reading. One type of experiment Burroughs lauded is called a color walk. When he would go out, he would choose a color beforehand and would look for everything along the way that was that color. He felt that this really defined and added detail to his writing. And this way, even if he took the same walk every day, he would find something different. He would be focused on a different color; there's going to be different cars passing by, different people walking down the street. Another exercise he would do was to go to a park or sit down somewhere and people watch, looking for intersections or connections. A lot of times he would run into someone that he didn't know and would note them as they caught his eye. Then, for example, he would jump on the train and see that person on the train, and then they would get off at the same stop. His theory was that we have to be paying attention to these things, because we are not going to notice the connections unless we are paying attention. He would not have noticed the synchronicities that are occurring if he hadn't noticed that particular person; the eye must be focused on detail.

This leads us to the concept of intersections. In an article written about David Bowie following his death, "Lessons in Time Travel: Intersections with the Starman," Foisy discusses the concept of intersections:

I remember her handwriting, blue pen turned to black marker as she scrawled the following sentence on sheets of lavender paper...

"The black candle is secretly providing the white candle with wax and wick. Eternally I may sleep. I don't want to Kate."

That was the last thing my cousin Holly wrote to me before she died, a poetic offering of what was to come. It crossed my mind as I first listened to the lyrics of Bowie's *Blackstar:*

In the villa of Ormen, in the villa of Ormen   Stands a solitary candle, ah-ah, ah-ah   In the centre   of it all, in the centre of it all   Your eyes

This is what William S. Burroughs describes as an intersection: a piece of writing, art, sound, or music that reminds you of something you or some one else has created and amplifies it. The example Burroughs uses to illustrate this phenomenon is the moment a piece of his writing from 1957 intersects with a newspaper article in 1964:

"An old junky selling Christmas seals on North Clark Street. ... The 'Priest' they   called him. ... And just here is a picture from Newsweek, May 15, 1964 ... plane wreck. ... The 'Priest' there hand lifted last rites for 44 airliner dead including Captain Clark (left). Left on North Clark Street."

The news article he is currently reading parallels something he has previously written, causing an intersection. The position of the priest in the two pieces, on the same street, their movements mirroring one another.

Holly's last words had intersected with Bowie's last album. While they related at the time, I didn't know it would be his last album. As a young girl, I practiced intersection by taking walks, photographing and recording what I saw around me. Later, I reflected on what I was thinking at the time I commemorated the moment. This practice continues to be a part of my daily life. Bowie's *Blackstar* acts as a link to what's known as a Black dwarf star (what happens when a White dwarf star has cooled and lost both it's heat and light) once it was revealed that the album was Bowie's parting gift to his fans and a reference to theoretical cosmology from the Starman himself. It is also a reference to Elvis's little-known song *Black Star* which was released in the 1960s.

Every man has a black star
A black star over his shoulder
And when a man sees his black star
He knows his time, his time has come
Black star don't shine on me, black star
Black star keep behind me, black star
There's a lot of livin' I gotta do
Give me time to make a few dreams come true, black star

Bowie shared a birthday with The King and was fascinated by Elvis' song. There are hints and references to it in his video for *Lazarus*, which was released on the day of St. Lazarus of Bethany. In the video, Bowie sits at a desk frantically writing while a figure representing Death creeps up on him. This was a lesson in time travel – in which quotes from the present reflect or intersect with writing and art that had been created earlier, bridging memory and the present in real-time. I think of Holly's last letter once again, subconsciously she knew death was approaching as she wrote out her own future.

Certain exercises can be done to promote these intersections. Exercises broaden perception, facilitating synthesis, allowing for concise clear thought.

Land has memory. Take Coney Island, a place that has written history from the early 17th Century, and well known for its late 19th Century and 20th Century historical value. Although the face of Coney Island has changed, much of the energy or land memory there has remained. Any place is going to go through changes over the years, some areas gain more popularity during certain eras than others. In Time Travel you are working with both land memory and time, creating a fusion of the two. This becomes the cut. The concept of Time Travel is to encounter places and land with embedded history experiencing multiple time frames. The experience in itself is time travel. Walking along the boardwalk you are there at one point in time, what you photograph intersects with what you are thinking at that moment, all while understanding the history and events that have taken place there. These exercises ingrain the history into your being, further expanding the understanding of time, space, and people, and connecting the dates and times to what you are experiencing at that moment. By taking an Ansco No 3 to the boardwalk and photographing, the simple act of creating an image with film is creating a cut and merging the two times. Taking film footage and playing with the images creates a piece that merges multiple time frames within clips.

Films are magical spells. Sigils are cut-ups, the deconstruction and reconstruction of language quite literally. Paintings as magical workings. Foisy has created a painting of William S. Burroughs, an altar actually. In the following passages, she describes the process of the creation of this work:

When painting Burroughs, I lost ten days thinking it was three. I was over saturated and had under slept. The soundtrack for this piece: cut-ups with Brion Gysin; Burroughs' interviews; the spoken word of Burroughs, Kerouac, and Ginsberg; Anaïs Nin's *Henry and June*; Hasil Adkins; Gil Scot Heron; SUSPENSE; Antonin Artaud; and Edith Piaf. I was playing my friend's grandfather's mistress in a play, a cruel woman in love with someone else's husband. Everything was rich. I wore velvet, took   a trip to Sleepy Hollow, lit dark incense and worked in front of my boveda with candles lit.

Before I started this piece I asked him what he wanted, how he wanted to be painted. You have to ask someone how they want to be painted before you start, at least in my case you do. You see, I have this altar and it's changed over the years but one thing has remained constant. There was always a place for Burroughs.

A NOT SO BRIEF HISTORY

One of my best friends in high school was Nicole Gonzalez Knowlton. We loved Burroughs, Ginsberg, Kerouac, Patti Smith and Jim Carroll. We travelled to Seattle and San Francisco to see spoken word events and music festivals. She was the writer and I was the photographer, the painter. I wanted to be the writer. I never was. Instead I did cut ups, including my words with those of people I admired. Each time I cut our words together I would meet them in real life. Some would become acquaintances, like Jim Carroll, and give me pointers on writing, others I would meet in passing over and over again on different occasions. Nicole and I introduced each other to Burroughs' books on dreams. I wrote my senior year paper from the headspace of him. I received an 'A' with the comment that the way I could channel his writing style and thoughts was 'creepy'. My mom brought me to the library so I could research his paintings from an art book that had become out of print. I tried to walk out with it. I lived and breathed Burroughs. I would dream about him too. Sometimes we would be sitting in grass surrounded by millions of moths and butterflies. I remember it was a hill in San Francisco, and I thought it was weird to have a dream about Burroughs and San Francisco. Other times it was darker. I once had a dream he was hiding behind doors and waiting for me. He'd jump out and attack me. It would take two-three people to get him off of me. I would wake up with large bruises on my legs.

The summer of 1997, I decided I would finally write him a letter. The day I was to mail it he died. I was heartbroken. August 1997, I moved to New York. The first person I met was Orien and oddly enough he was Burroughs' godson. He introduced me to his father Malcolm McNeill, a close friend of Burroughs'. A man that worked with him on a number of different projects. A confidant. I spent a number of days with Malcolm asking him about the friendship. He told me Burroughs had given him his former apartment; an apartment that would become a home of sorts for me in NYC. Later, while going through *With William Burroughs: A Report from the Bunker*, I found a passage and a small picture of old Bill in that very home. I closed my eyes.

Orien and I started dating in 2006. We made an altar to Burroughs and took note of odd coincidences. Orien's mother had ferrets; much to our surprise we found out old Bill had a fondness for the animal and kept them in the home. We set up strange altars, which we later found to be deities that he worked with. We skimmed the bookshelves while smoking rolled cigarettes. Often we'd find ourselves in exact locations mentioned i n *Junky*. We wrote and worked and lived our lives in a drunken haze. Once we found what looked like a curse on an old piece of paper. That curse has since disappeared. We drank vodka and played out scenes from the old boy's life. We broke up a year later. Sometimes relationships can be too intense for your own good. We remained close friends afterwards.

Burroughs' Ghost

In 2008, I went to England for a gallery show. While there, I took a side trip to Orton Longueville to visit someone I had never met. Her name was Sheryl and we had had many conversations on Vodou and espiritism. The first night at the pub she was flooded with messages. I was shocked at how good she was, as I hadn't told her anything really personal about me or the connection to Burroughs. He came through with messages and insight and some helpful advice.

Going mad

I started painting the piece on October 12th. I placed the sketch down and started to mix paint. I knew with Burroughs I couldn't listen to just anything, so I put on some interviews with him. The paint brush dipped and swirled in the paint. I remembered carrying around a tape recorder experimenting with my own cut ups as a teenager. I lit a candle on the altar and let the words and brush guide me.

But this painting was different than most. I had to step away from it a lot. It made me dizzy to look directly at it. Something was playing with me. I started to document everything.

From an email: It's putting itself together, slowly with thought, like the piece itself is thinking of the direction in which it wants to go. So I started to think of my Amy Winehouse piece and I started to realize there was a connection between the two. In the Amy piece I added a key. Like I felt I had to because somehow she was the key to something. Well I found this weird looking rusty key the other day and felt like it needed to be on this painting. And then I thought that there is something to all these keys, I mean I know Eleggua is my daddy but these people and keys and Eshu are all connected. So I painted more. I painted Burroughs and those who saw it said "It seems like it's alive, Katelan. The way he looks at you is a bit creepy." People have said with the Amy piece that they felt like her spirit was in it. I digress. So I'm painting, and it's coming along great. And last night I go to Cynthia's reading and Dean Haspiel and Chris Miskiewicz are there and we all go out to dinner after and I'm sitting next to Chris and I keep noticing this key around his neck. So I ask him about it because it's odd and I've been feeling the need to wear a key, plus two people that I've given keys to both had strange things happen to them after I gave them the keys, and oddly enough it has a tie to Australia, but that's another story. So Chris tells me it's from his grandmother's house and I touch the key for a moment because it's exactly like one that I have that showed up out of nowhere. So now I'm just thinking of keys and Eleggua.

I get home and I start painting more until I fall asleep, and I wake up and my mind is racing. I go to the park and start writing feverishly because I have a story in me, except it's a comic and not a story and I'm trying to write things down as fast as they're coming and all I can think of is "Ah Pook is here, Ah Pook is here" and I'm like "oh shit I'm channeling." So at this point I go home and I start to paint, and the painting is making me dizzy, and I can't look into Burroughs' eyes because I start to space out and lean closer into the painting. I'm losing myself in this painting, and I can feel it. The snake disappears as I paint him; Burroughs eyes seem to guide my hand. I know I'm going absolutely mad. So I start painting symbols. The ones used in chaos magic but I paint them secretly into the painting under layers of paint. I paint the hanged man, and I realize that's Burroughs' card. I always want to paint him as the High Priest but he's the hanged man, and then I start painting Eshu symbols and another symbol and I'm like, why am I painting these? And I realize that so much of magic has to do with Eshu, the crossroads. And it dawns on me that Burroughs talked a lot about Vodou but he wasn't in the religion and it all makes perfect sense. Orien and I also found that weird curse in the book shelf, so that also makes sense. Malcolm was the one that illustrated Ah Pook is Here. It was supposed to be a comic. The funny thing is Dan Goldman and I were having drinks the other night and he was like, Katelan you have got to do a comic. I'm seeing it. And then this happened. All of these paintings are Eshu related. Eshu opens the doors to talk to the dead, and each of these people I'm painting has some sort of Vodou or Eshu connection. Found out after Amy's death that she dabbled in Vodou. So it's been a whirlwind of a day and I'm not quite sure if any of this makes sense.

I started to crave sugar and tea. I don't drink a lot of tea so this is odd to me. I'm drinking tea throughout the day and into the evening replacing my two-three cups of coffee with it. This very same time I receive a photo of the Chelsea Hotel from my friend Robin. It's one she took while on holiday here. We were walking past it. I was reminiscing. I feel like these cravings aren't my own. I google "Burroughs and tea or coffee" and discover an article that goes into Burroughs' obsession with tea (Turnbull,   1962). Now I'm understanding that something much bigger than me is at work. I call my mom. "Don't worry about it," she says, "You're just channeling."

> "[...] the only people for me are the mad ones, the ones who are mad to live, mad to talk, mad to be saved, desirous of everything at the same time, the ones who never yawn or say a commonplace thing, but burn, burn, burn like fabulous yellow roman candles exploding like spiders across the stars and in the middle you see the blue center light pop and everybody goes 'Awww!' What did they call such young people in Goethe's Germany?" – Jack Kerouac, *On the Road* (1957)

OCTOBER 21

All of this happened between the last hours of October 20th and October 21st. I stayed at home painting in a frenzy and writing down everything. I listened to Kerouac and Ginsberg non stop, only to take breaks in between for the sparrow or whatever else would take me out the trance. I finished him on October 22nd after signing his name to the piece. My friend Mani messaged me that day.

"I kept thinking there was some significance about Oct 21 and why everything was happening on that day. I looked it up, it seems his friend Kerouac passed away that day."

I tell her that makes a lot of sense and that there was a lot of energy charged up in that day. I tell Mani what is happening and how I've been looking up a lot of stuff about chaos magic. I've never really looked into it, before but it makes a lot of sense to me. It makes sense why Burroughs was into it. There is something to be said for letting yourself explore madness.

> Working with any magical system can lead you into madness, if you're up for it, as it were. The trick of course, is getting out of madness again, or at least learning to disguise it to everybody else. The fear of insanity when doing magic has to be confronted head-on. It will come whether you're messing with 'things with tentacles' or the most basic book on new age witchcraft.
>
> But if you want to stay the same, why are you doing magic in the first place? Consider instead that becoming 'obsessed' or dwelling

on 'lurking things' might actually be good for you. In some ways, it is not dissimilar to childhood fantasies and fears about things under the bed. Whilst going into these states is undeniably weird, they are also intensely magical. I feel that part of the issue which makes these states problematic for some people is that as one tips into these weird states of mind, one begins to feel that one is losing control of what is happening. More accurately, one is losing the illusion that one is in control of what happens to one. It is the fear of what might happen, where one might go, that is often worse than the process itself. The fear holds us back from surrendering to the embrace of derangement. – Phil Hine, *Prime Chaos* (2004).

Mani sends me this article after the painting is finished. "I think you should read this," she says. It's an interview with Burroughs on magic and painting and dreams. At the end, the interviewer asks him if he thinks at some point he'll come through someone else's paintings.

Simone Lazzeri Ellis: Do you feel that you have checked into the unknown – the nagual – and come back out again?

William S. Burroughs: I do indeed, at least sometimes. You know the story about the Zen master who appeared before the emperor with his painting, bowed three times and then disappeared into it?

SLE: Will that ever happen to you?

WSB: I hope so.

References

—⟶— Burroughs, W.S. & Gysin, B. (1978). *The Third Mind.* Viking Press: New York.

—⟶— Burroughs, W.S. (2012). *RUB OUT THE WORDS: The Letters of William S. Burroughs, 1959-1974.* Morgan, B. (ed.). Ecco: New York.

—⟶— Ellis, S. (1990). *A Conversation with William S. Burroughs.* Contemporanea International Art Magazine (via RealityStudio.org).

—⟶— Hine, P. (2004). *Prime Chaos.* New Falcon Publications: Las Vegas.

—⟶— Kerouac, J. (1957). *On the Road.* Viking Press: New York.

—⟶— Sobieszek, R. (1996). *Ports of Entry: William S. Burroughs and the Arts.* Los Angeles County Museum of Art.

—⟶— Turnbull, G. (1962). *A Visit to William S. Burroughs at the Beat Hotel in Summer, 1958.* MICA Magazine #5 (via RealityStudio.org).

BEDS, BODIES, AND OTHER BOOKS
OF COMMON PRAYER

A Reading of the Photography of Nan Goldin

Claire-Madeline Culkin

1

I encountered *The Ballad of Sexual Dependency* like a prayer—like something which orients you in some way to a kind of faith at times when there is no basis for believing. I had spent some time at a hotel bar talking to a stranger named Ash—a visitor of the city—whom I felt like I'd known forever and did not know how that could exactly be. By some stroke of luck, he felt the same; a notion which I had no real reason to believe except for the way his face felt familiar-like: familial.

He packed his things for his flight to LA while I lay on the bed questioning how on earth I would manage to keep him around with the distance, and the time difference, and everything else. When he said goodbye I told him I'd fight for him—for the whole of him—despite the distance, and the past lives we've led, and all the rest of it that separates both strangers and even the best of friends.

When I woke up, the previous week seemed to be a dream that lifted leaving me wondering how to sustain this surreal sense of connection with this stranger. Before returning to the life I lead in the city, I sat in hotel's library with a cup of coffee. I selected, from its stacks, a book of photography, the cover of which pictured a man and a woman in an anonymous room, the woman laying down in its bed looking on at the man sitting upright on the far side of it; his eyes closed and turned away from her, their faces abrasively yellowed in the intrusive light of morning.

The collection of what has been called 'snap-shot photography,' titled, compellingly and also curiously, *The Ballad of Sexual Dependency*, is about this fight for familial others. In it, photographer Nan Goldin asks why we have to wage a war to wield a sense of togetherness in what feels to be some kind of dream in which the light of day always seems to intervene and rupture it.

Goldin, in her introduction to the collection, explains "[this books is about] the history of a re-created family" (*Ballad*). She explains, "In my family of friends, there is a desire for the intimacy of a blood family, but also a desire for something more" (*Ballad*). It is in this 'something more,' that something strange intervenes that both stimulates and stunts the effort to sustain it, something like the light of morning, and the distance between bodies in a bed.

As I turn the pages, I see, in my minds eye, a hallucinatory slide-show of memory.

MEMORY

I remember when he believed my body, touching his body, was closer than it really was. If this believing in bodies when they touch is what we call love, then I remember when he used to love me: I remember when he didn't just fuck me.

He had put on Philip Glass. The notes, I remember were slow. Each one of them came together, like droplets of water: separately. Listening to them was like listening to words: the sound felt close to me.

He told me to take my shirt off.

It was strange.

It wasn't like the times he seemed to manipulate my body as though arranging it on a display. I didn't feel like an instrument.

I felt like skin. I felt like bones and the blood that runs through them.

That was when he took his hand and touched me. He just touched me.

2

The Ballad of Sexual Dependency came out of a series of images Goldin had taken of a man named Brian, her boyfriend of three years from 1981-1983. Goldin's work at this time focused on, as she calls it "people's external behavior"; in particular, both during and after having sex (*In My Life*). In this series, she explores her own sexual life through her camera's lens: using a tripod and cable release, Goldin photographed hers and Brian's sexuality as it unfolded in real time, as well as the sexual lives of her family of friends.

In the photos of *Ballad*, Goldin neither functions as her-self, nor as another. She is simultaneously observer and observed. She is, at once, herself and *the effect of an other*. As Goldin explains "The way the show [out of which, came *Ballad*] is constructed at the Whitney the critics have accused it of being narcissistic… and self involved. If I hadn't constructed it in such a personal manner they'd be accusing it of voyeurism and vicariousness. It's neither narcissistic nor voyeuristic. It's something else" (*In My Life*). Her work, as she tells us from the outset, says something about *dependency*.

Though she describes this dependency as 'sexual,' the bodies of *Ballad* are distinctly not erotic. There is an intimacy to them that reflects a desire that is not strictly bodily. Insofar as the material is overtly sexual, it is not *pornographically so*; there is not the *contact* that characterizes sex; there is nothing in them that indicates the *pleasure* of togetherness. When two figures appear coupled in the photographs, they are framed in a way that is both related and unrelated: they are touching, but not looking at one another; they are situated meaningfully in the frame but doing separate activities; they are standing side by side, together, but looking, separately at the camera, like two glaciers (I think of the word glacier, and then of ice—of isolation.) Goldin tells us, also, that this work is about *alienation* (*Ballad*).

In *Ballad*, the bed, like the body, is a place where we both come together and separate. The photographs represent some limit and simultaneously refuse it. Goldin, in going back to the rolls of film produced spontaneously, finds, in her process of editing the images, a way to stage a separation; it seems, as a means of structuring it: rendering it comprehensible.

Goldin describes the photograph, introduced earlier, which would become the cover of *Ballad*—its snap-shot anthem: "I found this picture that I thought was really meaningful, in the ambivalence of my gaze, and sort of the distance between us right after sex—the fact that he's turned away from me and smoking, and I'm still looking at him for intimacy" (*Interview, Part 2*). Regarding the next photograph in the series, which does not appear in the book, Goldin comments on their sad estrangement—about the way sex separates. The words that stand out to me are: *ambivalence, estrangement, sad.* In her voice, as she describes this body of work—this period in her life as this *body*—I notice her sad estrangement *from it*—from herself.

In Freudian psychoanalytic theory, the ego-ideal is a precursor to the super-ego and to castration anxiety. In the construction of the ego-ideal, the ego is able to take itself as its own object, and treat it as an other. For Freud, this is the threat of human sexuality, desire, and subjectivity: it is *dependent*. Importantly, this dependency exists at a limit—in particular, the limit of the self, at the sight of the other. In this dependent borderland, desire has always the powerful and precarious capacity to turn round into violence (*Three Essays*).

MEMORY

I was listening to Band of Horses. The album, *Infinite Arms*. That one came after we no longer occupied the same space; when it was in music that I sustained our shared existence—imagined it into it. It was the album after *Cease to Begin* and after *Everything All the Time.*

Infinite. Everything. Cease. These words all suggest something absolute, something imposable: this always forever—this never again—we condemn ourselves to being in and out of love.

It was in music that I fell in love with him. It was in our mutual listening—in our shared silence—that we were first intimate.

That was when I couldn't imagine the sound of his scream. When he wanted my wanting.

3

The bodies of *Ballad* fail similarly as does the body in Freud. In "Instincts and Their Vicissitudes," Freud theorizes a relation between the body and mind that is structured around a fundamental separation. For Freud, the instinct exists "on the frontier between the mental and the somatic" (122). The instinct is generated from within the body, and places a demand on the mind to direct the aim of the instinct to an object, which satisfies it.

The body necessitates a demand on the mind that is fundamentally impossible. The impossibility exists on the frontier between mind and body, and between instinct and object or, to use terms more fitting for our discussion of the failure of the sexual relation, between self and other. The sexual instinct, which directs the self to the other, orients bodies in some way, but it is an orientation that is precarious, at best.

The peculiarities of this precariousness exist, in Freud's theory, in the relation between a series of paired opposites, all of which verge on this frontier. It is a frontier between the mind and the body—between my body, and your body.   That Freud uses the word frontier here is particularly interesting, insofar as the word suggests a space, constituted by a limit that is unidentifiable; it is one that we simultaneously strive for, one that we refuse.

There is desperation to desire that gives it a violent edge. The intimate verges on the catastrophic. This is a precipice our relationships verge on; it is a risk we do not know, and which, when we do, we refuse. The libidinal drive, in Freud, invests itself in objects—in others; it transcends; it moves beyond the body—beyond the self. It is in the way the drive approaches this frontier—a point of externality that both corresponds to the instinct's aim and is also different from it—that sexuality is organized in a split.

Desire, in Freud, is essentially perverse. By perversion, Freud means it is contingent. In "Instincts and Their Vicissitudes" he writes "the object of an instinct is the thing… through which the instinct is able to achieve its aim." (214). In "The Three Essays on the Theory of Sexuality" he tells us that anything that is not genital is perverse. Our dependency on the other, in sexuality, *is* what makes it perverse. Love is inherently pathological. The overwhelming sensation of the other leads to the extension of the sexual aim into its love object, its other. The over-valuing of the sexual object to a position of *contingency* in the satisfaction of the sexual aim elevates the object to the level of perversion.

The Ballad of Sexual Dependency is an anthem of this contingency. It is a contingency that perplexed Goldin and with which she became obsessed. Goldin explains, "My work for years was about sexuality as an addiction. I'm not a sexual addict but the idea that you could become sort of sexually addicted to someone who was inappropriate with you on many levels and why this need to couple is so strong" (*In My Life*).

MEMORY

A photo snapped in the subway station. Light cast down the stairwell illuminates his face beyond recognition. He is wearing that plaid jacket—the red one I ruined in the laundry—and his hair is a mess with bed head, which I had loved—I had loved that we had slept and woken up together and, having thrown on any old thing, were getting breakfast on a weekend morning.

At the diner he said something I can't remember. Something about if I had loved him—if I had really loved him—for who he was; not merely because he was a body near to me, who wore the clothes I ruined in the laundry, whose head was a mess from the bed in which we both slept.

I never noticed how badly he wanted to want me. Or how long it had taken him to accept that a long time ago I had gotten untraceably lost in a past that came before him—that he was unqualified to direct me to find myself there.

4

This something more, in Freud, is a narcissistic demand that is *impossible*. What Freud classifies as normal or primary narcissism is distinguished from pathological or secondary narcissism. In the latter, desire is withdrawn from objects, either real or fantasized, where as in the former desire is cathected to the object. Normal and pathological narcissism are *similar* insofar as it is in this object—either present or absent, real or fanaticized—that one experiences a sense of self (such is the contingency).

In love the boundary between self and other, through desire and its fantasy, is not this clearly elaborated (such is its violent edge) ("On Narcissism"). The basic impossibility is both necessary to the relationship and has nothing to do whatsoever with it; it is essential to the relationship and it also *pre-dates* it; it extends beyond the other and into the past. This violent edge—this frontier toward which we are always striving, and from which we must necessarily be retreating—threatens desire with ambivalence.

Goldin's photographs came out of a radical confrontation with this failure. She explains, "[Brian's] concept of relationships was rooted in the romantic idealism of James Dean and Roy Orbison… We were addicted to the amount of love the relationship supplied. Things between us started to break down, but neither of us could make the break" (*Ballad*). Eventually the break came and it came down on Goldin's body—the physical site of this failure. After reading (and then burning) Goldin's diaries, he beat her, brutally. In Goldin's understanding, "confronting [her] normal ambivalence had betrayed his absolute notion of romance. His conflict between his desire for independence and… the relationship had become unbearable" (*Ballad*).

Desire gets stuck. Freud explains that a fixation—the kind that constitutes a perversion—is a renunciation of this unbearable impossibility in the form of an "intense opposition to detachment" (*Three Essays*, 122). It is hard to love unconditionally because love *is* conditional; it is conditional on an*other* and it conditions a sense of *self*. Desire is always narcissistic. Desire is unconscious. That which is unconscious is fantasy. Fantasy is always failure. Importantly, though, it is a narcissism that is essential and a fantasy that finds a way, in its failure, to function as *desire*. This narcissism and this fantasy are bound up in the mythological Freudian mother and in the symbolic agency of the father.

What Freud thus describes is an experience that approaches Goldin's idea of 'coupling.' Both ideas contain in them the wish for a togetherness that is total. (I told him I would fight for him—for the *whole* of him). It is a wish that will always fail, as all wishes do. For Freud, the first failed wish is the wish for the mother. In Freud, we learn that we *want the mother completely*. In Lacan, we learn that this wish reflects a desire to *be the thing that makes love complete*. This desire *turns round upon itself*: from mother to me, from voyeurism to exhibitionism, from masochism and sadism. We are both the subject of desire and the object of it. Goldin is both the one looking on and the one being looked at.

There is something about this simultaneous function of, as Goldin observes, narcissism and voyeurism that makes her photography function as *something else*. So is love: it is, at once, both and neither. Just as the bodily instinct places a demand on the mind that does not accord exactly with its capacity for meeting it, so too does the instinct place demand on the other that does not always accord exactly with his (or her) capacity for desire.

MEMORY

It is important for me to remember that people and places lose their meaning; that people lose the meaning we invest in them; that sometimes desire can't hold up.

I knew from the get go that he was, to me, an empty thing: a prop, an image constructed into the structure of my denial. As I get farther away from the events, I can't tell the story of how this came to be, but I know that he couldn't live up to the task. Yet I hoped in vain that neither of us would see that a surface that deflects is none other than a mirror.

5

The fantasy of relationships does not coincide with the reality of coupling. These relationships between self and other, and between reality and fantasy, are inexact. More than being oppositional they constitute a gap. Goldin's photography tells us something of its nature—of the way the self and the other switch places in it. They both annihilate, and are annihilated by it.

Goldin's photographs can be understood as an attempt to capture this distance between bodies by arranging it in a frame. It is as though by framing an image she organizes a nothing that is incompressible into a something which can at least be represented. In this incomprehensibility there is a brutality. Some of the images are overtly violent—Goldin's self-portrait, for example, after she was battered by her boyfriend—but all of them are difficult to look at.

The violence of the impossible nature of desire is pictured in bodies engaging with other bodies, or trying to, laying on top of one another, flaccidly. Nothing is happening. Nothing at all is happening. It is brutal. It is banal. The unbearableness of Goldin's photography is the unbearable failure of love. It is the *mereness* of it that makes it so severe. The bruises on Nan's face that border on the fatal are not nearly as difficult to look at as those bodies, alive, but barely verging on love.

MEMORY

It all comes back like a bomb exploding. I'll be reaching for the soap in the shower—bending down to grasp it, mindlessly—when, in my mind's hallucinatory minefield, a bomb is detonated—a memory explodes in a flash and then is gone.

He and I are on the phone. It is night-time. Everyone else in the house sleeps while I sit with the phone to my ear on the living room floor. It is empty feeling: all of the un-used furniture in the dim table-lamp light. The moment is silent, mostly, except for the occasional sound of his voice on the other end. It is sorrowful, feeling: his silence.

I don't know—will never find out—if he had been dating that girl, or if he had called her, like he said he would that night, to end it. Or if she happened to beat him to the punch, and if this had anything at all to do with the weekend he did not spend with his buddy in New York, when instead he watched hockey with me on the couch which, with the phone to my ear that evening, no one was using.

After he made this superficial promise I listened to him say nothing for a little longer and conceded to the fact that he, in his sadness, was in a world all his own which I could not—would never be—a part of, before deciding to say a mute goodbye and hung up. It was uneventful: a memory of nothing at all happening.

They all are. In each and every one of them, I feel like no one: I feel X-ed out and no one notices.

6

It is an unbearableness that verges on loss. *The Ballad of Sexual Dependency* did not just chronicle Goldin's relationship with Brian, but also a decade of what has been called 'the counter-culture of the 80's.' The subjects of Goldin's photography are bi-sexual, homosexual, transsexual and transgendered. The book, to some, is about the tragedy of drugs and of the AIDS virus. Goldin didn't just experience a love that was sliced with the violent edge of ambivalence; she lost herself at this boundary, and she watched others around her lose themselves there, too. The losses in *Ballad* are the loss of the self to emotional and physical illness, and the loss of the self and the other, in sex and in death.

Curiously, these losses do not fracture love; *they constitute it.* For Goldin, her love for others is qualified by the fact that she is there for her friends in and through their emotional and physical losses. To use her own words: "because I photographed them when they were alive and death is a part of our relationship, I can't say I really love someone unless I am there for them as they're dying. So part of the love and the investment in the relationship when they were alive is carried over into the process of them dying and me witnessing that" (*In My Life*). There is an insistence in these pictures even as they fail to rectify this failure of bodies in relationship to sexuality and to their mortality.

"[Goldin] had thought that [she] could stave off loss through photography" but found that "photography doesn't preserve memory as effectively as [she] thought it would" (Ballad). In an afterword that was published in 1996 in a later edition of the collection, Goldin tells us: "a lot of people in the book are dead now… Cookie is dead, Kenny is dead, Mark is dead, Max is dead, Vittorio is dead… The book is now a volume of loss" (*Ballad*). As you move through the photographs, page after page, *this loss accumulates at the same time as it amounts to nothing.*

In Goldin's collection, the limit of love is represented not just at the boundary of the body, but also at the boundary between genders, between drug use and drug abuse, and between night and day. In the fight that ended her relationship with Brian, the basic impossibility of love collapsed at each of these boundaries, prompting a process of mourning. Importantly to Goldin's story, this intimacy was faced in her sexuality but formed in her family: in the loss of her sister to a suicide.

These two losses—of Goldin to her relationship and her sister to suicide—represent the loss of the feeling of *ownership* over one's experience. Goldin speaks of this in the afterword to her collection when she writes: "I don't ever want to be susceptible to anyone else's version of my history. I don't ever want to lose the real memory of anyone again" (*Ballad*). She goes on to explain the way she lost her sister to the revisionist history her family and her psychiatrists constructed about her sadness and about her fate. In a way, Goldin in her break-up and subsequent sobriety, and her sister in her suicide are intimately related in their attempt to achieve *some relationship to desire that is their own.*

As is fitting with the frames of *Ballad*, life and death structure love. Goldin, briefly and in vague generalities that ask us to take her at her word, describes the way her family law was defined by a basic and pervasive denial of reality. In Goldin's understanding, her sister took her life, not as in *took it away*, but as in *claimed it as her own*. "By the time she was eighteen," Goldin tells us, "she saw that her only way to get out was to lie down on the tracks of the commuter train outside of Washington D.C" (*Ballad*). In her suicide, Goldin's sister escaped escapism, similarly as in Goldin's photography, Goldin flees from fantasy. I see Goldin's photographing effort similarly as she sees her sister's suicide: "as an act of immense will" (*Ballad*).

When Goldin entered rehab, she had brought with her a copy of *Ballad* as comfort, and company, but it was removed from her by the staff who argued that the images were threatening. Her camera, the professionals thought, posed the same threat. When her camera was returned to her after she moved from rehab to a sober-living facility, she began photographing herself in order to familiarize herself as someone alone, un-drugged, and in the light of day. Prior to her sobriety, Goldin lived mostly at night. In her new life she literally found the light of day. She discovered herself anew, realizing in the way that light affected photography. Goldin admits, powerfully, "I did not know that available light could mean anything other than the red light of an after-hours bar" (*Interview Part 2*).

The sexuality of Freud's psychoanalytic theory is, at best, fragmented. It is transgressive. It runs the risk of alienation in the other, or in the self as fantasy. One can approach it, and one can transgress it (Goldin knows this), but one cannot define it (she knows this too). And yet one refuses to accept this impossibility, and so one tries (such is the function of her photographs). In the tragic dual function of Goldin's photographs, we see an effort to define something that is impossible to identify and in this effort, an attempt, also, to find some way beyond it.

This boundary between self and other indicates another boundary: between the somatic and the psychic—between the body and its meaning. All of these boundaries are at odds with one another, but they also structure, in their impossible relationship, a *possibility*. Goldin's photographs picture neither the fantasy of love, nor the way in which it fails, but something else—something more than this. Goldin perhaps describes it best: "I've been called a snapshot photographer and that's fine with me because snapshots are the only form of photography that are completely inspired by love" (*In My Life*). Her photographs are inspired by love and inspire love; they picture the way that love inspires. Like I said, *The Ballad of Sexual Dependency* came to me like a prayer: in its failure, I found a faith.

The book ends with a moment of lovers' alienation and then with an empty bed. It ends with a Valentine's table prepared for love's ceremony but empty of its lovers; with an elderly couple standing idly along side one another on a house patio; with a photograph of lovers' adjacent graves. It ends with corpses, lifeless, embracing, bone on top of bone, fated forever to be *as close as mere bodies enable us to be*. It all makes me wonder what it is we get from seeking proximity to the other only to be alienated in their presence. Goldin tells us that failed fantasy results in either violence or alienation—in either narcissism or loss. So does Freud. So do my narratives.

We move from the other to an I that is both God-like and barely believable, at its best. We love, and we document this love, as though staving off the loss it began with. And when our wish to do so fails, as it will, we fantasize it anew like we are praying, as we must. Goldin's photographs have the power of something that moves—the quality of something like desire. She explains, "I'm very interested in the continuity of relationships and the history of people's lives. I never believed that a single image said anything about a person. I believe in the accumulation of images." She says, "[I believe] in the narrative" (*In My Life*).
So I write. I just keep writing.

REVERIE

Yesterday was Cinco De Mayo, which means nothing at all except that it was sunny, and I wanted a glass of sangria. I wanted a reason to simultaneously escape thinking of Ash, on the other coast, and share a fake holiday with him in spirit, from mine. We sent each other pictures of our mustaches: mine drawn on a piece of paper and held up to my face for a snapshot, his pinned to the end of his beer, taking a swig so it sat there like some sort of Spanish pun above his upper-lip for the flash. This is the function our fantasies, isn't it? A means of flight: a means of finding?

I want the color blue: chlorine chartreuse. A pool. I want a white one-piece bathing suit, a purposelessly enormous black straw hat, Chanel sunglasses blocked black and white. I want oppressive sunlight.

I want LA: that anonymous city, itself a signifier. I want relief: a reprieve. I want to feel gorgeous; good enough; stunningly deficient.

I revel in my reverie—in the triumph of memory.

REFERENCES

—⁓— Freud, Sigmund. "Three Essays on the Theory of Sexuality." Trans. Array *Freud on Women: A Reader.* New York, NY: W.W. Norton and Company, 1990. 89-145. Print.

—⁓— Freud, Sigmund, Joseph Sandler, Ethel Spector Person, and Peter Fonagy. Freud's "On Narcissism–an Introduction". New Haven, CT: Yale University Press, 1991. Print.

—⁓— Goldin, Nan. "From the Book The Ballad of Sexual Dependency." Production of Images. N.p.. Web. 19 May 2013. <http://productionofimages.files.wordpress.com/2009/10/nan-goldin-ballad-of-sexual-dependency.pdf>.

—⁓— Goldin, Nan. In My Life. Web. 19 May 2013. http://www.youtube.com/watch?v=KwDUWJAACqY.

—⁓— Goldin, Nan. Interview, Part 1 and 2. Web. 19 May 2013. http://www.youtube.com/watch?v=wQ9-aSRvdf0.

On the Dance of the Occult and Unconscious in Freud

Steven Reisner

Historically, much of the view of Freud and the occult comes to us from Jung. Therefore, part of my emphasis is to reclaim Freud's position from Jung's gossip about Freud. So I will get to that, and I also would like to claim a piece of the review of the history of Freud's interest – and other people's interest – in the occult; I want to claim some piece for psychoanalytic theory. I believe it's important to move the ball forward in terms of psychoanalytic theory; if we are going to speak about psychoanalysis, to keep things fresh, and also to keep myself interested. I think that the great thing about Freud's theory, and Freud's personality, is that he was always curious. He saw himself like a conquistador; he was claiming new territory. He was expanding the realm of psychoanalysis, and let me explain what I mean by psychoanalysis, and why I don't see it as a kind of archaic narrow theory of therapy, but actually as a way of thinking about just about everything; everything human.

Foucault described Freud and Marx as unique in some ways because they created the discourse within which they taught and researched. They each actually created a language, a grammar, a mode of thinking and speaking about the topic that interested them. For Marx, of course, it was economics and politics; for Freud it was the human being in a social context. It was subjectivity itself. You could even say that it was the form that the discourse would even take; the way we think and communicate, and how that may be aligned or misaligned with being a human being.

So that the essential piece of what Freud was talking about when he spoke about the discourse of psychoanalysis. When he spoke about what it means to be subjective – a subjective, aware human being that communicates with other human beings – this had to do primarily with the different modes of the possibility of thinking. One mode being primary processing, one mode being secondary processing. I think all of psychoanalysis can flow from the streams of that particular concept; what it means to have an individual separate kind of almost physiological self: the primary process, and transforming that into a communicable knowledge: the secondary process.

That requires kind of a transformation, a kind of a turning of the mind, if you will. Freud used 'the soul' in German more than 'the mind.' But a turning, that allowed things to be thought, and then it also prevented certain things from being thought. And that – I think, the fact that things were allowed to be thought and prevented from being thought in the communicable discourse – leads us into some of the issues that I will get to, having to do with occult phenomena and Freud's interest in occult phenomena.

So let me now go back and give a little piece of history – which we could call a little bit of gossip – about the beginnings of Freud's relationship to the occult, the reputation of Freud and the occult, and Jung's role in this. There are many Freuds. If you read popular views of Freud, if you read anything that is do with Freud, including my own ideas, you find that you get a very particular Freud, and that might be very different from other Freuds.

I mean there's the classic Freud of television and New Yorker cartoons, where he sits behind the couch and doesn't say anything. There's the Freud who believes that everything is sexuality, and that all we are looking for is pleasure. There's Freud who is the pessimist about the possibilities of civilization, and thinks that the entire world – by virtue of us living in groups – is neurotic. There are many different Freuds that we could claim.

But there's a particular Freud that Jung describes. And he is part of the discourse on establishing Freud as being sex, sex, sex and nothing but sex. And he was. Jung particularly separated that Freud from his own explorations into phenomena beyond sexuality, including phenomena beyond what we can perceive with our senses, and so Jung tells this story, which I'll read. Because it's fun to read, and because it's so succinct, and such a lie.

So this is Jung writing 50 years after the fact: "I can still recall vividly how Freud said to me, 'My dear Jung, promise me never to abandon the sexual theory. That is the most essential thing of all, you see we must make a dogma of it, an unshakable bulwark.' In some astonishment, I asked him, 'A bulwark against what?' To which he replied, 'Against the black tide of mud of occultism.'"

Jung goes on to say, "This is the thing that struck at the heart of our friendship. I knew that I would never be able to accept such an attitude. What Freud seemed to mean by 'occultism', was virtually everything that philosophy and religion, including the rising contemporary science of parapsychology, had learned about the psyche." Jung says this happened a day in 1910. So, now why did Jung tell this story? Because he needed to explain what the territory was that he was bravely embarking to conquer and to bring to the world, and that Freud was too frightened to do that.

Jung is in good company. Freud did exactly the same thing to his mentor. And that was Josef Breuer. Breuer was really to Freud what Freud was to Jung. And Freud was to Breuer what Jung was to Freud. Breuer was a doctor in Vienna, at the turn of the last century. He was known to be a brilliant doctor, but he was not academic. He had a circle of young Jewish physicians around him, and he was relentlessly curious, and quite brilliant. He treated a lot of what at the time were called hysterical women. And of course, the most famous hysterical woman of all, Anna O., was a patient of Breuer's. Freud was the smartest student of them all, and Breuer befriended him and took him home, gave him cognac, and they would sit up all night and talk. Breuer would tell him about Anna O., who was a close friend of Freud's fiancée – there wasn't much confidentiality back then. But in any case, Freud was very excited about the story – it opened up a whole world of thinking and theorizing – and he asked Breuer if they could write a book together, which they proceeded to do. Breuer wrote the theoretical section, which was quite extraordinary, full of ideas about the world of sexuality and areas of conflict and trauma and dissociation.

Eventually, Freud broke with Breuer, supposedly over the sexual theory. But he broke with Breuer because Freud was very ambitious, and he didn't want anybody to think that anybody had influenced him and given him his ideas. And so he retells the story of Anna O.'s treatment – also about 30 years after the fact – in a way that does to Breuer what Jung later does to Freud. He did the exact same thing.

So we know the story of Anna O. Supposedly, she created the talking cure; she named the idea. She taught Breuer how to do it. And then she was cured at the end of the case. But when Freud tells the story – he related it to Jones, and Jones dutifully wrote it in A Biography of Freud – that the case was not a success; that the night after the case was resolved, in fact, Breuer was summoned back to Anna O.'s bedroom. She was in the throes of a hysterical pregnancy, saying, "Doctor Breuer's baby is coming!" According to Freud… I'll read it to you:

> On the evening of the day when all her systems had been disposed of, Breuer was summoned to the patient again. Found her confused, and writhing in abdominal cramps. Asked what was wrong with her, she replied, 'Now Doctor B's child is coming.' At this moment, he held in his hand the key that would've opened the doors to the mothers. But he let it drop. With all his intellectual gifts, there was nothing Faustian in his nature. Seized by conventional horror, he took flight, and abandoned the patient to a colleague.

"The doors to the mothers" comes from *Faust*. I mean, it's so much fun, I'll just read you the little piece of *Faust*. Mephistopheles says to Faust, "'Take this key.' And Faust says, 'That little thing?' And Mephistopheles says, 'Take hold of it, don't undervalue it.' Faust says, 'It glows, it shines. It increases in my hand.' And Mephistopheles says, 'How much 'tis worth, thou soon shall understand. The key will send the true place from all others, follow it down to lead the to the mother.'

So for Freud, the key that Breuer let drop was this key of sexuality; the key of transference; the key of the Oedipus complex; the key of all knowledge. And poor, conventional Breuer was horrified and ran away. And Jones, in the biography, adds a whole new chapter to this. In his biography of Freud, Jones says, "The profoundly shocked Breuer managed to calm Anna O. down by hypnotizing her, and then fled the house in a cold sweat. The next day, he and his wife left for Venice, to spend a second honeymoon. Resulted in the conception of a daughter. The girl born in these curious circumstances was, nearly 60 years later, to commit suicide in New York."

So you can see that each one is destroying the influences that might take some credit. By the way, the whole story of Anna O.'s hysterical pregnancy is bogus. There's a full record of Anna O.'s treatment to be found in the Bellevue Sanatorium in the outskirts of Vienna. And there's no record whatsoever of a hysterical pregnancy. And in fact, Breuer's daughter was born three months before the treatment with Anna O. ended. And she did commit suicide. But it wasn't in New York, it was in Vienna, when the Gestapo came to her door to take her to a concentration camp. So the story has been twisted in a kind of horrendous way by the Freud biographers.

Anna O. actually had a huge career. She became the creator, pretty much, of social work in Austria. And she was never a fan of psychoanalysis, as you can imagine. But she did have a very successful life helping children particularly.

Why do I tell this story? First of all, because it's really a great story. But secondly, because Jung, we have to take with a grain of salt. The categorization of former mentors, and that attempt to narrow them down to make room for oneself; Jung did that with Freud. And as a result, Freud's work on the occult is completely undone. We have this idea that Freud was frightened by new ideas. The idea that Freud was afraid of things that were not open to perception is a denial of everything that is psychoanalysis. Psychoanalysis is all about that which is outside of our perception, and what its origins are, what we do with it, how it affects us. For Freud, the occult was to be treated a bit like sexuality. Some piece of knowledge that we need to present carefully to a skeptical public.

So let me talk a little bit about the Freud that I've constructed, from my reading of his writings. I think that it's helpful to expand our view of Freud, so we can include what I would call the shamanistic aspects of Freud's curiosity and practice. Let's understand that Freud believed that there were things in experience that were not available to consciousness. He believed that in order to get at those – that material, one had to take a certain kind of a journey. What kind of a journey? It changed over his career.

He started believing strongly in the effects of cocaine. And he later believed in what we might call going into trance, because he became a hypnotist and started hypnotizing his patients. He was really willing to try quite a few things in the interest of what he observed. Let's remember that, let's take the story of Anna O., a hysterical woman of the day, who seemed to not be able to know certain things. But those things had to come out and came out in ways that could, in a sense, be disavowed. So symptoms were knowledge that was denied, usually associated with trauma, and it required some kind of a process to bring this information into awareness.

Freud's interest from the beginning had to do with freeing separated-off, denied or unknown aspects of self-experience. For Freud, freedom, health had to do with the integration of the most and access to the most self-experience and self in relation to other experience as possible, and so that is kind of the aim of the psychoanalytic journey. We can understand the occult experiments in that context, just like we can understand everything else that Freud did in that context.

You can always find quotes in Freud that support any view of Freud. The people who see Freud as this narrow anti-occult Freud have found some quotes where he rejected it, which he did do early on. But he also wrote to a colleague, "I want to remove a misunderstanding. A psychoanalyst refraining from taking part publicly in occult studies, is a purely practical matter and a temporary one. Not at all an expression on principle."

Freud believed that the world wasn't really ready to accept these studies, but he did pursue those studies. Similarly, he warned his disciples – if you want to call them disciples – his students, about the power of sexuality. Ferenczi was known for kissing his patients. And Freud thought that was a terrible idea, especially if it got out, because these were very powerful forces that they were playing with, and he thought that they really had to be handled in an objective, scientific, and reasonable way, taking into account the effect on the public. Don't give them more than they can handle.

Jung wrote a letter to Freud when he was in America. "Americans are really wildly accepting psychoanalysis." Freud wrote back, "And you think that's a good thing?" So Freud was very careful about how he wanted psychoanalysis disseminated; too careful in many people's minds.

But the point I want to make is that when Freud was with Jung during 1910 and 1911, when Jung claims that Freud set a bulwark against occultism, Freud wrote to Jung and said, "I'm not going to touch these studies right now, but I would like you and Ferenczi to pursue them." And then after the break with Jung, Freud encouraged Ferenczi to continue to pursue it. In fact, Freud, Ferenczi and Anna Freud did researches in telepathy, in thought broadcast, and they were successful experiments. Freud believed quite completely that thought broadcasting, that alternative modes of communicating internal processes from one person to another, was possible. In fact, he wrote to Jones, "The three of us carried out experiments in thought transference. They were remarkably good, particularly those in which I played the medium and analyzed my associations." So, like with cocaine, Freud experimented on himself, and he believed that he was quite successful. Cocaine was very successful, too.

I could give a whole aside about why Jung fled from Freud; not only because of his need to establish a grounding of himself independently, but I think he was a little freaked out by Freud's love for Jung.

And then the famous book case episode. I don't know if you've seen the movie *A Dangerous Method*, but there's this famous book case episode that Jung writes about in his memoirs. And there's letters from Freud about it. It actually happened. Jung said, "That book case is going to creak." And it creaked. And he said, "That book case is going to creak again." And it creaked again.

But this was during a weekend that Jung spent with Freud, where Freud said, "You are my son, you are my heir," and really wanted to sort of take Jung in. I think Jung fled from that over-involvement, that love that Freud had for him. Jung mentions in his letters that he also had a bad sexual experience with a previous mentor, a priest. So I don't know, but I really do get the feeling that Jung fled from Freud, in a number of ways.

The thing is that Freud was always a scientist. When he studies these occult phenomena, he's studying them with a scientist's eye. He knows that you can use all phenomena, including occult phenomena, including extra perception, parapsychological phenomena, for knowledge or for defense. I mean you could think of drugs in the same way. People use drugs for esoteric knowledge, and they can use drugs for defense. Addiction is all about using drugs as a defense.

So this issue is whether you're going to use it for knowledge or defense. The danger of course is to think of a communication that is parapsychological, esoteric, and say it must be true. Freud actually challenged that. He believed that you had to have the same critical view of the use of, for example, thought transference. It could be used for denial, as well as it could be used for knowledge, and I will get to that in a little bit: some of Freud's researches that absolutely convinced him that parapsychological phenomena were real, based on his study of fortune tellers who made incorrect predictions.

But first I wanted to talk about his idea of whether the occult is used in the service of a defense or a denial, or a contextualization of insanity. This is quite important, especially for those of us who are clinicians who are interested in these phenomena. For example, later in his memoirs, Jung talks about this dangerous hallucinatory period where he was faced with the possibility of losing his grip on reality, and his esoteric experiences, his images, his archives, his visions. This frightened him. And he asked whether this was madness, or whether this was another type of perception. The question of how to navigate that became very important for Jung, and should be important for us. And I think it was important for Freud.

Because we have to be very wary of romanticizing psychosis, as if it is a conduit to occult phenomena. Being a clinician, I see that happen a lot. That it gives a mode of explaining certain kinds of delusions or hallucinations. And being able to tell the difference. I had a patient who came from a small village in Puerto Rico. This was like something out of One Hundred Years of Solitude. He would describe how he would wake up in the morning, and there would be stones, huge stones in the living room of his small house. And at times the television would be screaming at him and accusing him of being homosexual. At another time, it was dark in the middle of the day, and all the neighbors came out and said prayers. It was difficult to me to separate out the cultural from the psychotic. And so we were finally able to determine, together, that if he shared what he was seeing with others, then it was cultural. And if it was only him, then we might think of it as psychotic. He was so relieved to understand that the voices from the radio and the television were different than the stones on the living room floor.

I just say that because the psychotic experience is a terrible experience. It's a terrible, lonely, dead, deadening experience, and it is not to be romanticized in any way. The goal is to help reconnect the psychotic with the social discourse, not valorize their separation from the social discourse.

Jung is talking about the time when he was working on his fantasies, on The Red Book. He says, "I needed a point of support in this world, and I may say that my family and my professional work were that to me. It was most essential for me to have a normal life in the real world as a counterpoint to that strange inner world. My family and my profession remain the base to which I could always return, assuring me that I was an actually existing, ordinary person. The unconscious contents could have driven me out of my wits."

Now I would like to talk about the concept of resistance. It happens to be a concept that I've been spending a lot of time thinking about lately, mainly because of my political work. I think that it is very relevant if we're going to understand the processes of incorporating occult phenomena, and how to understand certain kinds of sensitivities.

But I just want to start with, and elaborate on, a theory of resistance. I think there are some pieces of this that are kind of new, that are claiming some new ground. I became interested in resistance because of my political work. As a psychologist, I was kind of shocked to discover that the American torture program was a program created and overseen – and in some cases, actually run – by psychologists. That's true in the CIA. That's true in the Department of Defense. I would say there are about 20 psychologists out there who were associated with American torture, enhanced interrogation, interrogation abuses.

And I worked very hard with a community of dedicated activist psychologists to expose this. It took ten years, and we succeeded. But before we succeeded at exposing it, there was a point where I thought we had pretty much exposed it, but I discovered that even PhD psychologists are remarkably adept at resisting knowledge that they don't want to know.

Upton Sinclair said, "It is very difficult to get a man to think about something if his pay check is dependent on his not thinking about it." That's kind of the Marxist view. I was interested in exploring the psychoanalytic view – how people could be so resistant to this knowledge. At the same time, I was curious about why I was resistant to the dominant story I was being handed: that psychologists were actually there to protect the detainees; that they were the safety officers; that they made sure that the tortures didn't go too far – all that bullshit that we now know is not correct. I was allergic to the story that they were telling, and yet, I couldn't convince most of the members of governance of the American Psychological Association otherwise – no matter what evidence I showed them.

I began thinking a lot about the development of resistance. And so I thought about early development – and this brings us back to primary process and secondary process – but I was thinking about the child growing up in a family. Freud has this concept that goes all the way back to 1895, called the "Proton Pseudos". It's in his Project for a Scientific Psychology; it's the concept of the child's first lie.

Now, this turns out to be a very important concept. What does it mean when a child discovers that she can lie to the parents? Well, it means that there is a separate subjectivity in the child, and it also means that there's a kind of a separate ethical principle that the child is sort of working on. Or, at least, some form of shame, or something. "Why did I lie? And I got away with it. And so they can't read my mind. And so they are not omniscient. And they are not all powerful. And so, we are separate people. And they have an internal world, and I have an internal world." It's a momentous development.

And a lie, from my point of view, is a resistance. The parents say, "You can't do that." You do it, and you don't tell them… You have created some resistance to the norm that you've been handed. And to me, that is the kernel of resistance, and that leads to a very big cost. Because there's another resistance that is probably more dominant, unfortunately.

There's another resistance, which is the resistance to having a conflict with the most important people in your life. The idea that one disagrees with the rules – the law that they set down – can be very frightening, and so there's a kind of an internal challenge that comes at that moment. Do I suppress my resistant knowledge of separateness in order to maintain the relationship? Or do I hold my own value and my own idea, and separate myself from them?

Each one of those choices involves a certain kind of resistance. There's resistance to knowledge that shows the falseness of the dominant story, and there's the resistance to the dominant story. So when the government is exposed for torture, people who take a parental relationship with the government won't believe it, or they'll say it was necessary. But whatever it is, it's got to be consistent with maintaining that connection. But that leads to a kind of neurosis. That leads to a repression of the part of the self that would stand in contradiction to what one is being told, and then one has to not know what one knows. And one has to spend a lot of energy to defend not knowing what one knows. And that's generally the kind of neurotic process.

There is also a more severe version of this, and that is – and Freud separated these out – neurosis and trauma. The more severe version is when the knowledge that one gets is so severe that it challenges the belief in the order of the whole universe. So, if I am a soldier and fighting for what I thought was a good cause, and discover not only that it is not a good cause, but that everybody I know has been killed for what is not a good cause, the trauma is not only seeing the death and discovering mortality and fear, it is also not having any kind of a belief system that holds you up. And so there is a terrible traumatic experience there.

I'd like to talk more about trauma, because the theory of trauma has separated from the theory of neurosis in a very important way, and you know that when you read about all of the Freuds. One of the Freuds you read about is the Freud who betrayed sexually abused girls.

But the issue at hand though, is that Freud didn't quite get – at that point, when he gave up the theory that only sexual trauma leads to neurosis – that there was a fundamental difference between certain extreme traumas and most other kinds of trauma. And so he changed his theory to a theory that says life is full of trauma, and that's what neurosis is about: dealing with the trauma of everyday life. But there are actually very severe traumas, and that there is a difference in kind.

Freud finally wrote about this in 1920, in Beyond the Pleasure Principle, where he talked about how, when there's a trauma, the only thing that you can do is to try to repair the trauma. You can't deal with conflict, you can't deal symbolically whatsoever. And the other trauma theorists – including Breuer, including Janet – they would talk about dissociation. The people in contemporary trauma theory, who deal with the most severe trauma, talk about dissociation as a difference in kind from repression.

The question for Freud is always the same. And the question for those of us who are clinicians, and those of us who are shamans, I think is always the same. We have experiences that we have been cut off from. We have modes of knowledge that we can't allow ourselves to know. By what mechanisms can we free that knowledge, so that it flows once again? So that we take whoever we're dealing with, and expand their ability to know themselves; their dissociated selves, their repressed selves, and their ability to perceive terrible things in their environment, and wonderful things in their environment, but things that might challenge their view of the norms of society. How do we develop a therapeutic, or a shamanic, or some kind of process? The goal is pretty much the same. The therapy is pretty much the same.

I think it is often true in occult phenomena. I think it is true of drug experiences. I think it's true of sometimes in experiences of works of art. And it can be dangerous in paranoia. But we learn about what we don't allow ourselves to know, through discovering it in the world outside. In a pathological way, that's paranoia. In a creative way, it's how we deal always in a non-dissociated way.

If you look at infant studies, you see that the infant learns all about him or herself based on the response of, the observation of the self and the mother. So when the infant smiles, the mother smiles. The infant smiles, and the mother is smiling – and it keeps going. And so the learning about the self through the environment is an essential mode of self knowledge.

Freud loves to talk about learning about the self through disappointment in the other. Because Freud was basically a pessimist. Freud says that the baby is born in this narcissistic, wonderful experience, where every desire is immediately satisfied, and there's no separation between self and other. And the mother is all-knowing, and there's no difference in thought. There are no proton pseudos. It's all this sort of wonderful wash of responsiveness.

But if the infant gets hungry, and the mother's not there, then all of a sudden, the infant fantasizes the mother. And if the mother's still not there, Freud says that, "Experiences of hunger create an object out of the mother." The infant learns that there's a separate object through disappointment. That's where he's pessimistic. You might think of other ways, but that's one. So the whole point that I'm making is that on so many levels, we learn about what we don't know about ourselves. What Bollas calls the unthought known.

So, now let me talk about Freud's experiments and researches into bad prognostication. I'll read it for you:

A prediction has been made at a strange place, and by a strange fortune teller – meaning unknown to the woman – that something would happen to them at a particular time, which in fact did not come true. The prediction was for a woman – who was 27, but she looked much younger, and she took off her wedding ring – that she would be married and have two children before she was 32.

The woman was 43 when – now seriously ill – she told me the story in her analysis. She had remained childless. If one knew her private history, of which the palmist in the lounge of the Paris hotel was certainly ignorant, one could understand the two numbers included in the prophecy. The girl had married after an unusually intense attachment to her father. And had then had a passionate longing for children. So as to be able to put her husband in the place of her father. After years of disappointment, when she was on the brink of neurosis – she obtained the prophecy, which promised her the situation of her mother.

For it was a fact that her mother had had two children by the time she was 32. Thus, it was only by the help of psychoanalysis that it was possible to give a significant interpretation of the peculiarities of this pretended message from outside. But there was then no better explanation of the whole unequivocally determined chain of events, than to suppose that a strong wish on the part of a question, the woman. The strongest unconscious wish, in fact of her whole emotional life.

And the mode force of her impending neurosis had made itself manifest to the fortune teller. By being directly transferred to him, while his attention was being distracted by the performance as he was going. I have often had an impression, in the course of experiments in my private circle, that strongly emotionally occurred recollections can be successfully transferred without much difficulty.

Freud's idea is that there was this strong, emotional wish that had been transferred telepathically. But that the fortune teller misinterpreted it, and so made an incorrect prognostication. But the fact of the occult phenomenon, Freud believed was given evidence; it was proven. I love this. I love the fact that he takes what seems like it would falsify occult phenomena, and uses it to actually prove it. He wrote about this three times, this story; the last time in 1933. I think the earliest one is in 1922, but he told the story over and over again.

The interesting thing about this, is that in psychoanalytic theory, there is a theory that allows for what we might call thought transference. And I wouldn't say just thought transference; I can go much further in terms of subjective experience, emotional experience, bodily sensation transference.

It's been called "projective identification". There are number of what I would call sort of mystical psychoanalysts, who talk about projective identification – Melanie Klein was the originator of that idea. But I find it a rather paranoid construction. There's a resistance to the sensitivity that is required to actually pick this stuff up. And this is the problem – they will tell you – of working with borderline patients, who want to inject you into their discomfort, and therefore you become uncomfortable because you're picking up the discomfort that is denied and unbearable for the patient. And that's why this is, because they're putting this into you, and your job is to detoxify it and present it back to the patient. A kind of parapsychological communication. A communication of other sorts than simply by our general sense of perception.

Freud was way ahead of his time in terms of countertransference, and the use of countertransference. It has been theorized since; I just think that the way it's been theorized has this pseudo-scientific and rather paranoid language. But now Freud says something at the end of this article, that I felt was really interesting. He said, "On the basis of a number of experiences, I am inclined to draw the conclusion that thought transfers of this kind come about particularly easily at the moment at which an idea emerges from the unconscious. Or in theoretical terms, as it passes over from the primary process to secondary process."

Now to me, that is really quite a fascinating idea. That you turn something from a physical experience – which is where the primary process really lives – just at the point where it's becoming, before the pre-conscious, or it's beginning to be symbolized; where it's beginning to become imbued with meaning just at that moment, when one is battling whether to allow it into one's own thought or keep it out of one's thought. That it is so powerful; that it is coming up, it is erupting if you will from the primary process; that those moments are when sensitive people can pick it up. And who knows at what distance, but certainly it could be picked up by sensitive people.

I think Freud was onto something really, really interesting in terms of his own idea of what is primary process, what is this transition, and what is required in the bringing of that thought into thought and into discourse? Because it may not fit into the discourse. It may not be permitted into the discourse, but it's coming up. And certainly it's this moment of terrific meaning and conflict. And so, agitation of the soul, if you will.

Freud talks about it in dreams; the most vivid dreams are not dreams based on truth, but based on meaning. The biggest, most profound meaning is why you see color so vividly in a dream. I've actually written about trauma; that trauma is remembered so vividly; traumatic memories are recalled so vividly, not because they're real – in fact, research shows that they're very rarely real – but because of the meaning that is recorded; that moment of the challenge to one's belief system, and the new piece of knowledge that's coming up. And it is a kind of physiological sensation. And it's all happening at once.

And those are the moments Freud says, when transference is possible. And I would add that those are the moments that transference is possible in sensitive people. What do I mean by sensitive people? I want to take a little aside and talk about narcissistic parents; and truly traumatized parents.

There are a number of types of parents that create an environment where resistance is futile. Where it is really dangerous to be separate. Because first of all, they won't permit separation. Narcissistic parents do not permit separation; a separate entity of the child. Really, really traumatized parents generally only allow a recognition of the child, as a parentified child. As a child who's paying exquisite attention to the suffering and needs of the parent.

What I'm saying is that there are a whole number of constellations of parenting that make for very sensitive children. Children are so attuned, and a lot of these children become clinicians, and some probably become psychics. So I just want to talk a little bit about the children of suffering parents, the children of narcissistic parents, the children of violent alcoholic parents. There's a number of categories that we could talk about.

I woke up this morning from a dream, and I realized that it probably was influenced by this image. I was talking with Donald Trump. And he was wearing a hat. And he took off his hat, and there was no head. It actually looked like that.

I began thinking about Donald Trump, as an example of this kind of parent to this country. Because he is the perfect example. I mean, he is the paradigmatic narcissist. According to Freud, the narcissist believes that everything good in the world is part of them; that everything good in the world, they caused or they are a part of, or they are connected to; or they know the person, or they influence the person.

I mean, we've seen Donald Trump do that. Everything bad in the world, he tried to stop, is outside of him, has nothing to do with him. Even bad things in him are caused from the outside, and this is what makes the narcissist: the underside of narcissism, paranoia. Anything that might be perceived as bad in the South, has to have been caused by somebody externally. The bad has to come from outside, and you have to build a wall against it. And anything good in the world comes from inside, and you have to take credit for it, and welcome it. And if you don't accept that world view, you are destroyed.

The underside of that narcissistic charm is danger. If they're a loving narcissist, they'll ignore you. If they're an aggressive narcissist, they will want to kill you. And children who are raised by aggressive narcissists, work so hard to keep the charm going – keep the charmed relationship – and they deny the aggression, and they become exquisitely attuned to the nuances of the nuances of those parents.

Americans – many of them who are suffering – love the idea that Donald Trump is going to put us under his web of goodness and find the terrible causes of this suffering out there. But you'd better not turn on him, or be another ethnic group that he chooses to make outsiders.

So that's a kind of national version. This can happen nationally. It can happen personally. It can happen when the parent is scary. It can happen when the parent is needy. So my point is that there are people who are raised to be exquisitely attuned to these other modes of knowledge. And I think of patients of mine, who could not acknowledge their traumatic histories.

It really had to come in a dream. It had to come through extrasensory perception. It had to come from a coincidence, a synchronicity. It had to come from something where they could have deniability of knowledge. And then my job – it had to come through me – through projective identification, or through my perception. And yes, the whole point is to expand the knowledge of the self in all kinds of ways. It doesn't have to be psychological; it can be spiritual in all kinds of ways. It can be esoteric in terms of study. It can have to do with knowledge of history, of the great mystical texts. There are many, many ways of understanding one's soul and its place in the world of others. And there are many ways of being sensitive to that, and there are many ways of guiding people in that journey.

My job as a clinician, and those of you who are clinicians, or those of you who do this work one way or another – our job is to help navigate that passage of knowledge, knowing the two resistances. The resistance to knowing, and the resistance to buying the story of the other. And using those poles, and by using what we know that we don't know, we can expand the experience, the curiosity, the openness to new knowledge. That I think is what I would say is a sort of psychoanalytic endeavor: to help people through that. And it's not only a psychoanalytic endeavor, but I think that's why Freud was so accepting of occult phenomenon, and I want to end by just reading a passage. There's this unknown and wonderful case of Freud's. He had three conversations with a poet named Bruno Goetz when he was a student. Bruno Goetz was having what he thought was neurosis; Freud diagnosed it as hunger. Freud gave him money, and he went and ate.

But meanwhile, they had these three conversations, and Goetz was asked about these three conversations maybe 50 years later. He felt like he wasn't going to be able to do honor to those conversations, because it would be distorted in his memory. And lo and behold, he happened upon a box of letters that he had written. And in that box were two letters that he had written the night after he had those sessions with Freud. He published those notes. They talk about poetry; they talk about spirituality; they talked about the Bhagavad Gita. And so I'm just going to read to you his comments on Freud's comments on the *Bhagavad Gita*:

> The *Bhagavad Gita* is a great poem. It is deep and terrifyingly steep. Beneath me in purple darkness, I should have said in the diver, who did not come back after daring a second time. If you immerse yourself without the aid of a very sharp intellect, into the world of the Bhagavad Gita – where nothing seems to stand still, and everything dissolves into something else – then suddenly you are confronted by nothingness. Do you know what it means to face nothingness? Do you know what that means?
>
> And yet this nothingness also is only a European misconception. The Indian Nirvana is not nothingness, but the beyond of all opposites. That is not lustful pleasure, as one likes to think in Europe. But

a final superhuman, hardly thinkable; an everything encompassing ice cold insight. Or if one does not understand it, it is magic. Ah, these European dreamers, what do they know about oriental profundity? They rave, but they know nothing. And then they are astonished when they lose their heads, and thereby sometimes become deranged. In the literal sense, de-ranged.

I am a physician, and I would like to help the many people who live in an inner hell, as well as I can. Not in any kind of beyond – but here on earth, most people live in hell. Schopenhauer saw that quite correctly. My insights – my theories and methods have the purpose to make men aware of this hell, so that they can free themselves of it. Only when people have learned to breathe freely, perhaps will they experience again what art could really mean. Now they must use it as a narcotic, and rid themselves of their torture for a few hours. Art for them is a kind of Schnapps.

But then you're not an atheist, I exclaim. Stop, stop, not so fast, he warned me. I can't stand those big words. Nowadays they are filled to the brim with lies and filth. They have to be cleansed first before one may use them again. For that, we have you, the poets. But most of you don't want to know anything about that – and dance with the others, the dance of hell. It is a real dance of hell, and we can live to see where it all leads, and what will suddenly open up before our eyes.

Often, I can no longer hear the word, 'God,' and I don't like to use it. Perhaps it is different with you, but the older I become, the more distrustful I become also. I don't want to pretend to you. You are very young, and the devil knows where you will wind up. That's why I don't want to analyze you. You should find your own way, by yourself. As for my part, I shall remain, but as one they call an old honest atheist. And I shall try to help people to their own insight. That is my good conscience. You should try in your own way.

Now I've talked to you quite unscientifically, and it did me good to play a little with these ideas, and not always to be so stern with myself. Your seriousness is quite different, and your good conscience is of a different kind. Keep your courage – that's all that matters – and never let yourself be analyzed. Write good poems, when that is given to you. But don't cramp up, and don't hide yourself. Man stands naked in front of his God. That is the only prayer which is still among us.

The Twelfth House:
Art and the Unconscious

Katy Bohinc

Since my earliest studies as a poet I have sought to uncover unifying threads in human culture in order to understand human history with less bias and more permission; to understand with more truth. Poetry, a non-commercial and in this way non-regulated art (for better and worse), was one entrance. The other was astrology. Western astrology (discussed herein) is of course specific in cultural detail but the originating principles – math, measurement and scientific precision – are shared across astrological systems. The vast majority of early civilizations studied the literally sparkling unknown of the night, and with little more than the eye, a ruler and writing utensil, developed majorly complex measurement schemas; a feat which tells me all humans have the propensity and capacity to measure their worlds systemically. And let it be noted, that while certainly in the eye of the beholder I'll argue staunchly that the similarities in cross-civilization astrological symbolisms overwhelmingly outweigh the differences. Astrology has fundamentally taught me how similar we are.

In this spirit I will say further that when I talk about astrology I have little patience for the ones who say "but if this one thing isn't true doesn't this disprove the whole?" Or really, this is what they mean but it is phrased something like "but my sister is a scorpio and she isn't vindictive!?!?" My response to this is very seriously "call Becky with the good hair."

Herein's expose of astrology is not in any way meant as a proof to indoctrinate you. I am not here to show that astrology is scientifically valid, whatever you may think scientific means. I see astrology much more poetically: as providing a window of vision for a possibility of reality. I see it as a historical study of the foundations of ancient civilizations and cross-cultural similarities. And, to the logical positivists out there, there does exist the incompleteness theorem and yet we have not completely rejected mathematics. So if finding one or many logical loopholes is your project, I dare say you are missing the big picture for a penny or your ego.

My own interest in astrology began a few years out of undergrad. I was – swear to god – thinking back to my undergrad math courses which frequently covered early Greek mathemes – and wondering "why were they so interested in, of all things, Triangles?" Imagine the Greek landscape: a very busy metropolis, with some large-scale structures but not too many yet at 3 B.C., bustling trade and markets in dirt and stone streets, fancy silks on overcrowded wheelbarrow carts, more or less stinky fruits, some Plato and Aristotle sitting around. What geometric shape would be most useful to this society? Probably wheels for carting and transporting things. Maybe squares for building large structures. But triangles?! Trigonometry just seems rather out of place. How, operationally, the triangular shape would become such a multi-century obsession of study as to give rise to Trigonometry – which I assure you was not something that fell out of the sky – it took some serious earthly effort – until I realized: It completely came out of the sky.

What I'll term "Triangle Obsessive Disorder," arose from an obsession with the starscape, those fantastical night time creatures which made patterns and, if planets, caused dramatic speculation with their traveling. Recall that originally there was no linguistic difference between astronomy and astrology. Further, the astronomy/astrology term also frequently indicated what we differentiate today as "Mathematics." A great example being the incredible Hypatia, an Alexandrian woman who by studying the stars developed several complex geometric formulae which would not be proven accurate until centuries after her death. (Only freak egoists like Aristotle and Plato branded mathematics with a unique linguistic term, denying math's affiliation with astrology and confusing historians. One of these jerks also banished poetry.) Today of course we cull out linguistically "math" from "astrology," because astrology layers symbolism on top of math. In this sense, astrology was the original "Tao of Physics," putting human meaning to mathematic structure.

So we have established that study of the stars developed trigonometry. But what was the rhyme or reason to the great symbol of astrology, the Zodiac? How did this grand and infamous zodiac come to be? It was not whipped up willy nilly by early proponents of LSD, dreaming stories about star creatures. Although astrological symbolism is frequently interchanged with the term "mythology," it developed quite differently from the faith-based mythologies of other major religions, like say, the one around the Christ dude.

The Western Zodiac was born not by faith of miracles, but of the world's largest dataset – world's largest until Google and the NSA. For three millennia the largest data crunch in the world was the zodiac. For 600 years every single day, day in, day out, the Sumerians wrote down the position of all the planets and the constellations at least five times a day. It was these tablets of data which bore the data patterns that generated the zodiac.

Interestingly enough, every day since the big data boom decisions are made based on empirical analysis. Today it matters what the data says; The "why" it is true is irrelevant. Google constantly revamps its hiring practices because the data says "being friends outside the office increases team performance." The methodology for generating the zodiac was the same as the practices leveraged by Google and contemporary data science. Astrology can be deemed true based on whether it works, especially in the absence of a greater "why". As for the "why": if the moon can give me my period and make the tide come in, I see no reason why the planets' gravitational pulls aren't affecting my chi, except that chi is not studied by Western science. This is all to say, simply because the "why" has not yet been discovered, it doesn't render a thing false; in the absence of a Newtonian "why", I'm most concerned with whether it "works."

If one is not willing to consider astrology within the science category, well that is fine and dandy, you are not the first! A mid-point would be to consider it a thought system much more scientifically-based than the faith-based miracles of Christ.

What differentiates astrology (ancient and modern) from being a simple mathematical system is its propensity to be used as a divination tool, which allows people to grant it an almost deistic power. (Trust me, it's addictive.) Hence, in ancient times astrology directly competed with authority, particularly mono-deity Christianity. Astrology was thus banished. Like most banishments, it was genuinely ideological and directly related to power.

In an interesting sidenote, even after Christian rulers completely outlawed astrology, for centuries throughout the Dark Ages the vast majority of Western medical advice still held elements of it. For example: if you have a stomachache take ruddy metallic medicine on Tuesday because the gut is related to Taurus and indicates a lack of redness in the liver. I find it pretty astonishing that astrologically-related medical advice lasted so late in the game. But then again, "Modern Western Medicine" is so preeminent we don't consider how recent a development it is.

Anyway, I'm not advocating the use of astrology to treat cancer. I mean to elucidate how deeply ingrained astrology was in Western culture. More examples: The Three Wise Kings who found Jesus under three stars? The Three Wise Kings named Magi? "Magi" is the Egyptian term for Astrologer. And the three stars? Even fundamentalist Christians today use the rare conjunction of the three stars (believed to be Jupiter, Venus and Mars) in order to date the birth of Christ.

To make a long story short, astrology was super potent in the ancient West. However, (largely Christian) authorities were not as keen. So, Astrology was outlawed, exiled and practitioners burned alive time after time – the first expulsion of astrologers from Rome being in 139 B.C. Alongside the astrologers were also "Witches" and "Shamans". Also "Spells," which were deemed "the Devil's Art" and subsumed into private corners of the Catholic Church where they became the worst grimoires ever written – by popes. (A grimoire is a book of magic spells.) When I look at it this way, it seems like the yin of Christ's love, spawned the outright yang totalitarianism of Christian Rule.

Which, and I swear to god this is all relevant because it dovetails into understanding the rejection of the modern astrological experiments of Michel Gauquelin.

In 1955 French statistician and astrologer Michel Gauquelin published the book *Les Influences des Astres* which was the first modern study of astrology presented formally and publicly to intellectual journals and committees and so on. It used the modern form of mathematical inquiry: statistics (itself a field of mathematics about 100 years old).

Gauquelin ran a whole bunch of statistical tests on a fairly small dataset –

around 2,000 sample size. He was analyzing natal charts. Natal charts are the bed-rock of astrology.

A natal chart is comprised of the position of the planets at the moment of an individual's birth. The theory is that the position of the planets, and the angles these planets make to one another comprise a sophisticated set of meaning which determines a propensity towards a certain personality. This personality is not set in stone; it is not one's fate. It is the energy that we each have a tendency towards but is in no way finite.

Gauquelin studied natal chart data from all possible variables to see if any planetary patterns indicated professional success. In other words, he looked to see if anything in a natal chart actually mathematically correlated with real world outcomes. The results were clear, counter-intuitive and, unsurprisingly, contested. Controversy went on for decades – the official complaint was the math was faulty. However, from a political view, it is not shocking that "Enlightened France" (home of the Pope Grimoire) officially rejected Gauqulin's results, official body after official body, despite repeated evidence to the contrary. In my opinion the controversy around statistical methodology is moot anyway because the sample size should have been much larger. Today this is possible. What should be done is additional studies leveraging "big data" – and I do mean big, like millions of natal charts. The Astro. com database is a place to start.

Gauquelin's findings were not at all intuitive. The answer was nothing to do with a planet and nothing to do with the zodiac. It was to do with a house.

The houses are one of the least well known parts of astrology in contemporary culture. Today, we all know sun signs. Sun sign horoscopes – essentially the cheapest, most reductive form of astrology – entered into popular consciousness in the 1800's as a way for newspapers to make money. True astrology is based on a much more comprehensive analysis which considers all the planets, not just the sun. Again, the thing being analyzed is called "the natal chart."

The houses in astrology are based on the precise minute of one's birth. There are twelve houses, each with a different meaning: The first house of personality; the second of money and values; the third of communications; the fourth of home and family; the fifth of romance, creativity, children and risks; the sixth of work and health; the seventh of deep relationships; the eighth of inheritances and taboo; the ninth of study and travel; the tenth of professional standing; the eleventh of dreams and friendship; and the 12th house of the unconscious.

Gauquelin's findings were surprising on many levels. One would assume planets in the 10th house of public standing would most likely correlate to professional success. However, Gauquelin found that the 12th house of the unconscious was the leading indicator. Sublimely weird, because in ancient astrology, the 12th house was associated with prisons, mental hospitals, monasteries, orphanages, places of solitude and general underworldliness.

In contemporary astrology, the 12th house, the last house, is the house of Persephone's underworld. It is the house of Carl Jung's *Red Book*. It is the house of contemporary poetry. It is the house of our dreams, secrets and fantasies. It is still the house of our solitude, our truly individual adventures, or our solitary mental adventures which render us truly unique individuals. The 12th house is the house of prophesy. It is the house of the unstructured zeitgeist. It is the space we go when truly alone. It is the house of the soul.

And, the twelfth house was the only aspect of the natal chart Gauquelin found to have any bearing on a person's "IRL" professional success. So at first, while seeming highly unlikely that this lonely, damned house would make us great, on second thought, that the section of the chart which ultimately stands for true individualism would reckon us notable figures, makes a damned lot of sense to me. I think of it like this: it is each of us who makes the choices to become notable figures, but with 12th house planet(s), one is so original that they differentiate from the rest of the famous fucks out there. In short, being famous isn't enough. One must produce something of value via connection to the unconscious and truly independent thought. And, one must have put oneself in a public position (been able to make a mark on the world.)

Gauquelin's findings were incredibly specific to the planet and the exact vocation. However, in my personal investigations of the 12th house, I find it useful to broaden the search to any planet in the 12th house and particularly, multiple planets in the 12th. Let's look at some examples, beginning with my favorite example of the 12th house archetype: David Bowie.

Bowie was the best example of the 12th house. He had "David Bowie" versus "David Jones" denoting an deep understanding of public versus private selves. He could cull from the Zeitgeist a public desire even before the public knew they wanted it. He was an utter individual, weird and unpredictable. He was a phoenix, constantly re-inventing. He was remarkably honest. And he had soul.

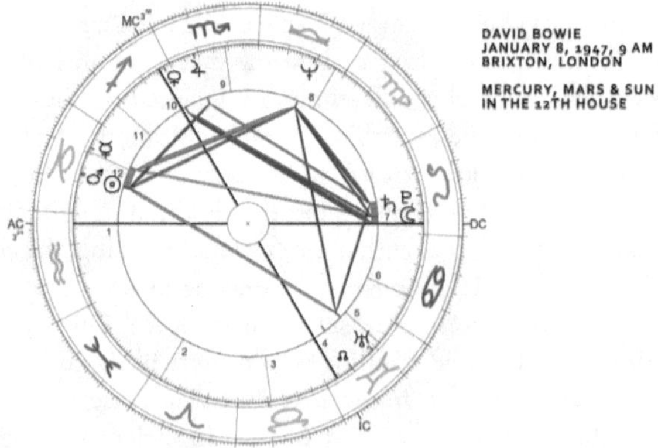

David Bowie natal chart. Sun and Mars conjunct in the 12th house. Mercury on the cusp of the 11th house (planets on the cusp of houses typically interpreted as part of the next house.)

Another deeply archetypal example is Gertrude Stein. Stein infamously began her intellectual career studying under philosopher William James. But the first paper she published was on psychology (titled "Normal Motor Automatism"). It theorized that an action can be completed by a second "unconscious" personality. Or, in other words, that the unconscious can act. Stein then flunked out of medical school where she studied neuroscience (the unconscious) before becoming "The Genius" she was known as in Paris. Little surprise this "stream of unconsciousness" poet has not one but four planets in the 12th house.

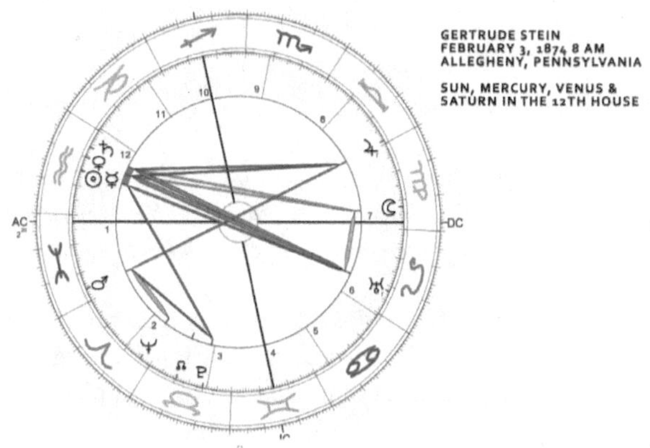

Gertrude Stein Natal Chart. Sun, Mercury, Venus and Saturn conjunct in the 12th house.

No wonder she wrote like this!

A kind in glass and a cousin, a spectacle and nothing strange a single hurt color and an arrangement in a system to pointing. All this and not ordinary, not unordered in not resembling. The difference is spreading.

GLAZED GLITTER.

Nickel, what is nickel, it is originally rid of a cover.

The change in that is that red weakens an hour. The change has come. There is no search. But there is, there is that hope and that interpretation and sometime, surely any is unwelcome, sometime there is breath and there will be a sinecure and charming very charming is that clean and cleansing. Certainly glittering is handsome and convincing.

There is no gratitude in mercy and in medicine. There can be breakages in Japanese. That is no programme. That is no color chosen. It was chosen yesterday, that showed spitting and perhaps washing and polishing. It certainly showed no obligation and perhaps if borrowing is not natural there is some use in giving.

A SUBSTANCE IN A CUSHION.

The change of color is likely and a difference a very little difference is prepared. Sugar is not a vegetable. d

from *Tender Buttons*, Gertrude Stein, 1914

Outside those typically associated with the avant garde, there are some 12th house celebrities.

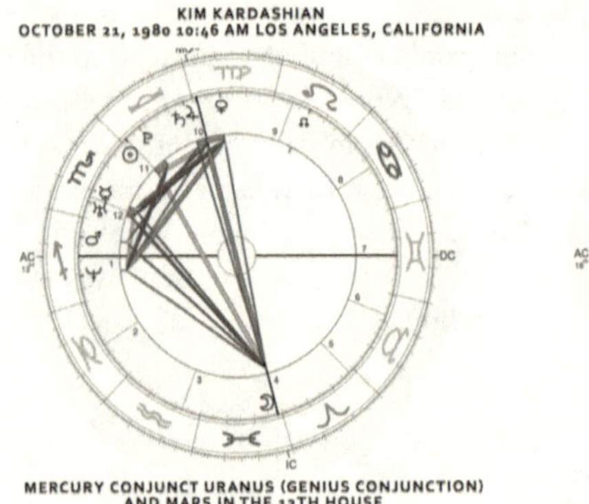

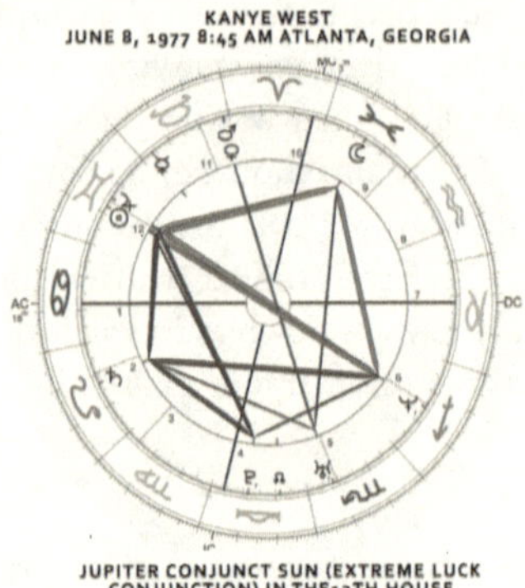

Kim Kardashian and Kanye West Natal Charts. Kim (left) has the genius conjunction and Kanye (right) the conjunction of extreme luck. Both are cusp placements, which per Michelle Gauquelin were the most potent of 12th house positions.

I really do believe Kim is a genius. Her selfie book is proof. Kanye? Who else could make such a jerk of himself time and again without failing except the truly lucky.

Striking is a very small list of notable figures with planets in the 12th house.

Prominent 12th House placements:

- JOHN CAGE – MERCURY
- GHANDI – SUN
- MADONNA – SUN, URANUS, MERCURY
- NICK DRAKE – SUN, URANUS, MERCURY, VENUS
- PRINCE – NORTH NODE, NEPTUNE
- HELENE CIXOUS – SUN
- ALAIN BADIOU – MOON & SATURN
- KANT – SUN, MOON, MERCURY
- BLAISE PASCAL – SUN & MERCURY
- ORSON WELLS – SUN & MERCURY
- HITLER – URANUS
- MARTIN LUTHER KING – JUPITER & URANUS
- GEORGE WASHINGTON – VENUS & SATURN
- NELSON MANDELA – MOON
- PICASSO – MARS
- HEMMINGWAY – MERCURY
- GINSBERG – JUPITER, MOON, MARS
- JOHNNY CASH – SUN, MERCURY, MARS
- TOM WAITS – SUN
- ARTHUR CONAN DOYLE – SUN, URANUS, MARS
- FREUD – ZERO
- MARX – ZERO
- JOHN COLTRANE – JUPITER
- THELONIOUS MONK – JUPITER
- MILES DAVIS – SUN & MERCURY
- SUN RA – NEPTUNE
- NINA SIMONE – MOON
- BILLIE HOLIDAY – MOON
- TAYLOR SWIFT – SUN & MERCURY
- MERYL STREEP – SUN & MERCURY
- CHARLIZE THERON – SUN, MOON, MERCURY
- JANIS JOPLIN – SUN, MERCURY, VENUS
- GEORGIO ARMANI – SUN, MERCURY, NEPTUNE
- THE DONALD (DUCK!) – PLUTO (SEEMS EVIL)
- HILARY – SUN & MERCURY
- OBAMA – JUPITER & SATURN
- JOE BIDEN – SUN, MERCURY, VENUS, MARS
- DAVID CAMERON – PLUTO & URANUS
- MARGARET THATCHER – SATURN
- TONY BLAIR – SUN, JUPITER, MARS
- GEORGE W. BUSH – SUN & SATURN
- MAO ZEDONG – SUN & LILITH
- JOSEF STALIN – SUN & VENUS
- SADDAM HUSSEIN – SUN, URANUS, MERCURY

Note a few things beyond the unsurprising Nina Simone with a 12th house moon. Of course that woman had soul. Beyond that, however, consider that nearly every single major contemporary politician – Obama, Hillary, George W, Trump, Biden, Cameron, Thatcher – all have 12th house placements. Frightening even.

Finally, I note with irony that Freud and Marx, arguably the two most influential Western intellectuals of contemporary thought both tally zero 12th house planets. Our fates are not entirely created by 12th house planets. Then again, maybe I'm correct when I also say Freud and Marx are the two most overrated Western intellectuals of contemporary thought. I suspect their function is primarily as "summarizer" rather than creator.

Another example of someone I loathe as a wife-murderer, but dear friends in the audience adore, so I'll let them know: your muse William S. Burroughs was 12th house psycho:

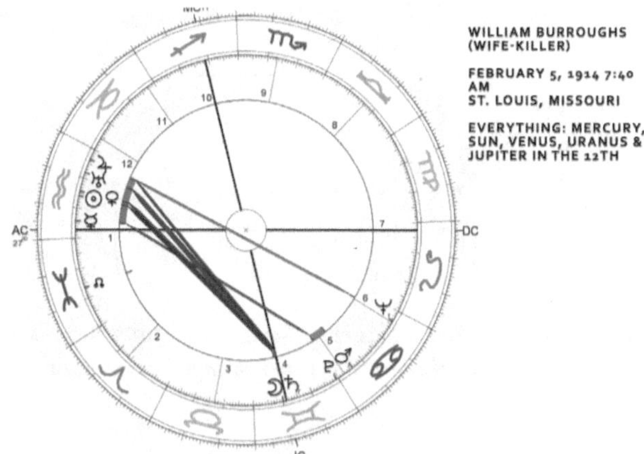

William S. Burroughs' Natal Chart. Five planets in the 12th house: Mercury, Sun, Venus, Uranus and Jupiter.

Planets in the 12th house clearly do not correlate to moral performance.

Just to keep the tension going, a genuinely shocking find: the king of the unconscious world, Carl Jung, is absent of planetary influence in the 12th. This one would genuinely debunk me except to acknowledge Jung's childhood in a house filled with mysticism, astrology and meditative studies inclines me to believe he knew the 12th house not by planetary default but by learned awareness. In short he spent his life overcompensating, trying to experience what he knew others could experience but did not come naturally to him. That or Carl Jung's recorded birthtime is wrong.

Nonetheless, I cannot help but continue my party trick with my favorite example of a major 12th house presence. Beyonce is still the queen:

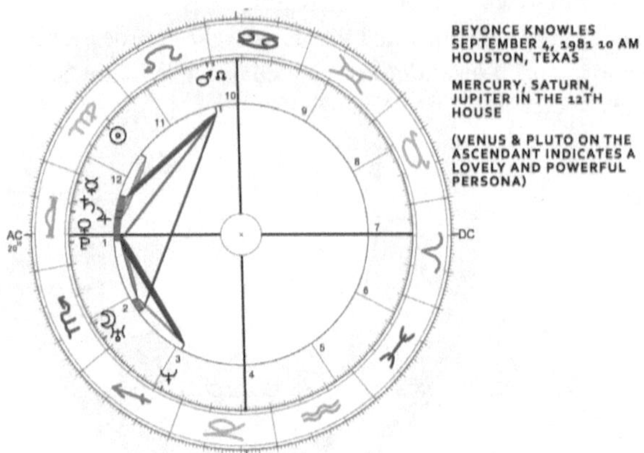

Beyonce Knowles' Natal Chart. Saturn, Mercury and Jupiter conjunct in the 12th house. (Venus and Pluto on the ascendant, which signifies she is an intensely powerful and adorable persona.)

What we poets write when we write about chaos, when we verbalize the fantastical or impossible, when we examine the connectivity of all things, when we expose our singular strangeness: these are all machinations of the 12th house. It is comforting to know the unconscious has been one twelfth of the world view since antiquity.

In a sense, the 12th house is universal suffering. It is the place where by seeing beyond ourselves we become ourselves. By leaving ourselves and seeing the whole, we find our singular reference. The 12th house is the Koan. The Zeitgeist via solitude; the individual via the collective. The 12th house is perhaps the fundamental basis for art.

As for astrology as science, we have the technology available today to examine this beautiful and fundamental knowledge of our civilization. It should be studied further.

Until then, astrology is a fabulous party trick, the 12th house an awesome metaphor, and both a portal into incredible insight. In a way, it doesn't matter if astrology is "true", it matters that it works as a vehicle to truth.

When shall we three meet again?
Psychoanalysis, Art and the Occult:
A Clandestine Convergence

Olga Cox Cameron

> *I am the necessary angel of earth,*
> *Since in my sight you see the earth again*
>
> *Cleared of its stiff and stubborn, man-locked set.*
>
> *Necessary, according to the poet Wallace Stevens, but nonetheless*
> *hovering on the perimeters of our representational field;*
> *Am I not*
> *Myself only half of a figure of a sort*
> *A figure half seen , or seen for a moment, a man*
> *Of the mind, an apparition apparelled in*
> *Apparels of such lightest look that a turn*
> *Of my shoulder and quickly, too quickly I am gone?* (Stevens, 435)

From forever this perimeter has exercised a powerful magnetic pull on both the arts and occult branches of research. As Paul Valéry remarks, the intrication of creative writing and these esoteric systems is one of the oldest of all literary forms. "It belongs to a department of literature remarkable for its persistence and astonishing in its variety," he writes. It includes sacred books, admirable poems, outlandish narratives, physico-mathematical researches, all of them, as he says, "full of beauties and absurdities." Valéry is benign in his assessment of this ongoing infatuation, seeing it indeed as something essential to the human spirit. "It is the glory of man," he asserts, "and something more than his glory, to waste his powers upon the void… the role of the non-existent exists; the function of the imaginary is real and we learn from strict logic that the false implies the true." (Valéry, 123)

So a strong link exists between art and the occult. But what of psychoanalysis? Despite his well documented fascination with this domain I think Freud might have been surprised to see psychoanalysis lined up alongside art and the occult in the title of our congress. His career began under the auspices of scientific positivism with his most influential teacher Ernst Brucke insistent that "No other forces than the common physical and chemical ones are active within the organism."

(Jones, 45) However, it is not irrelevant that the very beginnings of psychoanalysis coincide exactly with the late 19th Century craze for all things occult, and that the first English review of *Studies on Hysteria* was published by the Society for Psychical Research in 1894. And this too was the era when Poe, de Maupassant and Hoffmann were thrilling readers with evocations of the horror-studded thing that lies beneath the semblance of the thing. So a historical convergence is visible. Also, already in *Studies on Hysteria*, Freud whose other great teacher Brentano asserted that the psyche *is* representation, is pushing his readers towards the perimeters of the representational field when he speaks of unconscious memory as "thoughts which never came about, which merely had the possibility of existing." (S.E.2, 300) It may be that the convergence is not just historical but also conceptual. Freud returns a number of times though not very systematically to this question of the perimeters of representation throughout his work, but to get it more clearly in focus and as a result to line up psychoanalysis with art and the occult we must turn to Lacan.

To the Lacan of a specific era. It is difficult to overestimate Guy le Gaufey's archeological reading of Lacan where he tracks the exact places where mutations occur which leave the Lacanian vocabulary intact but angle its terms in new directions. Helped by Le Gaufey, in trying to think about how these three fields might converge I have been drawn to re-read the seminar on Identification. In the eight years between the Seminar on Desire and The Logic of Phantasy, Lacan returns again and again to the topic of the representational field, specifically in relation to the status of an innovative concept, the "o-object". He does this via difficult demonstrations, using the Moebius strip, the Klein bottle and the Cross-cap in topology, the vanishing point in Perspectivist painting, the zero and the Fibonacci series in mathematics. Since he was not someone who simply repeated himself year after year, the wide and ever changing terms of his inquiry reflect the difficulty of what he was trying to do. Each seminar picks up and recalibrates the themes of the previous one but it can also be useful to read each as an isolated document with its specific accents and avoidances. The seminar Identification seems particularly apt in today's context because of its emphasis on occultation and on the way in which the o-object can menace or even collapse the everyday representational field which we inhabit. While it may seem annoyingly smart-ass to read the word occult as o-cult this is primarily where I see the connection between the three themes of this congress.

In this difficult seminar, the question of occultation bears firstly upon the nothing of Leibniz' seminal question, "why is there not nothing?", now imported into psychoanalytic theory, and secondarily upon its relation to indeterminacy. Three years earlier, in Desire, Lacan had spoken of a necessary not knowing, of the essential veiling which ensures that one continue to be a subject who speaks. And in that seminar he invoked one of the foremost citizens of the occult, the Ghost, to show how in the absence of this essential not knowing, the structure of subjectivity itself collapses. Because the Ghost in *Hamlet* knows, Hamlet must founder under an impossible knowledge. As Lacan says of the ghost's revelation, "something is lifted, a veil which weighs precisely on the articulation of the unconscious line." (27/5/59 p.11)[1] "What is laid bare is the irredeemable and unplumbable betrayal of love," (8/4/59 p.6) a beyond of pact and of possibility identical to that evoked in seminar 7 for Oedipus and in Seminar 8 for Sygne de Coufontaine. Speaking of Hamlet, Lacan's language is stark and uncompromising: "The betrayal is absolute, representing a radical cancelling out of anything resembling goodwill or fidelity. The truth of Hamlet is a truthless truth." (8/4/59 p.8) In the three seminars which precede Identification, Desire, Ethics and Transference, Lacan is in tragic mode, focussing on the nothing as an absolute and unmodifiable *ne phunai*.[2] This accents shifts in Identification.

What we now encounter is not the nothing of unplumbable betrayal, but an oscillation between the nothing perhaps and the perhaps nothing which together constitute a question and a message. The *nothing perhaps* as question opens out onto possibility, onto the unforeseeable, while the *perhaps nothing* as message functions as uneasy reassurance. But Lacan insists on their intrication. As he puts it in the lesson of 21/3/62: "the message manifests itself in the middle of the question", elaborating further on "it is through the question itself and not the answer to the question that the message comes to light." (21/3/62 p.8)

To what does this essential but unstable oscillation respond? To the demand for meaning, the demand for a final definitive explanation with respect to which, as he puts it, every approximation would be insufficient. But the whole point here is that approximation and insufficiency are the only things on offer. While in the earlier spond more adequately than this, its impotence as guarantor is troped as "a common tragedy", in Identification it is troped as absolutely essential to ongoing existence. I quote:

> This Other who guarantees precisely nothing qua other, qua locus
> of the word it is here that it takes on its instructive incidence. It
> becomes the veil, the blanket, the source of occultation of the very
> place of desire. (21/3/62 p.9)

There is nothing simple about this assertion he tells us, since what he calls "this dimension of the hidden" is, he says, the most contradictory one that the spirit can construct once it is a question of the truth." (21/3/62 p.10)

These are not just difficult abstract concepts or serious brain teasers for leisure time cerebration. While this whole domain represents what Lacan calls that which is most veiled and most difficult to articulate in our experience (13/6/62 p.11), it is everybody's business and everybody's business every day. This is what each of us must grapple with concretely in his or her own way, and in this regard, as he says,

---

1 The Seminars of Lacan quoted have not yet been published in English. References are to page numbers of individual lessons.
2 Taken from Sophocles' *Oedipus at Colonus*, this phrase, differently inflected, recurs in Lacan's work during these years.

the neurotic, the pervert and the psychotic are only faces of the normal structure. Lacan is certainly not thinking about the occult here but he does gesture towards the arts remarking that what he is engaged in is a kind of aesthetics.

So is it valid to suggest that the three domains around which our congress has been organized – Psychoanalysis, Art and the Occult – are three different types of involvement with the equipoise required to cope with the nothing perhaps/perhaps nothing. One can see how the occult, in more or less exalted and degraded forms, preoccupies itself with the message and the question as distinct from but related to each other. Whole swathes of esoteric ritual exist in order to question the thing that lies beneath the semblance of the thing, and often in the midst of this questioning, messages issue forth in thrilling and variously decipherable guise. In its various modalities the occult does indeed engage directly with the nothing perhaps/perhaps nothing. The necessary indeterminacy outlined by Lacan can be courted, disavowed, or shunted towards certainty by elaborate cabbalistic calculations, and the veil can be excitingly or terrifyingly lifted by sudden irruptive manifestations which perforate the normal surfaces of representability. Across the enormous range of the occult, stretching from divine apparitions to the Friday night horror movie, the various permutations of the nothing perhaps and the perhaps nothing surge up in menace or sink uneasily into near invisibility. And this is often brought about by unchartable infractions of the ordinary laws of specularity. As a kind of aside I find this intriguing since Lacan's mighty attempts in these middle years to find ways to demonstrate the non-representability of the o-object saw him foregrounding shapes which also broke these laws. The moebius strip, the Klein bottle and the cross-cap all do in fact possess a specular image. If you put them in front of the mirror something will appear there. They just do not invert so the image is odd. Not enough reason to line them up with the ghost's games around specularity but I am intrigued nonetheless.

Again, in terms of the possible convergence suggested by the title of this congress, one might note that the oscillation between the nothing perhaps and the perhaps nothing is also that which underpins every work of art. While art glories in creation and creativity, it has also always known what George Steiner calls the "provocation of non-being". The making of the poem, of the painting, of the sonata, remains contingent, and in every case, as Steiner goes on to say, it might not have been, emerging from the vortex of zeroness to challenge Leibniz's question: "why is there not nothing?" The work of art carries within it the scandal of its proximity to the nothing, the trace of its hazardous emergence *ex nihilo*. Steiner, speaking of what he calls the compelling needlessness of art, suggests that it is to be situated at the exact synapse where being at its most vivid joins with extinction. (Steiner, 30)

So it may be that art and the occult represent two different ways of playing with the oscillatory rhythm of the nothing perhaps/perhaps nothing which specifies the human condition according to Lacan in this seminar. Freud recognized an elective affinity between the two fields, pointing out how fiction does better than real life when it comes to the hair raising effects brought about by pushing this oscillation into danger zones. Turning again to the seminar on

Identification, one can perhaps see something of how this occurs.

It is only certain sections of art and the occult that push this oscillatory rhythm toward the frisson of excitement and danger. In literature, the great literary critic Roland Barthes distinguishes between what he calls *textes de plaisir* and *textes de jouissance*, defining the latter as bringing about a loss of one's bearings, putting the reader into a state of loss, "rocking her historical, cultural and psychological foundations." (Barthes, 25) This is what is in question here – a risky engagement with the perimeters of the representational field. What Lacan is at pains to emphasize in the final lessons of the Seminar on Identification is that what he calls the big Other is itself this representational field which is there to be a veil. At the point where this big Other fails, where it has nothing to offer it becomes itself the veil, the blanket, Lacan says , the source of occultation. Veiling what? Not necessarily the utter devastation laid bare by the Ghost in *Hamlet* but the hidden wellspring of desiringness, a force not amenable to the ordinary laws of representation. A view with which Yeats and other practitioners of the occult would be in entire agreement. In the last lessons of this tough topological seminar, Lacan speaks of the illusion of the cosmicity of the world, and of the conditions under which this cosmicity can be sustained, explicitly designating this force as "that which must be renounced so that the world as world can be delivered to us." (27/6/62 p.7) Alain Badiou calls this "cosmicity" the phantasm of the reality of the world.

In our everyday living the big Other, or Lacan's cosmicity, takes the place of this force, and is indeed specifically designed to keep it at bay. As Lacan says, "the whole of humanity as such, the whole of humanism is there to make us miss it." (27/6/62 p.10) Conversely, when it does erupt, the symbolic itself fades and founders, undoing the contours of both the self and the world as we know it. Bracha Ettinger puts it well; it is as if the subject and this o-object are like the front and back of the same piece of fabric, the recto and verso of the same sheet of paper. "When the subject appears (as in everyday life) the o-object disappears, and when the o-object finds a way to penetrate to the other side… signifying meaning (symbolic and imaginary, exchangeable through discourse) disappears and goes into hiding." (Ettinger, 41)

Lacan is equally eloquent: "Everything retreats, everything is effaced in the signifying function in face of the rise, the eruption of this object." (13/6/62 p. 10) Obviously no-one is thinking of ghosts here but one can see how certain exercises in occultism such as ghost stories and horror movies can bring this about out in a perhaps populist but compelling way. In a wider sense, Bracha Ettinger links this momentary fade out to the blinding hit one can experience in the presence of all great art. Speaking of how this breakthrough can occur Lacan buttresses his own highly poetic formulations with the vocabulary of classic psychoanalysis. This force is "being insofar as it is missing from the text of the world ," he tells us, adding rather formally, "and that is why there can slide around it everything that is called the return of the repressed," (27/6/62 p.9) before succumbing again to poetry in order to indicate its place in our lives: "We know from our experience that nothing has any weight except something which makes an allusion to this o-object of which the big Other takes the place in order to give it a meaning." (27/6/62 p.10)

It is by no means difficult to line up the final lessons of this seminar with certain aspects of the occult, and in particular with gothic art. Lacan ends the year with an obscure reference to obscure mirrors and the relation of the o-object to horror, citing Blanchot's *Thomas l'Obscur*. In English, examples abound, none more telling than the great gothic scenes in *Jane Eyre*. This is a particularly interesting novel in terms of the representational field which is rigorously controlled by Jane's own righteous and self righteous vision, so much so that the reader's seeing is never allowed to exit this frame. The oedipal desire that shimmers through the novel is located always and only in the other, in Rochester who indeed will be blinded and lamed as a result of this transgressiveness. In the two places in the novel where this oedipal desire is indexed to Jane herself it can only appear as the infraction of the uncanny, the looming of gothic otherness. The return of the repressed in the form of the fantasized father's love and mother's jealous rage blanks out the entire representational field as Jane's vigilant consciousness gives way. The two gothic scenes in question are explicitly linked in the novel.

In the first instance, the encounter is with the father's love. Locked up as a child in the death chamber of the uncle who had loved her, what Jane fears is not a hostile but a loving visitation from beyond the grave. Glimpsing her own dim image in the shadows of a darkening mirror terrifies her because of the possibility that this little distressed object could solicit fatherly attention; might "waken a preternatural voice to comfort me, or elicit from the gloom some haloed face, bending over me with strange pity." (Brontë, 48). And it is the proximity of this upsurge, the looming lineaments of the hidden spring of her desiringness that entirely blanks out the everyday world for Jane. This must not be., and as she puts it herself, "unconsciousness closed the scene" and she faints. (Brontë, 50)

The exact counterpart of this moment and explicitly linked to it in the novel is the scene where Jane just before she was to marry Rochester woke from sleep to see in her bedroom mirror, the image of the mad Mrs. Rochester, purple faced and huge, wearing her wedding veil, then rending it violently in two, and bending down to look into Jane's eyes, not with the gaze of pity but with the glare of outrage. Here too Jane is object – indirectly – of the father's desire via the mother's outrage:

> Just at my bedside the figure stopped: the fiery eyes glared upon
> me – she thrust up her candle close to my face, and extinguished it
> under my eyes. I was aware of her lurid visage flamed over mine and
> I lost consciousness; for the second time in my life – only the second
> time – I became insensible from terror. (Brontë, 312).

In both of these two great gothic scenes, using the seminar on Identification as a springboard, one can see that there are indeed specific instances where psychoanalytic theory, art and the occult can indeed converge.

I changed the topic of my paper because these instances are specific and limited.

A lot of occult phenomena in Ireland are simply troped as the activities of a parallel but relatively quotidian universe. My own family has its resident troublesome ghosts but they do not activate either the eruption of the o-object or the vacillation of the representational field. However, their longevity – one of them has just recently departed after more than 100 years – suggests that either they are indeed necessary or that they see themselves as necessary and this is the point Lacan makes in this great seminar when he asserts:

> Nothing of the reality of man, nothing of what he searches for nor of what he follows can be sustained except by this dimension of the hidden insofar as it gives the guarantee that there is an existing object… (21/3/62 p.10)

The necessary angel is indeed necessary.

References

—⁓— Barthes, Roland, *Le plaisir du Texte*. Paris, Editions du Seuil, 1970.

—⁓— Brontë Charlotte, *Jane Eyre*, London, Penguin, 2006.

—⁓— Ettinger, Bracha, *The Matrixial Borderspace*. Minneapolis and London, University of Minnesota Press, 2006.

—⁓— Freud, Sigmund, *The Standard Edition of the Complete Psychological Works*, London, ed. James Strachey, London: Hogarth Press and Institute of Psychoanalysis,1953-74.

________ (1896) *Studies in Hysteria*, S.E. 2.

—⁓— Jones Ernest, *Sigmund Freud: Life and Work*. London, The Hogarth Press, 1957.

—⁓— Lacan, Jacques: Unpublished Seminars: All quotations in English unless otherwise specified taken from typescripts of translation by Dr. Cormac Gallagher, circulated privately in St. Vincent's University Hospital, Dublin 4.

________ 1958-9 *Le Désir et son interprétation*. Le Seminaire 6

________ 1961-1962. *L'Identification*, Le Séminaire 9.

—⁓— Steiner, George, *Grammars of Creation*. Yale University Press. London and New Haven. 2001.

—⁓— Stevens, Wallace, *Collected Poems*. London. Faber and Faber 2006.

—⁓— Valéry, Paul, *Selected Writings*, New York, 1950.

WAIRUA: FOLLOWING SHAMANIC CONTOURS IN PSYCHOANALYTIC THERAPY AT A MĀORI MENTAL HEALTH SERVICE IN NEW ZEALAND

Ingo Lambrecht

INTRODUCTION AND CONTEXT

As a consultant clinical psychologist I work at Manawanui, a state-funded Māori Mental Health Service of the Auckland District Health Board, which has adopted the indigenous Māori mental health model of *te whare tapa wha* (the house of well-being) as a holistic model of Māori health or well-being. This model formulates four major pillars or aspects of well-being, the corners of the house of well-being, namely *whanau* or the family health, *hinengaro* or mental health, *tinana* or physical health, and *wairua* or spiritual health.[1] These four pillars hold the protective space of health and well-being for Māori and in fact, it could be argued, for most people.

Distress is the result of an imbalance of these four aspects, and healing would require ideally the involvement of all four cornerstones. In this manner, Māori mental health is more clinically sophisticated than the common Western psychiatric medical model. For example, schizophrenia or psychosis within a Māori mental health model is not merely addressed as a brain disease with medication, or is only considered to be an intra-psychic process (*hinengaro*) engaging talking therapies, but rather requires the addition of understanding the *whanau* (extended family), the whole body (*tinana*), and the spiritual (*wairua*), which leads to an integrated intervention of healing the whole person.

This clinical-cultural interface avoids reductionism and also enhances clinical depth and range. So we can run emotional regulation groups using the *atua* or the gods, or we can facilitate a Mentalization Based Treatment (MBT)[2] group for over three years within a cultural framework. It is beyond the scope of this paper to articulate the personal-political-sacred complexities of colonization, how the sacred and the political intersect with intergenerational trauma, and I have addressed this elsewhere.[3]

---

1 Durie, M. (2001). *Mauri Ora: The Dynamics of Māori Health*. Auckland: Oxford University Press.

2 Bateman, A., & Fonagy P. (2004). *Psychotherapy for Borderline Personality Disorder: Mentalization-Based Treatment*. Oxford: Oxford University Press.

3 Lambrecht, I. (2014) "Healing Transgressions of Tapu: Re-Membering the Body Sacred". O'Loughlin, M. & Charles, M. (Eds.). *Fragments of Trauma and the Social Production of Suffering. Lanham*, MD: Rowman & Littlefield, pp.45-63.

The *Whare Tapa Wha* model gives me as a therapist the opportunity to access thinking that Western psychoanalysis and psychology struggle with, such as body-mind issues, political-systemic processes, as well as working with 'anomalous' or exceptional experiences that belong to the *wairua* or spirit aspect of the model.[4] The *wairua* part can incorporate the findings of parapsychological research and spiritual practices. Māori mental health professionals and clients are often grateful that their worldview and 'anomalous' experiences are not dismissed or considered to be 'crazy'. Here the paranormal is normal.

WAIRUA

The term *wairua* is made up of two parts, first *wai*, which means unique, special, unprecedented. The second part of the word *rua* refers to abyss or container. *Wairua* then is that which is unique, special, which is contained within. Importantly, *wairua* is not to be understood in a religious, ritualistic, or intellectual manner.[5] It is not *tikanga* or cultural even; it is utterly unique. In other words, it needs to be experienced to be present. To move cross-culturally for a moment, *wairua* as a unique container and abyss within us resonates with the complex mystical definitions of Advaita Vedanta[6], notions of Zen[7], the negative path of the Christian mystic Meister Eckhart[8], as well as with the Jewish mystical concept of the *Ayin Soph Or* in Kabbala[9].

In New Zealand, the *tohunga* (Māori shaman) considers mental health difficulties to be the result of intergenerational afflictions between the living and the *tupuna* or ancestors.[10] This is not so different from genetic, psychoanalytic or attachment theories of mental health. With this in mind, it is worth mentioning an intervention, shared with me by a *tohunga*, namely Wiremu NiaNia. He was working with a young Māori woman who heard distressing voices, being diagnosed as psychotic at a mental health service. He was able to see and become aware of another ancestral figure in the room: the deceased grandmother. Thus the healing included working with all persons present, the living and the *tupuna* or ancestors. The healing occurred as the relationships became healed.[11] Healing meant that the

---

4 Randal, P., Geekie, J.; Lambrecht, I. & Taitimu, M. (2008) "Dissociation, psychosis and spirituality: Whose voices are we hearing?" In Moskowitz, A.; Schafer, I. & Dorahy, J. (Eds.). *Psychosis, Trauma and Dissociation: Emerging Perspectives on Severe Psychopathology*. John Wiley & Sons Ltd, West Sussex, UK, pp. 333-345.

5 Bidois, E. (2012). "A Cultural and Personal Perspective of Psychosis". Geekie, J., Randal, P. Lampshire D. (Eds.) *Experiencing Psychosis: Person and Professional Perspectives*. London: Routledge, pp. 35-43.

6 Deutsch, E. (1969). *Advaita Vedanta: A Philosophical Reconstruction*. Honolulu: The University Press of Hawaii.

7 Watts, A.W. (1957). *The Way of Zen*. Middlesex: Penguin Books

8 Fox, M. (2014). *Meister Eckhart: A Mystic Warrior of our Times*. Novato, California: New World Library.

9 Scholem, G. (1960). *Zur Kabbala und ihrer Symbolik*. Zurich: Rhein-Verlag.

10 Durie, M. (2001). *Mauri Ora: The Dynamics of Māori Health*. Auckland: Oxford University Press.

11 NiaNia, W., Tere, Bush, A., & Epston, D. (2013). 'I Will Not Leave My Baby Behind': A Cook Island Māori Family's Experience of New Zealand Māori Traditional Healing. *Australian and New Zea-*

ancestors, whether external or internalised, achieve a positive, engaging, empathic holding function.

In my therapeutic work with a Māori woman at a personality disorder specialist unit in Auckland, similar issues arose. She struggled with severe dissociative features due to significant childhood and institutional abuse and neglect. One day, after several months of therapy, she hesitantly and with trepidation told me that she regularly sees people in the street walking through bus stations.

She was concerned that I would send her to an inpatient unit due to such so-called hallucinations. This was not an unreasonable concern, as from a psychiatric perspective, such visual hallucinations would raise concerns of her mothering, and maybe her child should be removed. However, I saw no concern in regards to her mothering capacity. Through collaborative exploration, it emerged that for her, and true to her cultural background, these were people, who had departed. Using skills of normalization and distress tolerance, mentalizing, as well as validation, she was able to down-regulate her emotions, avoid dissociation or 'splitting', to use a psychoanalytical object relation term. She was able to accept them for who they are. It needed neither denial of her exceptional experiences, nor paranoid terror of the dead (the paranoid-schizoid position[12]). It was more helpful to support my client to engage with the *tupuna* respectfully, as well as setting limits of how the dead may speak to her. In this regard, it is worth asking in which manner psychoanalysis can be of value to those that have exceptional spiritual or psychic experiences.

THE VALUE OF PSYCHOANALYSIS FOR THE SACRED

Although the Māori mental health services acknowledge *wairua*, how to integrate this value into a psychoanalytic practice is not always clear. It is beyond the frame of this paper to consider the full extent in which psychoanalysis has engaged with the occult and/or spirituality. However, I consider two main approaches or discursive positions of psychoanalysis in regards to exceptional experiences, namely the interpretative approach and therapeutic approach, which certainly overlap.

The interpretative approach commonly holds a stock standard psychoanalytic reading of occult practices, psychic phenomena, or mystical experiences as being only the result of defenses, projections of underlying processes, as well as being symptomatic of cultural compromise formations. Freud, despite his ambivalent position on telepathy, for example considered mystical experiences to be a regressive process seeking the oceanic feelings of the womb.[13]

In Freud's writings such as *Totem and Taboo*[14], as well as *Civilisation and its*

---

land Journal of Family Therapy. Vol.34, 3–17.

12 Klein, M. [1946] (1975). Notes on some Schizoid Mechanisms. In Money-Kyrle (Ed.) *The Writings of Melanie Klein.* Vol. 3. London: Hogarth Press, pp. 1-24.

13 Radin, D. (2006). *Entangled Minds: Extrasensory Experiences in a Quantum Field.* New York: Paraview.

14 Freud, S. [1913] (1983). *Totem and Taboo.* London: Ark Paperbacks.

Discontents[15], Freud experimented with understanding psychic and spiritual experiences as being the result of compromise formations due to conflicts between unacceptable pleasures that are repressed, and the function of managing inner and group conflicts to sustain a functioning culture or society. This approach is reductionist, typical of Western dominant discourse of its time, and holding on to an unconscious materialistic epistemology. But then Freud was steeped in his own time, as we all are.

However, I would consider that the value of this approach is important not so much in regard to the reductionistic interpretations that Freud provided, but rather, it allows us to wonder more deeply about the personal and group unconscious processes that clearly affect psychic and mystical phenomena. It is possible to enhance the psychoanalytic discourse by moving away from a materialistic epistemology, to a more structured approach in which psychoanalysis can be taken up as a methodology, neither reducing nor elevating spirituality. This allows for understanding personal, group, as well as socio-political dynamics that are involved with spiritual experiences. For example, it cannot be unimportant that intergenerational trauma of colonization leads to generations living with higher dissociative capacities, which in turn can be part of altering states of consciousness, usually in the pathological sense, but also opens up people to positive states of consciousness. With colonization, much knowledge in regards to discernment and distinction about such states of consciousness, held by the shamans of different cultures, has been lost, thereby leading to confusion and unresolved processes.

The second approach, which I call the therapeutic approach, highlights actual experiences in therapy and provides a psychoanalytic means to process and think about spiritual and psychic events developmentally and therapeutically. This ranges from Jung's transcendent function[16] to Fromm's positive psychoanalytic reading of Zen[17]; from Winnicott's sense of the mystical experience being an ecstatic and a deeply still reflection of a true core self[18] to Bion's Neoplatonic mystical notion of the unknowable O[19]; from Grotstein moving on from Bion to formulating a transcendent position[20], from Symington's considering meditation and contemplation to be beyond ordinary thinking[21], leading to a higher, healthier mystical truth to

---

15 Freud [1929] (1985). "Civilisation and its Discontents". In Dickson, A. (Ed.) *Sigmund Freud: Civilisation, Society and Religion*. Middlesex: Penguin Books, pp. 243-340.

16 Jung, C.G. [1916] (1957). "The Transcendent Function". *The Collected Works of C.G. Jung*. Vol. 8. New Jersey: Princeton University Press.

17 Fromm, E. (1960). "Psychoanalysis and Zen Buddhism". In Suzuki, D.T.; Fromm, E. & De Martino, R. (eds.) *Zen Buddhism and Psychoanalysis*. New York: Harper & Brothers.

18 Winnicott, D.W. (1965). *The Maturational Processes and the Facilitating Environment*. New York: International University Press, p.187.

19 Bion, W. (1984). *Attention and Interpretation: A Scientific Approach to Psycho-Analysis and Groups*. London: Karnak Books, p.92.

20 Grotstein, J.S. (1996). Bion's "transformation in O', the "thing-in-itself", and the "real": Toward a concept of the "transcendent position." *Journal of Melanie Klein and Objects Relations*, Vol.14:2, 109-141.

21 Symington, N. (2004). *The Blind Man Sees: Freud's Awakening and Other Essays*. London: Karnak Books, p.11.

Eigen's direct work with meditators and those with mystical experiences, moving them through death and rebirth, exploring ecstasy and Kabbalistic notion of *tikkun*, namely repair or healing.[22]

Engler[23] and Washburn[24] have used psychoanalytic understanding to elucidate more specifically the developmental stages related to meditational practices. Lazar recently attempted to integrate more modern quantum physics into the thinking of psychoanalysis, thereby creating a scientific space to re-consider psychic phenomena.[25] More recently in this millennium, Totton, in his psychoanalytic writing on telepathy and the paranormal, highlights how the mind-body split can be understood.[26]

Long before Freud, indigenous cultures have recognized this overlap of personal struggle and spiritual development. It occurs most commonly in the calling of becoming a shaman. The initiation illness or crisis could be understood as a spiritual emergency[27]. Spiritual emergencies or shamanic crises as a transitional phase are the overlap of personal and spiritual events filled with struggle and pain. Psychoanalytic or psychodynamic therapies provide a means to work through such complex difficulties and overlaps.

The value of psychoanalysis then becomes less about the attachment to materialistic or transpersonal beliefs. Rather, psychoanalytic thinking is then freed to function as a lens, a means to understand personal and group dynamics. The power of this model is that it is able not only to explain the positive but also the negative and painful expressions in the form of spiritual emergencies and initiation crises common in shamanic training. In this manner, early psychoanalysis can be re-read as seeking to explore how the unconscious becomes conscious in psychic and spiritual events. Speaking and writing as shaman and psychoanalyst, nothing in the topographic, energetic, and structural psychoanalytic insights needs to be sacrificed except defensive closemindedness.

SHAMANIC SKEPTICISM

Equally, in other cultures besides the Anglo-Saxon and European cultures, there is not necessarily a blind acceptance of psi effects without discernment. In fact, in my experience well-trained shamans, similar to Freud, are very concerned about

---

22 Eigen, M. (1998). *The Psychoanalytic Mystic*. London: Free Association Press.

23 Engler, J. (1984). "Therapeutic Aims in Psychotherapy and Meditation: Developmental Stages in the Representation of Self". In *The Journal of Transpersonal Psychology*. Vol. 16, pp. 25-62.

24 Washburn, M. (1994). *Transpersonal Psychology in Psychoanalytic Perspective*. Albany: State University of New York Press.

25 Lazar, S.G. (2001). "Knowing, Influencing, and Healing: Paranormal Phenomena and Implications for Psychoanalysis and Psychotherapy." *Psychoanalytic Inquiry.* Vol.21:1, 113-131.

26 Totton, N. (2003). "Each Single Ego": Telepathy and Psychoanalysis. In Totton, N. (ed.) *Psychoanalysis and the Paranormal: Lands of Darkness*. London: Karnac Books. Pp.187-208.

27 Lukoff, D. (2011). "Visionary Spirituality and Mental Disorders". In Cardeña, E. & Winkelman, M. (Eds.). *Altering Consciousness: Multidisciplinary Perspectives. Volume 2: Biological and Psychological Perspectives*. Oxford: Praeger., pp. 301-326.

wild analysis or pseudo shamans. Let me present you with a vignette of shamanic skepticism I experienced myself.[28]

During my three day sangoma graduation in Bushbuck Ridge, not far away from the Kruger National Park in South Africa, I was introduced to the main event or test, namely the locating of hidden objects through trance states. This is a test of validity and reliability. If I do not find the hidden objects during my trance state, then clearly I am not ready to be a sangoma, nor am I sufficiently accessing the ancestors, and this occurs in front of the whole community, so no pressure… I danced in front of the community, which is drumming and singing, and at the same time watching closely. After I had danced and achieved a trance state, I was able to pick out the person in the crowd who had hidden my objects. I had to name the object and state where it was placed. The object was my bundle of beads which was hidden in a calabash to the right of a hut's entrance.

When the object is hidden, my sangoma teacher was not told where the object was hidden in order to avoid a bias, namely the teacher wanting his student to succeed. This not only as a test of the apprentice but also the teacher. I was petrified about this test, for I did not share my teacher's belief that I was ready, and the chances of failure seemed obviously high to me. I found out later that this is a common experience for apprentices. After the test, I was relieved that it was over. For me it felt the worst was over. However, in the afternoon my teacher came to me and said that they could not believe I had passed the test as a white man, and so they wanted to set up a second test the next day. I said half-jokingly: "Hmm, is this shamanic skepticism?" My teacher did not know what I meant, but he continued to be soothing with his words and voice. He was far more confident in my abilities than I was. I was clearly upset.

I quickly realised that my response held some of my anger, born out of a defense in terms of a deep anxiety of failure and possible shame. Psychic states are not easily switched on and off, and I had not slept for three days, which of course is the whole idea in order to allow for easier trancing. However, this meant that also my more primitive defenses were activated. After passing the final test, I had to stay in the hut all day, as I was considered to be 'newly born', and therefore needed to be protected from sunlight. At that time whilst lying on the matt on the floor, I remember reflecting on being newly born or being re-configured, tired and grateful for my own psychoanalytic therapy before my graduation.

The Occult and Psychoanalysis

The value of psychoanalysis finds its early support amongst prominent Western occultists already in the 1920s. Western occultism is nothing but a form of Western shamanism with its Kabbalistic tree of life and trance states achieved during rituals. Israel Regardie was deeply troubled after he left Aleister Crowley as his secretary. He went to Dion Fortune, and at her dinner table heard about Freud and Jung, later

---

28 Lambrecht, I. (2014) *Sangoma Trance States* Auckland: AM Publishing.

even undergoing psychoanalytic therapy, as well as Reichian therapy. Dion Fortune even integrated the notion of the psychoanalyst in her writing in the form of her fictional figure of Dr Taverner[29].

Israel Regardie later became a prominent author and practitioner in the field of Western occult practices. Already in the 1930s he valued psychoanalysis, believing that it could prevent the inflation or bloating of the ego as the shaman accesses powers through trance states in the climb towards so-called higher states of consciousness[30]. No doubt affected by his interactions with Aleister Crowley, he thought it was essential to undergo analysis in order to avoid the common narcissistic pitfalls of shamanism.

Regardie I think was right when he eventually concluded that it was such unresolved developmental issues that accounted for most of the chaotic group dynamics of earlier and I contest later esoteric fraternities. This would lead him to insist on the necessity of psychotherapy for anyone seriously practicing any spiritual discipline. Spiritual practices are not without their mental health issues and risks, and "narcissistic strivings" as Epstein would call it.[31] Ecstatic, mystical and meditative states have been conceptualised within the psychodynamic framework as regressions in the service of the ego[32], and it seems on occasion, this may be the case.

On a psychodynamic developmental level, these problems appear to arise particularly with those individuals who have a vulnerability and disturbance around identity as well as intersubjectivity[33] – a fact also openly acknowledged amongst shamans. This would explain the high attraction of such meditative or spiritual practices to late adolescents and people undergoing a mid-life crisis[34]. At the earliest developmental level, such difficulties could be explained by the pathologies of the self within Kohut's understanding[35].

In fact, an insecure or disorganised attachment in childhood produced by the trauma of neglect or sexual and physical abuse, leading to a failure of good-enough holding[36], will result in difficulties in self-regulation[37], which in turn leads to a propensity to dissociation[38] – a form of altered state of consciousness to escape

29 Fortune, D. [1926] (2011) *The Secrets of Dr. Taverner.* San Franscico, CA: Weiser Books.

30 Regardie, I. [1938] (2010). *The Middle Pillar: The Balance between Mind and Magic.* Woodbury MN: Llewellyn Publications.

31 Epstein, M. (1990). "Psychodynamics of Meditation: Pitfalls on the Spiritual Path". In *The Journal of Transpersonal Psychology.* Vol. 22, pp. 17-34.

32 Shaffi, M. (1973). "Silence in the Service of Ego: Psychoanalytic Study of Meditation." In *International Journal of Psycho-Analysis.* Vol. 54, 431-443.

33 Stolorov, R.D.; Brandchaft, B. & Atwood, G.E.; (2000). *Psychoanalytic Treatment: An Inter-Subjective Approach.* London: Routledge.

34 Engler, J. (1984). "Therapeutic Aims in Psychotherapy and Meditation: Developmental Stages in the Representation of Self". In *The Journal of Transpersonal Psychology.* Vol. 16, pp. 25-62.

35 Kohut, H. (1971). *The Analysis of the Self.* New York: International Universities Press.

36 Winnicott, D.W. (2005). *Playing and Reality.* London: Routledge.

37 Schore A.N. (2003). *Affect Dysregulation and the Disorders of the Self.* New York: Guilford Press.

38 Granqvist, P.; Reijman, S.; & Cardeña, E (2011). "Altered Consciousness and Human Development". In Cardeña, E. & Winkelman, M. (Eds.). *Altering Consciousness: Multidisciplinary Perspectives. Volume 2: Biological and Psychological Perspectives.* Oxford: Praeger, pp. 211-236.

the terror of the brutal moment. All of this begins to re-emerge during spiritual practices as the 'return of the repressed'[39]. Also, in the attachment as well as transferences to spiritual teachers, such as gurus, teachers or shamans, as well as within occult groups, much earlier unconscious processes are played out, at times intensely painfully and pathologically. Therefore psychoanalysis really matters in regards to spiritual practices.

Shamanic or Paranormal Value for Psychoanalysis

The anthropologist Lévi-Strauss stated that the shaman is the first psychoanalyst, the analyst being a 'medium for transference'[40]. Today I would like to emphasise that a *tohunga* or a shaman is not merely a healer or a therapist. Shamans work with clients using words and medicines, but more importantly they enter altered states of consciousness or trance states. They access other worlds, and they are the messenger between two worlds. Hence the comparison of psychoanalysis and shamanism can be misleading if the shaman is merely equated with being a healer.

The trance states are deeply embedded both in the roots of the term 'shaman', as well as in the shamanic view of the cosmos, namely travelling in a usually three-tiered universe made up of upper, middle and lower worlds populated by spirits, and the middle world corresponding to our earth. These worlds are connected by an *axis mundi*, often a cosmic mountain or a tree of life found in the stories across the world from the Siberian tent pole to the Kabbalistic tree of life of Jewish mysticism in Western shamanism or occultism[41]. It is during such trance states that often paranormal experiences can occur.

The Paranormal

I would like to address an edge where I have certainly experienced a taboo not amongst shamans but amongst many academics, intellectuals, and psychoanalysts. Many academics and intellectuals can just about remain neutral because they can be politically and culturally correct when it comes to indigenous cultures. However, when engaged in thoughts on the paranormal or extrasensory perception (ESP), many respond with either denial or attacks on linking[42] and therefore on thinking. If not denial, then derision and dismissive approaches are common, despite all the hardcore scientific and statistical evidence supporting paranormal or psi phenomena[43]. It is not more science we need; it is more psychoanalysis we need that can analyse these defenses.

39 Freud, S. [1939] (1985). "Moses and Monotheism". In Dickson, A. (Ed.) *Sigmund Freud: Civilisation, Society and Religion*. Middlesex: Penguin Books, p.382.
40 Levi-Strauss, L. (1963). *Structural Anthropology Vol. 1* Middlesex: Penguin Books, p.219.
41 Eliade, M. (1964). *Shamanism: Archaic Techniques of Ecstasy*. Princeton: Princeton University Press.
42 Bion, W. (1984). *Attention and Interpretation: A Scientific Approach to Psycho-Analysis and Groups*. London: Karnak Books.
43 Radin, D. (1997). *The Conscious Universe: The Scientific Truth of Psychic Phenomena*. New York: Harper Collins.

When considering psi phenomena, any serious contemplation of paranormal phenomena or psychic research is not acceptable in academic and intellectual discourse[44], and evidence remains unspoken and or in fact becomes repressed. I know from my own experiences that many psychoanalysts will only whisper about their psychic experiences in dark corners of cafés, and won't even take it to supervision for fear of ridicule from colleagues. There is also an entangled and ambivalent history of shamanism and psychoanalysis, as is evident in the relationship of Freud and Jung.

This came ahead for Freud personally and ideologically during a psychic or occult event that led to his split from Jung. The separation of Freud and Jung could be understood as a split based on the occult and the shamanic. Freud accused Jung of being preoccupied with the 'occult', which was how psi phenomena were called then. Jung felt heat built up in his diaphragm and then a loud noise was heard from the bookcase. Jung predicted another loud noise would occur, which of course happened, and Freud turned pale, accusing Jung of having a death wish against him, and ended the relationship between them[45]. Freud responded typically, namely with anxiety in the face of psi phenomena, for it is challenging on many levels. To Freud's credit, he always remained interested in psychic phenomena. His papers on telepathy in dreams were more dismissive in the beginning, but became more openminded in later writings, after 1921[46].

Jung himself had contact with Philemon, a spirit guide, and he believed the dead need to learn from the living[47]. He had poltergeist activity, experienced déjà vu, precognitive dreams, clairvoyance, telepathy. He began experimenting with mediums, which are in fact Western shamans. Sandor Ferenczi, who then became Freud's favourite disciple, also became interested in ESP. When Ferenczi wished to present a paper on telepathy in 1919, Freud advised him not to as it would be very explosive. Ferenczi and Freud went to visit Frau Seidler in Berlin. She was a clairvoyant or a Western shaman. She could read letters blindfolded. They thought it was trickery until they met her. Freud swore Ferenczi to secrecy when he admitted he thought Frau Seidler had some clairvoyant powers[48]. It could be said that there was a battle between his superego and what Nietzsche called his intellectual conscience, and his superego held court. However, Freud liked to tell Jones about uncanny experiences. Jones, being a skeptic, resented Freud's connection with Ferenczi and Jung, and he felt that Freud's interest was "unfortunate and regrettable"[49]. He was worried how this would affect the science of psychoanalysis – a commonly held concern.

---

44 Lazar, S.G. (2001). "Knowing, Influencing, and Healing: Paranormal Phenomena and Implications for Psychoanalysis and Psychotherapy." *Psychoanalytic Inquiry.* Vol.21:1, 113-131.

45 Lazar, S.G. (2001). "Knowing, Influencing, and Healing: Paranormal Phenomena and Implications for Psychoanalysis and Psychotherapy." *Psychoanalytic Inquiry.* Vol.21:1, 113-131.

46 Radin, D. (2006). *Entangled Minds: Extrasensory Experiences in a Quantum Field.* New York: Paraview.

47 Jung, C.G. (1965). *Memories, Dreams, Reflections.* New York: Random House.

48 Lazar, S.G. (2001). "Knowing, Influencing, and Healing: Paranormal Phenomena and Implications for Psychoanalysis and Psychotherapy." *Psychoanalytic Inquiry.* Vol.21:1, 113-131.

49 Eisenbud, J. (1974). *Psychologie mit Psi.* Bern: Schweiz.

Balint[50] was also more open minded about such phenomena, occurring especially in highly charged transference and countertransference dynamics, which I can attest to in my own practice. Jule Eisenbud[51] was far more positive about such phenomena, and he paid dearly for it. His extensive descriptions of "telepathic cross associations" between analyst and patient led to attempts to have him kicked out of the New York Psychoanalytic Society. This failed, but some withdrew their referrals to him because he was considered to be dangerous. Ullman noted that patients who function on schizoid or obsessional levels manifest psi abilities in therapy more than other patients. Ullman hypothesized that they use language to distance themselves to such an extent that telepathy occurs in order to seek a meaningful communicative bond with the therapist[52]. Ehrenwald in the seventies postulated that the early mother-child relationship is the source of telepathy and it plays an important role in that early relationship. Hence, maybe not surprisingly, telepathy often occurs between family members or in intimate relationships. More recently, Dennis Farrell in the eighties considered some of his own dreams, as having telepathic importance, and he equally pointed to the resistance in psychoanalytic thinking towards telepathy.[53]

The edge between shamanism and psychoanalysis is an abyss if the classical physics model of reductionist materialism and positivism, basically the physics of the 18th and 19th centuries, is held. For shamans, it would be easier if some would be able to not merely know about quantum physics but to begin to think in terms of quantum physics of the 20th and 21st centuries, such as the non-local effects over distance, in which entangled particles have what Einstein called 'spooky affects over distance'[54]. So there is no need to give up materialism; it is the level of sophistication, i.e. moving beyond Victorian empiricism, that may be worth considering. Just because psi events are unusual does not mean they are not deserving of integration and of course discernment. What I am wishing to highlight is that the communication between analyst or therapist and client may have more aspects than has been considered previously.

DISTRESS AND THE SACRED

It is not always easy to distinguish between distress and the sacred. I have worked with some who have had intense *kundalini* emergencies, *qigong* psychosis, *matakite*, a Māori term for hearing voices and seeing visions, as well as in South Africa with *ukuthwasa* (shamanic initiation illness) and *amafufunyana* (possession and psychotic states). These distinctions are not always clear, and this would need more space

---

50 Balint, M. (1955). "Notes on Parapsychology and Parapsychological Healing". *International Journal of Psychoanalysis*. Vol.36, 31-35.
51 Eisenbud, J. (1974). *Psychologie mit Psi*. Bern: Schweiz.
52 Ullman, M. & Zimmerman, N. (1979). *Working with Dreams,* Los Angeles: New York: Tarcher.
53 Farrell, D. (1983). "Freud's "thought-transference," repression, and the future of psychoanalysis". *The International Journal of Psychoanalysis*. Vol.64:1, 71-81.
54 Radin, D. (2006) *Entangled Minds: Extrasensory Experiences in a Quantum Field*. New York: Paraview.

than this paper to unpack the complexities.

One way, and not the only one, is taking Lukoff's model[55] into account. Lukoff is a psychiatrist with his own personal experiences of mental health issues and spiritual transformation. He notes that there are important overlaps when comparing psychosis, mania, and mystical states. These overlaps or spiritual trauma have been termed 'spiritual emergency' or crisis. The differential diagnosis between madness and spiritual crisis is not always easily made. In indigenous cultures, the shamans usually determine how to distinguish between madness and spiritual crisis through divination, reality testing, and psychic abilities. Importantly, certain visionary spiritual experiences, if misdiagnosed as psychotic disorders, can lead to personal growth being interrupted by being pharmaceutically repressed through psychiatric medication and, even worse, through hospitalisation, and I have witnessed this.

Shamans in indigenous cultures make use of tests based on reliability and validity, just as psychologists do through testing. What this means is that, within indigenous cultures, often certain 'voices' will be tested. During my own apprenticeship, I was told by my teacher that as a *thwasa* (an apprentice to a South African *sangoma* or shaman), the pain would lessen as the relationship between the ancestral voices and the *thwasa* improved over time during the training. I recall asking my teacher: "How would I know whether the voices I heard are the ancestors or just me simply going mad?" "Ah that's easy," my teacher replied, "we test them"[56]. The 'true ancestral voices' would be those that in the eyes of the community are accurate, for example, in helping to find herbs and lost cattle, or in diagnosing and healing illnesses. Here voices or visions are the result of ancestor contact, validated and made reliable through training and testing the voices against reality, thereby engaging the 'reality principle'[57], to use a psychoanalytic term. The ones that fail to be related to reality deserve healing.

In my clinical work at Manawanui, this overlap between distress and the sacred was evident when clients present with paranoia and capacities for pre-cognition; when the cause of psychosis for another client turned out to be a cultural trauma triggered by overstepping the boundary of a cemetery, an act of taboo; or when with another client *mauri* or intense energy, expressed in fine shaking of the body, was related to affect dysregulation. Equally, this overlap was evident for a client with severe depressive features whose overwhelming pre-cognitive dreams came true. Many more examples come to mind of how it is necessary in the holding space of therapy to process both spiritual dynamics and distress mindfully and effectively. This leads to a notion I have been wondering about, namely 'spiritual holding'.

55 Lukoff, D. (2011). "Visionary Spirituality and Mental Disorders". In Cardeña, E. & Winkelman, M. (Eds.). *Altering Consciousness: Multidisciplinary Perspectives. Volume 2: Biological and Psychological Perspectives*. Oxford: Praeger., pp. 301-326.
56 Randal, P., Geekie, J.; Lambrecht, I. & Taitimu, M. (2008) "Dissociation, psychosis and spirituality: Whose voices are we hearing?" In Moskowitz, A.; Schafer, I. & Dorahy, J. (Eds.). *Psychosis, Trauma and Dissociation: Emerging Perspectives on Severe Psychopathology*. John Wiley & Sons Ltd, West Sussex, UK, p. 337.
57 Freud [1920] (1991). "Beyond the Pleasure Principle". In Dickson, A. (Ed.) *Sigmund Freud: On Metapsychology*. Middlesex: Penguin Books, pp. 269-338.

SPIRITUAL HOLDING

Importantly, spiritual holding, based on Winnicott's notion of 'holding'[58], requires acknowledgement not merely in terms of thoughts and religious rules about the spirit. It focuses on lived experience, namely sacred, 'anomalous' or exceptional experiences. Just being unconditional is not enough, just as unconditional love without effective limit setting is not good enough parenting. Real acceptance and knowledge is required to traverse this complex arena that is often a liminal space, filled with *Unbehagen*[59]. In Western psychoanalytic discourse exceptions concerning the sacred exist; this type of holding has some precedence, such as in Jung's "transcendent function"[60], or in Grotstein's "transcendent position"[61].

Spiritual holding could be said to allow for altered states of consciousness or trance states to occur in transitional spaces, as within the spaces of therapy, art or play. Equally for shamans, mind and space are closely related as a transitional space. Different from religious rituals, in which the form of the ritual is the meaning, in shamanic rituals the form not only holds meaning, but also creates a transitional space to alter consciousness. The repetition of ritual is in fact more like stepping into a field of resonance, the repetition becomes the ground upon which the mind takes flight, and new forms appear. This is true for music, art, psychoanalysis and trance states[62]. The ritual provides a specific spiritual holding that allows the trance state to be safe and effective – in fact is a part of the technology that alters the mind.

Another aspect of spiritual holding is trust and knowledge. It is important to actively explore certain exceptional experiences and validate their reality, for many Māori don't trust *pakehas* (Whites) in this regard. Such exploration requires an active respect and knowledge for the reality of their world. Such respect cannot only be based on 'unconditional positive regard', as conceptualised by Carl Rogers[63], but also requires sufficient expertise to distinguish between experiences of spirituality and distress, namely the complexities of spiritual emergencies. Spiritual holding often requires us to make space to talk about such exceptional experiences. However, it does not avoid or deny the necessity to test these experiences in regards to reality. All effective shamans do so.

---

58 Winnicott, D.W. (2005). *Playing and Reality.* London: Routledge.

59 Lambrecht, I. (2015) "Belonging: A Shamanic Tale of Death and Unbehagen". In *The Candidate Journal.*

60 Jung, C.G. [1916] (1957). "The Transcendent Function". *The Collected Works of C.G. Jung. Vol. 8.* New Jersey: Princeton University Press.

61 Grotstein, J.S. (1996). Bion's "transformation in O', the "thing-in-itself", and the "real": Toward a concept of the "transcendent position." *Journal of Melanie Klein and Objects Relations,* Vol.14:2, 109-141.

62 Sinclair, V. & Lambrecht, I. (2016) "Psychoanalytic and Ritual Spaces as Transitional – featuring Sangoma Trance States". In *The Fenris Wolf. Issue No 8.* Stockholm: Trapart Books.

63 Rogers, Carl (1951). *Client-centered therapy: Its current practice, implications and theory.* London: Constable.

CONCLUSION

My concern is that psychoanalysis in general may not be wild enough concerning the sacred, and that it may find when it comes to the shamanic edge one day, that the wild has been already cultivated, and that experts from other indigenous cultures have already cultivated the fields. Will psychoanalysis be leaning forward in this regard, or will it be left behind? I suspect it will be the neuroscientist who will show the way. They already are at the edge with their research on meditation, raising important questions about consciousness. I do see though that there are lights amongst the psychoanalysts, some who remain quiet whilst others are beginning to speak out, lights at the edge, and this is in fact a shamanic position, for shamans by definition hold a similar liminal space or a transgressional function in their own societies.

An Occult Reading of PAO!
Imagining in the Dark with
Our Vestigial Shamanism
in a Shade, Shadow, Wide

Elliott Edge

"Out of the blue an' into the black."
– American folk psalm

The imagination is a problem. The invisible is a problem. The hidden is a problem. Creation is a problem. Participation is a problem. Choice is a problem. The Soul is a problem. The planet is a problem. Reality is a problem. Being is a problem.

Existence, or, *the pressing matter of our shared circumstance*, is a problem. That we have anything available to us is a problem. That there is an *us* is one problem. That there is a *this* and a *here* is another. Our biggest problems are the very backdrop of our most casual, moment-to-moment experience of being alive. They are the wallpaper and our breath against it. They're what lies just beyond the wallpaper and into what we suspect in fact made it, and the entire universe, possible. It's the ant crawling across the floor and the elephant in the room. For these reasons, they are frequently skipped.

And the arch-problem reigns as "Mystery." Upon the forehead of all problems is the united name Mystery. Mystery remains pervasive. And Mystery is always ever-widening. This very room bulges with it. But, despite its promise and despite its omnipresence it is intuited by all animals in the cosmic kingdom that Mystery can be dangerous.

Knowing it can be dangerous and sensing that it is indeed lingering above us at this very moment, and all moments that become *very*, we're naturally encouraged to skip this very present experience, this Mystery that, if we were to push just the tiniest bit, would catapult us into a truly stellar vertigo. And, along with choice, it is this vertigo that is part and parcel with the pressing matter of our shared circumstance. This vertigo has plagued humanity under the names Despair, Terror, Armageddon, and Madness. So, to right out avoid the fate of the careless or the damned, we jump before we can truly move. We look past the room and the thing that's obviously everywhere; that baffling *this* that's here – "outer" space and "inner" space – and then we begin. We skip all we can, and then we start imagining truths.

Yet, if we were to court the Mystery in ways that would not mean our unmaking, we would see that pregnant in the very same vertigo that has lead us into new universes of pain, there is also within it Salvation, Awakening, Gnosis, Consciousness, and Love. It is due to this dual-toned discovery that practices like Art, Occultism, and Psychoanalysis rose from the dirt with us. Psychoanalysis, Art, and the Occult are awakening with us in the web of our microcosmic problems, as well as the arch-problem Mystery, that is on full cosmic display.

Try typing something meaningful, or insightful, or true at a keyboard with your eyes closed. It wipes away the "outside" world. There is only you and the mirror machine, and sense, and struggling articulation. Psychoanalysis, Art, and the Occult have been born from this primeval, struggling articulation.

To celebrate them is to touch their origin. Their origins are:

Psychoanalysis is Life and Soul – P.
Art is Creating and Doing – A.
Occult is The Hidden, the Invisible, the Unseen – O.

Psychoanalysis, Art, and the Occult are the fundamental forces of the universe. They indeed exist to deal with the fundamental forces of the universe as well. This is our gravity, our charge, and our spin. Psychoanalysis, Art, and the Occult is the universe, and reflects us as the universe itself. These are the pillars of all Nature for the purposes of this essay. Being so, we should begin by *affirming* Psychoanalysis, Art, and the Occult into a formula:

Reality itself is the Life-Soul (P) Creating and Doing (A) from the Hidden (O).

PAO and the Self as Magic

Psychoanalysis, Art, and Occultism overlap in many domains. One common ground among them is the Self. Theses are traditions aimed to examine, measure, probe, explore, wring-out, illuminate, express, and transform the Self.

PAO exists to find the Self, see the Self, to know the Self. This is frequently with the aim of healing it, or bringing it voice, or song, encouraging it to blossom meaningfully, and totally.

Ever-rebirthing the Self is the Magnum Opus of PAO. This is the goal of conscious reality; and this is the goal of PAO.

PAO is engaged in bringing forth the soul.

Psychoanalysis, Art, and the Occult all overlap in Magic. Magic in terms of the Self and the crisis of the World; a Self that seems to exist as a Reality seems to exist. That there seems to be an "outer space" and an "inner space"; and both are participatory – we discover, mold, and make in them – this too is Magic.

Magic in terms of understanding, wielding, and reflecting. In terms of willed action, change, the word, enigmas, vision, and sense. Magic in terms of Consciousness, holder of Magical Weapons. And Awareness itself, the greatest Magical Weapon of them all. Magic also incarnated as providence, synchronicity, understanding, wisdom, imagination, insight, gnosis, awakening, discovery, and dreams.

Indeed, "The Self" is Magic's name when it has burned itself awake.

The Self is the Magician of the Tarot. The Magician and the Self represent a willer, a doer, a wielder, a creator; the living focal point of experience, the one who makes its meaning, the change-maker, the mask-bearer, the interpreter, the discoverer, the speaker, the actor, and the master, and the Mage.

The Magician and the Self receive cosmic information (the World touch; sense data); generate psychic information (perceptions, languages, thoughts, social orders, fantasies, personas, imaginings, dreams); and become action itself – the One that Wills, (participation, behavior, relationship, legacy, alchemy). That is the Card's symbolic arena. It is the of Mind-Body-Action-World axis. The One we call "The I"!

Magic is folds of information that have become awake.

The Self is Magic that has become awake.

Psychoanalysis, Art, and the Occult are exploratory, transformative, and creative in their united opus of uncovering and altering the Self and uncovering and altering the World. But most of all, Psychoanalysis, Art and the Occult exist because the Self and the World are exclusively of Mystery. This is why they exist. The Self and the World are Mysteries that continually demand everything of consciousness. Ignore these Mysteries and face coma, con, and death. Despite the unending efforts of awareness, both our seeming "inner" court and seeming our "outer" court remains only vaguely illuminated, even on our brightest of days. Of this willful Self that's here and this willful World we're in, and the Mysteries that make and unite them – Psychoanalysis, Art, and the Occult stand as a vestigial relic of our now somewhat reclusive Shamanism.

For the Magician of the Pamela Colman Smith's Tarot is nakedly the Shaman.

Psychoanalysis is Shamanism by another name.

Psychoanalysis, Art, and the Occult are all the work of the Magician; The Magician is the Shaman. The Shaman is involved with dreams. The Shaman is involved with drama. The Shaman is involved with the invisible. The Shaman is in an act of dealing and communing. The Shaman is making the art. The Shaman is healing and guiding. The Shaman is using all their tentacles and actively growing new ones. The Shaman is making and remaking all the World, and making and remaking all the Selves. The Shaman is seeing very far and through fog. The Shaman is the Mother of Man; and the Mother of Invention.

This Shamanism, parent of PAO and all humanity, is the same Shamanism that made man man, worded the world, birthed religion, and inspired the sciences.

Freud saw what the Shaman sees – The World you see when you close your eyes *is a real world.* It is so real that it needs you to participate there. The survival of your soul depends on it. Freud and Jung were Shamans of the Analytic school. They both awoke to that most awesome and vital magical ability; the power to open and close your eyes. This is how we begin to move competently within worlds. With this membrane, we shift our attention and intent between interlocking realities.

The earliest Analysts, like the earliest people before them, saw quite quickly—

We do not stop seeing when we close our eyes.
We do not stop walking when we lay down.

Indeed, the Darkness we encounter behind the eyelid is really the light of the Other World.

Secretly, the eyes are always open and cannot be closed. A closed eye is only seeing what the light of this World, the "outer" court of Einstein's light, obscures. This is what the Shaman knows. We, our Selves, are the secret portals to Unseen Worlds. The Self indeed is an Unseen World. The Analysts and Artists know this as well.

The Shaman knows that the surface of all things holds the living Mystery. Any moment, any place, can awaken us to the All. Everything contains everything. There is no escape from the Shamanic consciousness once it is realized. The Artist will always transform a thing. She will always see into the thing, and she will see its life, and it will come alive, and it will be alive for her. The Analyst is but the Artist Shaman. The Artist is but the Shaman Analyst. Analysis is communion, art making, craft, and exorcism. Occultism and Art are the exact same enterprise. All three – PAO – are deep, baroque, and purposeful. All three are conscious of the inter-dimensional. Indeed, the Analyst, Artist, and Occultist are all in fact the same exercise only with slight bents in expectation and aesthetic. All play pitter-patter in the black seas of the Occult. For the Occult is why we're really in the room. The Occult is the cauldron, the web, behind everything. The Occult is the World behind the World.

Our universe is a stage for Mystery.
The World is Mystery.
And we are Occult in it.
For the Mind is an Invisible, Hidden Kingdom.
And we are of it.

Little is illumined, or "without a doubt." Less than a sliver is known. We helplessly dream at the feet of the living World. And we hopelessly believe things – and even barely these things alone are noticed or known.

This is why PAO exists – We have found ourselves and we have found the room. And PAO – all of them come from the Shaman.

The Self is the Magician. The Magician is the Shaman.
And the Shaman is in the Room.

RITUAL CHAMBERS

The Room. The Analysts call it "Being in the Room." That is where the world unfolds with the analysand – the secret other Self. The Room is where the whole of history joins them. Every life not present is actually with them like a phantom limb. The analyst is a subjective mirror for another soul when they are in the Room. They are in the universe of each other, bridged by the spacetime medium of Einstein and God. Here there is a dance of the microcosm and macrocosm; the universe (the room) and the humans. Life with life, in life, in the Room.

This is where our Occulted inner worlds unfold. With the Analyst. In the Room.

The Analyst's Room is the Occultist's Room but with human company. Occultists will tell you, "You are in a Great Room." Both are in the Room and the Room is all universes. And all universes are filled with rooms.

The cosmos is a
Ritual chamber.
The Ritual Chamber is the
alchemist's pot.
The alchemist's pot is the
analyst's Room.
The analyst's Room is
life in the cell.
Life in the cell is the cosmos.
The cosmos is a Ritual Chamber.

Christ teaches that we should pray alone in a dark closet, in a tiny room. Witches awaken the Sabbath under the blanket of night. Magicians cypher to maximize their spellcraft and their tradition within heavily glyphed walls. The analyst must keep the secret of the analysand, so that both may grow the Self. Artists toil like attic-bound mad scientists late into the creaks of sunrise. The alchemist stirs her pot until it is perfect and only until it is perfect.

Artists, analysts, and occultists gestate in their cells and from that imagined seclusion push their consciousness well beyond the walls of this universe and into the tissues of the Mystery.

This is always part of the Opus.

The Room, the Universe, is where all of consciousness and all of creation can be detected. Any and all rooms can only ever be in contact with any and all other rooms in the creation – Both the maintained rooms (universes) and the aborted ones are available. This is how hypnosis, and trance, and conjuring, and free association, and invocation, and memory, and distant healing, and telepathy, and remote viewing work. All rooms touch each other. All rooms are in the Great Room. We touch the invisible universe when we speak with the analyst, or the black mirror, or the skull. This is what the Shaman, the artist, the analyst, and the occultist all understand. With a twist of attention all rooms can be realized. From anywhere you can access anything, call anyone. Feel anyone. All things are magically detected and connected. Just because it is invisible, doesn't mean it's not there.

Jung called it all "an omnipresent continuum, an unextended Everywhere. That is to say, when something happens here at point A which touches upon or affects the collective unconscious, it has happened everywhere."

For the Room is the universe.
The Self is the true gateway to many worlds in the Great Room.
The kingdoms of heaven are within you. The kingdoms of hell are there too.

"Darken your room, shut the door, empty your mind. You are still in great company." Saint A.O. Spare said.

Of this "great company", it should be considered…

The early 20th Century's premier neurotic, phantasmagoriac, artist, anti-occultist, and Lord of the Dream Cycle Howard Philips Lovecraft hex-marked the aeon of the "Civilized" animal-man, who was at the time just tilting over the cusp of extending his data-phillic tendrils vastly deeper out into our grand cosmic circumstance with these resonating comments:

> The most merciful thing in the world, I think, is the inability of the
> human mind to correlate all its contents. We live on a placid island
> of ignorance in the midst of black seas of infinity, and it was not
> meant that we should voyage far.

"Merciful" in that if all the mind could see itself all at once… *"Cthulhu"* – all the worst Gods would come and tear the universe into bleeding sheets of madness. *"Cthulhu"* – that whisper from just below sleep and sanity. *"Cthulhu"* – the horror of the All. *"Cthulhu"* – the utter gravity of the true mirror upon our carelessly anthropomorphic souls and egos. *"Cthulhu"* – the imagination, the Self, in the face of the Mystery. *"Cthulhu"* – the mind seen clearly. *"Cthulhu"* – the lie we need to live. *"Cthulhu"* – The naked truth. *"Cthulhu"* – all the rooms. *"Cthulhu"* – all that can be uttered when everything is realized.

To live and endure without having to touch this truth is, to Lovecraft, "the most merciful thing in the world." We should not "voyage far," for the horrible truth of the Self and the World is that it is secretly *"Cthulhu."*

Generally speaking of course, this is the stead of the common, or the careful, or the dreadful. Yet therapists of all stripes, guides, healers, storytellers, and then patients, psychotics, depressives, the hurt, and the artists, creators, inventors, writers, musicians, poets, and finally witches, magicians, psychonauts, mystics, and the devout all answer to the call of the black seas of infinity. For the black seas make us be. We look at what few others have a desire to look at: our ignorance first, and then the black seas before us and inside us. And once you learn to sense the presence of both ignorance and the endless black seas, you can't help but detect both everywhere.

For both the black seas and ignorance are the provinces of the Occult. The Occult is the medium upon where the Analyst and the Artist do their bidding. The black seas are where the Shamans have their visions and strike their deals. Dip your hands in the colorless pool. Find out what's inside the empty hat.

On Occultus

Occult comes from the Latin word *occultus* meaning: *concealed, secret, hidden, obscured, invisible,* and *unseen.* Latin synonyms arrive as *absconditus, latens, abstrusus, arcanus, caecus, clandestinus, obcultus, obscurus, mysticus, imprensibilis, reconditus, opscurus, opertus.*

Occultus means: there, but not seen.

The Occult is never-ever *nothing.* It is always something that is hard or impossible to see. Its obviousness stolen away, or obscured, or naturally too obtuse or subtle. A trick is afoot – either the universe's, or someone else's, or our own, or all three. The Occult is all that is at the threshold of availability, as well as all that remains off in the utterly unavailable.

We are not so much strictly attuning ourselves to themed correspondences between planets, elements, numbers, and metals with this kind of Occultus. We are dealing with that which is Unseen. That which is Unseen beyond this room. That which Unseen even within this room. Everything undetected. Even what's just behind our head. What's in between the atoms. And what this room was long ago.

Occultism, Shamanism, Art, and Psychoanalysis have waking reverence for the Unseen. Reverence for the elves and demons that creep odd circumstances into our lives. Reverence for what magic happens in a dark and empty room. Reverence for what mechanisms, and planning, and actions whirl behind the stage. Reverence for the laws and rules of the cosmos that we tease out of mathematic formulas. Reverence for how the trick was hidden.

All we can see was once Invisible.
When something is discovered it is found from out from the Occult.

The Occult is a central, co-creative player in the alchemical swirl that results in the World; that results in Reality. The Unseen is as important as fire is to a cooked meal.

We know about 2-5% of the Universe thanks to our sciences. That's what we've thus far teased out of the otherwise Occultus Mundi. The Unknown, and the potential within it, is poetically and religiously referred to as the Pregnant Darkness. Anything could be born at any moment.

Thought is an Occult universe. We each have our own "inner" world. Inner – invisible, hidden, unseen, occult. Its impossible trenches are traumas cut out on the surface of our lands. Its monuments and landmarks tower toward the sun of our unfolding and becoming. Our skies flicker and change constantly with the erratic sway of our attention. Our planes are pockmarked with the hail of ideas. When we build our Memory Palaces, we create rooms within rooms in our mind to help us remember the waking world.

> Where are our palaces? Where are you?
> Where are we but utterly occulted?

We reveal our innerspace only in tickles as we reveal ourselves to others. Language and actions are the anagrams between us. All of this occurs under the depths, invisibly; though our faces point out our inner geography as helplessly as a compass points to north.

Alan Moore wrote in *From Hell*, "The one place Gods inarguably exist is in our minds where they are real beyond refute, in all their grandeur and monstrosity." This stage of our mind, upon which these gods must play, must also be grander indeed than they.

To this implicit massiveness of the mind, the folklorist and paranormal journalist Nick Redfern said:

> The word "soul" is derived from a combination of the Old English word, sáwol, the Gothic saiwala, the German sêula, The Saxon sêloa, and the Norse, sála. Suggestions have been made that all these words have a connection to the word "sea," which has led to speculation that the early Germanic peoples believed that souls of the dead resided in the deepest parts of the world's oceans. Notably, the Ancient Greeks used the same word for "alive" as they did for "ensouled," suggesting that the soul and the state of living are synonymous and conceptually linked.

Dream analysis fixes the Ocean as the unconscious. Ancient peoples saw the soul as like the ocean. Freud's self is a glacier that is mostly hidden. Psychoanalysis, Art, and Occultism have their roots in the circumstance of the invisible living soul.

All the functions, operations, processes that we could call "internal", we can also call Occulted. These are the tides and weather of our black seas of infinity. After all it must always be asked: *Where is thought?* Soul, mind, consciousness, Self—whatever you call it, everyone has an invisible universe. The invisible universe is central. We are the Hidden Place where meaning is made. The Occultist, The Artist, and The Analyst are all Masters of the Invisible. We sail the black seas.

Recollect, before 1910, the Latin *psyche* and the Greek *psykhe*, always meant *soul, life-animated,* or even *living ghost.* This use always implied something invisible but was revealed as authentic in the willed movement of bodies.

The authority of the Invisible is affirmed in our willful manipulation of our flesh.

We are the invisible illuminator at court between worlds.
Those who claim *there is no soul* have yet to see their own sight.

ABRACADABRA

Ptah and Thoth – Two self-generated, parentless, creator gods in the religion of Ancient Egypt. These gods are gods of language and magic. They speak the World into being. This idea of the word, the *logos*, being cast as the primeval force behind the universe is a central concept to the Western cannon. We find it in the Abrahamic religions, Hermeticism, and Witchcraft.

"In principio erat verbum et verbum caro factum est."
"In the beginning was the word and the word was made flesh."

Indeed, as children we learn by talking to ourselves. To the Ancient Egyptians, so did reality.

The word creating the world is the ultimate act of magic. What of magic, art, and words?

> There is some confusion as to what magic actually is. I think this can be cleared up if you just look at the very earliest descriptions of magic. Magic in its earliest form is often referred to as "the art". I believe this is completely literal. I believe that magic is art and that art, whether it be writing, music, sculpture, or any other form is literally magic. Art is, like magic, the science of manipulating symbols, words, or images, to achieve changes in consciousness. The very language about magic seems to be talking as much about writing or art as it is about supernatural events. A grimoire for example, the book of spells is simply a fancy way of saying grammar. Indeed, to cast a spell, is simply to spell, to manipulate words, to change people's consciousness. And I believe that this is why an artist or writer is the closest thing in the contemporary world that you are likely to see to a Shaman.

These are the words of Alan Moore, and they are ever succinct to PAO.

Stuart Chase detected the plastic reality that was being pushed on Americans through the saturation of mind control and black magic, executed in the form of advertising in the 1920s and 30s. On the magical power of words, Chase may have said it best; "Language is apparently a sword which cuts both ways. With its help man can conquer the unknown; with it he can grievously wound himself." This is from his 1938 book *The Tyranny of Words*, an effort to awaken (and thus heal) his fellow man from the new era of *created wants* that went on to seize the 20th Century mind. Advertising destroyed human consciousness; it created an indelible trench in our souls that we now try to stuff with stuff. It is a landfill that never quite fills. That was the goal of *created wants* all along. That is black magic.

Indeed, as any Analyst, Artist, or Occultist all recognize, words are often one of the most ultimate of tyrannies. What we call our selves and others guides our mutual destiny.

We are all authors.
All authors are godlike.
All words are magic.
It all goes in the great ledger that all life shares.
Sticks and stones may break your bones
but words will torment your being.

Psychoanalysis helps you read your book, and rewrite your book.

New Thought movement, a sister born of Spiritualism and Mediumship brought to the forefront of the American attention the tyranny and promise of words. Words, indeed words believed, are all powerful. Be careful what you think and what you say. Mind is like a garden; thoughts are the individual plants, flowers, and weeds; sprawling living fractals; and consciousness is the light that nourishes and grows them. Be aware of where your light shines. One need go no further than Neville Godard's classic lecture *Self-talk Creates Reality.*

Apropos of Everything, Abracadabra supposedly means "I speak it into being!" or, "I create it with speech!"

> One very important aspect of art is that it makes people aware of what they know and what they don't know that they know. Now this applies to all creative thinking [...] Once a breakthrough is made there is a permanent expansion of awareness. But there's always a reaction of rage, of outrage, at the first breakthrough. For example Joyce made people aware of their stream of consciousness at least on one level on a verbal level and he was at first accused of being unintelligible. I don't think many people now would have any difficulty with Ulysses. So the artist then expands awareness and once the breakthrough is made this becomes part of the general awareness.

Analysis, Art, and the Occult are all exactly as William S. Burroughs has laid out here. The Analyst is present to bring forth the hidden speech of the analysand. So too does the occultist and the artist bring forth the hidden speech of the Occult World Soul. It is all the same exorcize.

As any single book invisibly touches all the languages, all the books, written and unwritten, the whole Record, all our History. Words lock and unlock consciousness. Words lock and unlock the Self. A word echoes in the history of its own evolution; touching billions of souls, over thousands of years. "The New World" was not a new landmass; it was a new idea, a new planet, and a new Self to discover.

Psychoanalysis is a universe of words. Neuro-linguistic Programming, Cognitive Behavioral Therapy, indeed even the phrase "The Talking Cure", all underscore the power of words. We speak of our hurt, and hope, and hate, and then we are healed. The Word guides consciousness, and the Wound demands to be conscious. The Wound is made conscious, brought up from the Occulted Unconscious, with words and invocations and questions. Occultists use litanies of magic words. Artists claim new territory in the imagination with the poem, the prose, and the joke. The Analyst asks you how you feel.

The Analyst, the Artist, the Occultist speak; as we do we are intimately involved with the titanic forces of the word. Our Occult voice, the speech of our minds that no other ear can touch. The "inner" dialog. The speaker inside. The spellcaster. Speech before the spoken. Where is speech before it is spoken? Where is the voice that's read these shapes into words? Where is the ear that hears them? The answer is Occult.

All words come from the Occult.

That is what they have magic power.

SOME IMPORTANT QUESTIONS TO CONSIDER

The Question is not human. It is likely universal in Nature.

Imagine: "Is there water over there?" Or "Is the watering-hole still where it was?" And "Is this clean water?" Or "Can I drink this water?" Or "Is that large toothy asshole going to try and eat another one of us?" These are all questions, but deeper still, they are an experience – an experience that is far from remote or uncommon in the Animated kingdom. We are not at all the only creatures in the land of the living that have had these experiences – These questions. The Question is not just a homo sapiens phenomenon. All animals question. The Question informs survival. Indeed, Intelligence itself Questions. Nature Questions as it experiences, comes into living contact with, its "inner" and "outer" cosmoses, or conditions we could say.

The Analyst, Artist, and Occultist live in the womb of the Question.

Maturity develops in the womb of perception. The question guides the focus of perception.

Questions guide life and mind, as light guides plants and photosynthesis.

When light is cast on an object, doesn't it cast all else in darkness? When something is revealed, is not something else obscured? Doesn't the conscious mask the unconscious? Doesn't the daylight hide the stars? Doesn't the word *human being* disguise us from ourselves and discourage us from finding out what we really are? Don't we speak to hide the truth?

Now I'll guide you to the end.

Where are you?
Where are you really?
Where are you really is a two-fold question.

Where is your body?
Where is your Self?

Starting with the body. *Where is your body?* What we find is as simple and confounding as a child's interrogation, which is itself an ever-widening mirror of Mystery:

"Where are we?"
"We are on earth."
"Where's earth?"
"In the solar system."
"Where's the solar system?"
"In a galaxy."
"Where is the galaxy?"
"In the universe."
"Where is the universe?"

And our journey is already at an end, and it barely even moved. That is where your body is; in the universe. But then, of course:

Where is the universe?
Your body is in the universe, but where is the universe?
Where are you? In outerspace? What is outerspace in?
What contains outerspace? Where is outerspace?
We do not know where we really are.
Maybe, in a cosmic bowl or all within our head – Or godhead.
We do not know where the universe is.

Now that we don't know where the body is, because we do not know where the universe is, we can look at the second fold of *where are you really?*

Where is our Self?

Move your hand.
Now move that which moved your hand.

Can you move the mover? Can you move the Master of Thought?

Can you lift your house and all its Rooms?

Where is the silent voice that just changed these shapes into words?

Where are you experiencing this moment from? Where in the past, or future, or present?

Where are thoughts in this body? Where is meaning made? Where is the self that weeps at the presence and absence of love? Where is the imagination? Where are our dreams?   .

Jung said, "Somewhere our unconscious becomes material, because the body is the living unit, and our conscious and unconscious are embedded in it; they contact the body. Somewhere there is a place where the town ends meet and become interlocked. And that is the place where one cannot say whether it is matter, or what one calls 'psyche.'"

In terms of where we are, the only answer is *maybe somewhere.*

Consciousness is multidimensional – There is at once both physical stimuli and physic experience. Therefore, we are multi-locational, even during the most pedestrian exchange of footsteps and concepts.

Thought is motion when darkness moves.

What is the most Occult thing in this room right now? What right now here with us is the most Invisible thing? What's the hardest thing to see? What's the biggest paradox occurring right now?

It's this.

Where is this occurring? What is the most unseen thing? What is the hardest thing to see? The most Occult thing in this room, in any room, is always you – Most monumental and most hidden.

It's you.

Where is this you weaving meaning upon meaning; calling red sex, and black dead.

It seems to be "here", but where is "here"? And are we truly here with all that's here? Or does it only seem to be that way? Are we really "there" while this is "here"? Can even our wisest truly say? Can you even?

Where are you?

What are you?

Our body is in a universe
– "outserspace" –
Whose location is occulted.

The Fenris Wolf

Our self is in a universe
– "innerspace" –
Whose location is occulted.

Where you are seems, only seems, to be a private theater of experience. You and everyone else in this room are in the same position in terms of being in this room. But none of you share the same life experience. Each is different. Each is in a different position. We all see this Mystery space from an Occult location.

Wherever you really are, you're *definitely* all over the place.

Everyone and everything is a portal into the Occult, into the Hidden.

Oh my, oh me!
Aren't we walking in the dream!
As walking is dreaming,
micro-macro-cosm we!

The dream dreamed Art, Psychoanalysis, and the Occult in effort to ride the dream on the crest of this total Mystery. The waking world is dreaming and thus PAO exists.

We are here and we are not here. We are paradoxed within the mystery.

The real paradox of this Mystery is that the dream *is real enough*; real enough indeed to warrant the birth and work of magicians, artists, and healers. No matter where we really are, folks like us have been encouraged to show up. In the mighty darkness of sleep we all return to each other as the umbra black blanket that unites all worlds and bleeds profuse dreams.

Our orientation – *what are we really and where are we really* – is answered only by our imagination. Our imagination is our true orientation. We are only ever where we imagine ourselves to be because where we really are is a totally unknown Occult matter.

You are not on a planet.
You are in a fractal.
You are not a human being.
You are the history of evolution.
You are feeling the World.
You are feeling your Soul.

You, friend, are a fellow-fellow
amongst us other learner-creators
in the Alchemical Dream Lab
that we all call a lifetime.

All worlds, all platforms are illusory. Only souls and the communication between them, their relationship, their communion, is real.

The Interrogation of the Zen Man is the same as the Baby's; eventually it is revealed to all parties that no one has the answers. We only have semi-answers or non-answers on the way to Mystery.

Language has an obfuscating effect that makes us believe in the most basic, pure, existential, and immediate level that we actually know something. The simplest claims like, "We know we are human beings in the primate family. We know we are on a planet. The planet orbits a star. That star is but one of many in an eco-system of stars. Stars are flying through space. All of this is happening, depending on your point of reference, at tremendous speed." Every noun in these examples kind of deadens perception in its tracks. We don't really know what is this life process that we are. We don't know what livingness is. We actually experience it indirectly because *"human being"* as a thoughtform, an assumption, has stolen the show. It actually obscures the totality and both the awe to be existing and the awe of how very much in the dark we are about all of it.

Where are we in an occult universe.
We are an occult universe.
And we are the Gateway to both.

Truth is you aren't even in your body. Truth is you aren't even in a Room. You are in many rooms and made of many bodies.
This is what the Shamans
Analysts, Artists, Occultists see

You are in many universes all at once
There are many beings to be

We do not know our true address. Our address approaches infinity, and more than a single location. Our address is imagined.

We are in our imagination.
And our imagination is in the dark.
The dark very well may be someone,
Or something else's imagination,
Trying to see through.

This is why Lovecraft froze,
and found even his heroes murmuring,
The dreadful name,
"Cthulhu."

TENEBRIS TREMENDUM

The Self is an Interior Sun. Because it is Interior it is an Occult Sun. It is an Invisible Sun. What we experience is a way of indirectly experiencing it. The world, our hearts, and thoughts, and actions; exposure to this gives us a sense of Self over time. We know the Self only by how it paints our "inner" and "outer" world. The Self is revealed by *how* it rorschachs the Room. Our light can be seen on what our awareness illumines – pessimistic or optimistic glow – but our sun, our star itself remains invisible. We are the hidden focal point, the black hole of the universe at all times, in all places. We are the crossroads and all the rooms. For we feel it and make it out of feelings.

Paul Levy reminds us that Jung saw the Shaman's crossroads:

> 'abandon,' in Jung's words, 'causal descriptions of nature in the ordinary spacetime system, and in its place to set up invisible fields of probability in multidimensional spaces.

And all of science would in one way agree.

Any moment could be explored almost infinitely – fractally. You could be riding on the subway for five minutes. You could touch all those heartbeats singing softly there about you. Where are they going? Where have they been? What's the history of all that blood? They came from the union of their parents' syncopated beats. What did their lub-dubs sound like when they were in love? Or when they were in pre-vertebrate time – what did their body's music sound like then? What is their future? Are they walking towards whatever it is that makes their heartbeat scream with joy? Are they walking away from it? How much lovely can they touch? How much lovely can you touch? How much would you like to touch of the hanging lovely, lovely? We usually don't spend a lot of time thinking this way, often for fear of drowning asunder.

—◊— —◊— —◊—

Freud's great contribution to our endeavor was suggesting the presence of an Unconscious. The part of our total Self we cannot easily know. The black seas of infinity. That we gaze not through a window; we are many beams bounced off and split by a maze of prism-mirrors. And much is hidden. And the Unconscious moves our hand just as much as our waking willing self does. And our unconscious secretly tilts the glass. Our private world has a room that is even private to us. Even the unconscious hides from the equally invisible conscious. All we can do is press our ear to the door and try to make out a few words from the whispers and the shouting from the bottom of the glacier.

Is not the use of the word "God" but a placeholder for our vast and yawning ignorance as well as our suspicions that shimmer and stagger at just beyond its lip?

Indeed if "God" represents the creator, maintainer, or whole of Reality, Nature, is it not also telling that "God" is synonymous with "Mystery"? Jung's construction of the ego-Self axis seats the Self as being analogous to "God". The total Self and all of consciousness is more like "God" than just your persona. Your persona shifts. The "God" axis holds it all and molds it all. The "God" axis is the floor of the World. This Self as "God" to Jung can't help but bring with it "Mystery". The total psyche, all our consciousness, ego and all and all, at any point in the individuation process is always "God" in the background. It is the movie screen. We can rarely ever directly perceive the Self. To authentically and entirely make contact with the Self is to touch The Whole Show. The Whole Show is all Selves and all Rooms all Present and all Past together as One. The black seas made bioluminescent. The *coincidentia oppositorum* of the unit and the All – making thus the Unitary; the origin of religion, life, science, and reality, and the mind running through all of it; the One Mind occulted behind all the minds.

What this looks like Grant Morrison calls the Hyper-entity:

> I'll try and explain this as fast as possible; this isn't metaphysics, this is actual physical reality, when you think about it. Because most people don't think of the dimension of time in their lives, because the way we live is to see sections of time. So to try and explain it as quickly as possible in a way that everyone will understand. Right, you're standing here in front of me with your microphone, but in order to get here you had to come through that door, so can you point to coming through that door? You know what I mean?
>
> In order to get here today you had to be ten years old, can you point to being ten years old? No you can't, because in the way we experience time we can only see it in memory. We can't actually go there, even though we know there is a place called 'the past' where all this stuff happened, and where all those old comics came from, and from where you as a kid lived – You can't go there. You can't point. You can't show me a direction where the past is.
>
> But think of yourself as the leading edge of you, right? This is you, right now, you're moving forward through time, but behind you there's all these different versions of you going back and back and back. The same for all the guys in here, same for me – I go back through that door."
>
> "Well, imagine you could see that in time. It wouldn't just be a man with a back and a front. It would be a long trailing thing. And it contains all of you. And it has all these arms and all these eyes, and it moves backwards through the door and backwards through the stairs, and it's getting younger all the time through that trail. But, like I say, we can't see that. But if you could see it, it would look like a huge snake and it would keep going back, and there are lots

of these snakes and they all weave together. Every one of those kids running around, everyone here all starts going backwards through time, and eventually you get to be one year old. Somewhere in time you are right now one year old, because if you were not one year old you couldn't be here today. And that one year old then disappears up into its mother's womb, but you're still, still physical, you're still the same you – it's getting smaller and smaller, and it goes in there, and that same physical thing divides into an egg cell and a sperm cell. And the egg cell grows out of your mother, so it's still present, nothing's gone away there, the actual physical thing of you has now become an egg in your mother and a sperm cell going up inside your father, and the same thing happens to your mother and father, going back into their mothers and fathers. See? So you starting to see this?

"You take it right back so it's like everybody in the human race goes back to the same human root. Then somewhere along the evolutionary tree we're joined by apes, but it's still all one thing, the tree is the one thing, and the tree is rooted in three and a half billion years ago in the ocean, which is when the first living cell appeared and started to divide, and as I said in the other, the first mitochondrial cell, the DNA cell is still dividing in your body right now, it's immortal. It's never died it never went anywhere it just keeps dividing and making more copies of itself in all living forms. So what we actually are is this amazing divided single cell, which has grown itself across three and a half billion years into a gigantic… I imagine, I see it in my head as like an anemone made out of people, and bodies.

We rarely see life and time this way. Yet, this point-of-view is a physical point-of-view. As Morrison said, "This isn't metaphysics. This is actual physics." And it is. This is normally an unseen view of the matter. It is an occult reading. Morrison calls the anemone of we, the All, the Hyper-entity. This part of our Occult self. This cellular and temporal linage Morrison sees. This is what we are just a quarter of an inch under the psychic surface.

This is what it is. An Invisible Visible You. A Paradox in a Mystery. Many feet in many worlds, like jellyfish tentacles drifting, looking for something to touch, something solid enough to brush up against, in the black egg and the black seas of the Mystery.

SCIENTIFIC ARTIFACTS

Lévi reminds us in his *Doctrine*: "There is only one dogma in Magic, and it is this: The visible is the manifestation of the invisible [...]"

And soon after: "What, in fact, does man know? Nothing, and at the same time he is allowed to ignore nothing. Devoid of knowledge, he is called upon to know all."

It seems safe and honest to say that there will always be vastly more that is unknown than known – that is, if the unknown actually exists *before* it is known. Our blindness and constant surprise at the nature of the universe informs us repeatedly: *you couldn't even begin to know.* This is why the Artist, Analyst, and Occultist all bow in reverence to the Unknown and the Unseen.

A German study in 2013 (Steidle and Werth) found that creativity, the imagination, a room-filling aura of freedom, naturally surface and take hold of us whenever our bodies are in dim lighting or darkness. Recollect the theater, just before the lights fall completely. They are low, but they have stopped in mid air. They are on the way out. Twilight anticipating the dream to unfold. Observing from our seats. Waiting to unfold together. Imagine the street lamps of a solitary walk home, but that we are filled with love and the world. We admire the darkness so much so that it was also discovered that by merely thinking of dim lighting or darkness was enough to elicit stronger creative moods and imaginings from people. Think of what might be in the hidden shade and you'll be free. Of course the Germans noticed the beauty and merits of darkness.

The stars towering above assure us that we have many neighbors. Mind sees mind out there. Life sees life out there. We're all thinking the same thing. *"We see you."* (The Analyst does only the same – The Artist does only the same – The Occultist does only the same: *"We see you."* We all know at least that we're in the Room together. Or at least we seem to be.) Gulfs of darkness, but it is certain that once you notice your Sun is but one in the tundra of stars and darkness; you see what's in store for us all in the Room.

Medieval deceptions of the Christian Godhead or the Virgin often included a black halo, a black aura, vesica pisces, or a black egg surrounding them. This was a visual reminder that the closer you approached the Godhead, which for Christians the Godhead is Truth itself, the less your mortal being can know. The Divine, meaning the central reality, is always unknown. The highest Truth is unknown. We all bare a black halo, all universes metamorphose in a black egg, a black aura makes the environ about the crystal ball of all mind and being. This is why Faith is needed; God is Occult.

Today, our leaders in Science tell us the unmatched heavyweights of the visible universe are the Invisible. Dark Matter and Dark Energy, or Mystery 1 and Mystery 2. This "Dark Matter" has no radiation and no reflection. It is an invisible, yet utterly present monster that dominates reality. "Dark Energy" is an avalanche of magic that is equally present and equally untraceable. These forces are positively Lovecraftian in scale; 96% of our total known universe qualifies as either, and equally eldritch so far as their ultimate scientific description: "made of stuff astronomers can't see, detect or even comprehend." They are Lovecraft in name; "Dark" this, "Dark" that.

This is where the crisis of falling in love, of dreaming, of wanting, of creating, living, and dying occurs. This is our most basic observation. Incomprehensible, invisible forces tie our shoes together. Hold the Room in place. This is where all life lives. This is where the Artist and the Analyst attempt their Alchemy.

We don't know where we are. We don't know where we are at all. We can barely say that we are here at all. All we can sense at the summit of all Honesty is that we seem to exist; that the universe seems to exist. That the mountain itself seems sure, but only for now. That is all. Everything else is Mystery.

We might as well be standing
in the womb of the Witch.

**The obstacles have made who I am
I am the wound who speaks in light**

Alchemically speaking, the universe is the Prima Materia. What we do when we engage in therapeutic process, or create art, or practice magic is we transform the universe. We "create the soul" in the Ancient Egyptian vision of a dung beetle rolling up a large ball for its babies to grow in. Just imagine if Sisyphus's rock turned out to be an egg, and after rolling it back up aeon after aeon – one day, finally, the love of his life happened to break out of it. This is what the alchemist does; she stirs her pot until it is perfect. Every drop goes into Her cup. This is what the Buddhists do. They breathe until the act of breathing is magically transformed into an unparalleled spiritual reality; where healing and wellbeing are the norm, and boredom absolutely dies. The Artist and the Magician consciously create themselves and everything. Conscious therapeutic-art. Conscious art; Art as conscious. When Consciousness bears the load of co-creative Imagination, being Conscious itself becomes an Art. This what we're doing with PAO. We are working towards conscious competency. We are walking around the clockwork of our very daily lives, trying to tolerate the face of the Master. We are trying to see in every moment why there is any moment at all. And what it is *we*, as transformative forces ourselves, are doing *meaningfully* with it. *To be.*

Though we dwell in a Mystery, and the body is trillions of animals, and we know not where we are, and we cannot find the capitol of Thought, and less than a sliver is known to us – there is still *Us*. We! Life. The Animated. The Animated have arrived. And we are Willfully Animated. And we Animated have a variety of styles of existence available to us. We can be glorious insects, wide-ranging mosses, foe-less porcupines, or primates. We can be schizophrenic, psychopathic, morbidly obese, obsessive, horrified, or apathetic. We can also be great artists, imagination-wideners, lovers, teachers, explorers, and ingenious discoverers, and great caregivers of each other and reality Herself. This is the crisis of choice and the crisis of our shared circumstance.

To live, *to be*, is to necessarily muddy up the place with the artwork of your being passing through it. So what is your artwork? What is your art? What beauty are you leaving in the living of your wake?

Henry Miller shared in *The World of Sex*:

Real life begins when we are alone, face to face with our unknown self. What happens when we come together is determined by our inner soliloquies. The crucial and truly pivotal events which mark our way are the fruits of silence and solitude. We attribute much to chance meetings, refer to them as turning points in our life, but these encounters could never have occurred had we not made ourselves ready for them. If we possessed more awareness, these fortuitous encounters would yield still greater rewards. It is only at certain unpredictable times that we are fully attuned, fully expectant, and thus in a position to receive the favors of fortune. The man who is thoroughly awake knows that every 'happening' is packed with significance. He knows that not only is his own life being altered but that eventually the entire world must be affected.

The word *mood* spelled backwards is *doom*, your *doom* means your *fate*. Your fate is your mood. Your mood is your doom. Your *mood* spelled backwards is *doom*.

"It's not the job of the artist to give the audience what the audience wants. If the audience *knew* what they needed, then they wouldn't be the audience. They would be the artists. It is the job of artists to give the audience what they *need*." Once said Master Moore.

This is what the Shamans do.

—⁓— —⁓— —⁓—

All Analysts, Artists, and Occultists are adepts of mediumship and channeling. All states and dimensions are their oyster. All feelings and angles a living thing could possibly touch in a thousand lifetimes is their stomping ground. Their job is to taste all of being. It is their purpose in life to be the multitudes. They are here to navigate well, or well enough, the "inner" and "outer" courts. Analysts, Artists, and Occultists touch *everything* and they know it. They work to be Shaman, and Shaman are the ships on the black seas of infinity. We illuminate and bob up and down upon the tide of Mystery. We point to oases, small bits of land, flotsam, rock, and islands that can make do as useful shelter, until our people learn to fly or swim happily back into the Mystery again. And the Shamans heal, and help you grow your gnawed off broken wings back.

Artists and Occultists don't always suffer the black seas happily. Those who survive the black seas likely do so thanks to the cheer of a lover, a healer, an analyst, a guide, a friend, a mentor, or a devastatingly well-timed mirror. All the great shamans, heroines, leaders, artists, and cunning folk are healers in one form or another. Those who are Masters channel the Wound. They are mediums for the Trauma to speak itself whole, to dance itself out, to paint its pain upon the grass. Eventually it is universally realized that all beings exist to help heal the Wound. For the truth of the pressing matter of our shared circumstance is that secretly, secretly everyone is holding everyone else's hand. And very slowly, we've been overcoming our total fear of this.

The deep PAO sees the alchemy at play in this; the mixture of horror and healing.

You will know the Wound was finally free to speak when the voice of it is physically healing.

They say: *Nobody's perfect so don't play pretend. Burn ever picture of Buddha inside yourself and keep your stone warm.*

Oh what Great Zen cometh when we let out all the bees!

ARISE, THY DREAMING OTHER

Blake said, "The imagination is not a state; it is human existence itself."

Blake said, "The Eternal body of man is The Imagination, that is, God himself."

Jung said, "The imagination is perhaps the most important key to understand the opus."

Goddard said, "Jesus Christ is the Imagination; the power of God."

Booth said, "Imagination is the key."

He closed *The Secret History of the World* with that four-word paragraph.

Even *matter* is only what we imagine.

As is *death* imagined as well.

The Self and the World are imagined. PAO is engaged with examining and re-imagining them. We imagine the World to fulfill life's pact – as it has imagined us in first place, so we must imagine it back. We are created and thus we are fated to create. We are the creature that creates every moment's meaning. We are made and thus must make. We live in the Occult Mystery on a Scaffolding of Imagination.

Dreaming and Imagining are the all-sided coin.

Randolph Carter, the alter-ego of Lovecraft, is a master dreamer; A dreamer that knows how to commune and relate meaningfully with the dream beings of the Other World. Carter guides, knows the customs, the symbols and signs of the people and elementals and endless monsters that wander the Invisible. This is the goal of PAO – To be a Master Dreamer in an uncertain reality, in a living Mystery.

We are dreaming, enchanted, imagining in the Room of Mystery. This is why Shamanism, Mysticism, Magic, Art, Religion, and Analysis exist. The imagination is real, the Mystery is real; the feedback between the two (between the seen and the Unseen) is real. That is almost all we know of reality. Yet, there is much to hope. For the sooner you accept that dreaded co-creator status that you share with all reality, the sooner the walls around will turn to sponge.

Our Salvation is in competent dreaming. For we are always dreaming and in dreaming we co-create the world as we shed, polish, and peer into the Self. For the pain of society is due only to careless dreaming, as careless dreaming soon turns to nightmare – the galloping horse of horror. The four horsemen are bad dreams. Bad dreams make war on all scales. Careless dreaming makes demons of the dark. Soon there is only everything to fear and hate.

What we are reaching towards is not into space, nor into some other darkest trench immeasurable, but actually into the Mystery of the Self. We are using the seeming universe-dream apparently before us to do so. We grope outside ourselves to see what there is to find within.

Thus the sane and happy dreamer is always the dreamer who sees the Zen; you find out there is the Zen you nurture in here. The World is only ever as ugly as your mind is. Buddha is smiling because she sees she's always at the crossroads. It is the World that moves through her. She is the star that paints it.
She says:

> Try not to see yourself as a body moving through spacetime; bobbing about in an ocean of people, places, animals, and things. Instead see yourself living at an ever-fixed crossroads. Here evolves your conscious awareness as the circumstances of life pass by, make their comments, their claims, and wander. For they will always be your magical mirror as you both show each the state of your ongoing weather. They will always show you how far you've come and where you fumble. Linger and observe. At the crossroads meets the history of cosmic evolution. This is your unmoving reference frame.

Never disregard the role of boredom in the evolution of consciousness. Without it, we'd likely never change at all.

Nevertheless...

The great deception against perception was the suggestion of the mundane. There is no mundane to be found. Yet it is found religiously. The alchemist is to stir her cauldron, to clean her mirror, to walk through reality, until everything appears as the rainbow gold it is. That is what lives always-just underneath the low muck of assuming pontification. That's what's just under the deadening gloss of the "mundane" of the "answer". The rainbow gold of the living Mystery realized. The floor of the Room and all of the Room is made of living rainbow gold. For the energies in the room, the stardust, and light, and all the animals that you are; nothing is dull but our attention when it's removed from outer space.

For this Room, and we in it, is the Mystery most high. There is no need to divine our way into another celestial sphere or astral spirit world (valuable though that may be) to understand what is Occult; it is this World already that is totally

Occult. The most common is nakedly the most magical, the most nakedly Hidden. Seize the mundane and the black seas of infinity suddenly all shimmer.

For this ongoing cosmogenesis – the origin of everything evolving – can only be boring if your mirror isn't clean. Reality never gets boring; it's our own finely-tuned engagement with reality that becomes unbearable. Thus PAO exists.

Where are you really?
What are you really?
Do not answer.
Context is key.

Create context.
Thy Living Mystery.
Summon your All.
And See.

Stripped to the Core:
Animistic Art Action and Magickal Revelation

Charlotte Rodgers

Over the years I have been involved in a myriad of projects that blur any lines and distinctions between performance, magick and art: anthologies, zines, art events, films and film festivals. Things that I would personally call egregores; living entities that eventually assume a life of their own and generate an energy that was draining in the creation but can be directed to effect upon completion.

My sculptural work is about channelled hybrids and amalgamations, living cut-ups, evolutionary progressions and atavistic recreations; and other elements of my creative process have a similar basis and direction.

These creative processes were and are very much mirrored in my own life: a disparate person trying to find a way of expressing herself within mainstream society and being castigated and judged in the traditional time honoured manner. Ostracised, labelled, committed and institutionalized until I found a way of translating myself, my art and my beliefs in a way that is inherently strengthening and magickal; feeding my spirits, my guides, my gods, my creativity and thus strengthening and developing my core self.

I was born in New Zealand, first generation, no traceable family tree and no strong and identifiable family spiritual heritage.

This was before the internet, so in many ways New Zealand was a free floating land with little interference or interaction outside the country which in some respects allowed a lot more freedom, but freedom that brought with it, in my sphere anyway, a degree of chaos and experimentation. Sure, there was indoctrination and influence from Great Britain and a strong Scots Presbyterian ethos, and sure, there was suppression of the inherent indigenous belief systems but still... It was a country with huge tracts of empty spaces where it was easy to drop off the radar, and the 1970s/1980s was a liminal and transitional time that lent itself easily to wild and in some respects potentially dangerous, creative and spiritual explorations.

I always believed in magick, always, being the ability to effect change through will, and I also was always was fascinated by bones and remnants of death. These have both been constants in my rather messy and fragmented life.

In my earliest years I was brought up and educated under the umbrella of Roman Catholicism; something that never really touched me but it did impress upon me the transformative power of ritual and glamour when coupled with belief, both to good and to bad effect.

My mid-teens saw me already versed in palmistry and tarot, experimenting with creating sculptures from bones and remnants of death, using drugs and psychedelics for recreation and spiritual adventuring and searching various textual sources for magickal references which I could relate to.

There wasn't much out there at that time that pressed my buttons, although the work of Aleister Crowley moved me, partially because sexuality was essential to his practice.

My personal spirituality has always made a necessity of exploration of the physical. This is varied-fold in purpose; I see it as a necessary embrace of self because it breaks various taboo areas and conditionings which I felt limited me. These explorations of self have encompassed, among other things, utilising ritualised sigilisation through tattoo piercings and scarification; and in-depth exploration of the use of body fluids in ritual.

Being a long term adherent of the Hermetic doctrine "As above so below…", as well as a palmist, where the lines on the hands dictate the persona, and the persona in turn dictates the shape, structure and lines of the hands. It seemed natural for me to look at deliberately imprinting scars, and patterns upon my own body in keeping with changes that I desired to occur.

Eventually I dropped into a no man's zone of addiction for some years where creativity became part of a repetitive, tedious depressing repetitive loop darkly coloured by my opiate dependency. When I finally I cleaned up, my art and magick became progressive, challenging and experimental once more.

I'd never stopped working with the tarot and palmistry, both of which required stepping into a persona to deal with the public. Later I briefly did traditional spellcraft for people, and also taught yoga. All of which needed an assumed physicality in the way I related with the public; stepping into a glamour so to speak.

However, none of these roles I found comfortable and I eventually backed off from them.

I spent several years specifically focused on the use of blood in magickal practice, looking at ways in which its use could effect change on both esoteric and exoteric levels.

I interviewed, networked, wrote up questionnaires and sent them out, and enlarged my research to include sexual fluids and breast milk; breast milk being interestingly enough the most taboo fluid and the most difficult to find reference to.

I think this is because the mother/child bond is the most iconic, idealised and near sacred. There has been a much greater repulsion and negative reaction to the dolls I create than to any of my work with road kill, something which reiterates this point I feel about the perceived sanctity of the mother/child relationship.

But I digress, albeit a valid digression because confronting the most sacred of cows creates the most profound effects, the most impact and causes the greatest change.

Whilst I was doing my blood work, I was also creating art from clay and road kill, experimenting with channelling intent into said creations and feeding them various fluids, all the while writing up the results. One series of ritualised creative work that I did was orientated around the flowing residue, religious indoctrination and conditioning that I had been subjected to as a child into a series of clay dolls, then baptising the dolls in various ways, including with both my own venous and menstrual blood so I could reshape said conditioning into something more progressive and less restrictive.

I also wrote a book, co-founded a magickal discussion group that essentially was an egregore, and as an extension of this put on a Magickal Film Festival and A Magickal Art Fair. All of which were about active artistic creative expression that although magickal in premise had no specific desire for a result.

Initially I used the internet a lot. Not just for networking, information gathering and magickal e-groups but exploring the potentialities for the creative magickal and slightly chaotic play that was inherent. For instance, a version of the surrealist party game exquisite corpse where I would send a reactive statement around the world and ask for an automatic response embodied in any form that the recipient found necessary: sculpture, music, photography, text, film, performance. Then I cut and pasted the results in a magazine and put together what could be considered an oracular transmission starting. Omphalos of the dark cliffs.

From here I moved onto the next klesha or personal taboo: Death, and then my own history and past primarily focused on the aspects of the outsider expressions of sexuality and addiction.

My work became more centred around art and I moved away from the ritualised group work that I was doing, as I realised that the line between art and magick is so fine as to be near nebulous.

I agree that there is crossover of performance with ritual and there is a saying that a good actor is a great ritualist but I found that within established and structured magickal groups there could be a tendency towards narrowness and fundamentalist attitudes. As I have aged and accumulated layers of memory, issues, experiences and assorted crap I found the need to strip back and work without tools and without dogma.

This is one of the reasons that sculpture appeals to me as more able to articulate magick and intent without residue-conditioning attached. Writing and language are learned and even automatic writing techniques have a degree of indoctrination clinging to them, no matter how much one turns off their conscious mind.

I reached a point where I found I was learning more about spirituality from a visit to the indigenous tribal sections of the Pitt Rivers Museum in Oxford or the Hornimann museum in London than I was through reading books on the subject, be they archaic or contemporary.

Sculpture, especially clay, is atavistic and much easier to flow into, especially in my case as I have not trained as an artist and have less indoctrination about the right approach and technique to interfere with what I'm doing.

I can look at very early pieces of work that I did, before I learned more about practicalities such as structure, materials and technique, and see an inherent power and rawness, that I would, in all honesty, find it very difficult if not impossible to achieve now.

The work I do alone is ritualised in the way I consciously step into a sacred space, move into a trance-like state and swim in the collective magickal consciousness.

Another technique that I use both in my art and magick is the camouflage technique. On one hand I am taking something which has been used in warfare and subverting intention, direction and application; on another I am using light and shadowing to rearrange reality. Taking something that was previously not seen and making it visible, and vice versa.

The finding of the pieces that I use in my sculptures is also very indicative of working within a magickal consciousness. An awareness of death creates a way of looking at your surroundings that makes it easier to find bones, road kill, the discarded and the dead; a different way of looking at reality. You are looking for the memory or essence that is contained not the container, and that memory has a pull or draw to it. For me anyway, but I suspect it is the same for everyone if they allow it.

I give people fragments of bone which I always seem to be finding, and it often links them into that vision by opening them up to a new way of seeing, and many of these people say that theses fragments change them, and they, too, start finding sundry bones and remnants of death.

You don't need to see to have vision.

Some years ago I participated in Ron Athey's *Gifts of the Spirit* in Manchester. I attended initially as a magickian who saw the performance as a ritual that utilised many of the techniques that I have a great fondness for: glossolalia, automatic writing, chanting, mantra, and I was fascinated to discover that the performers and myself actually were aligned; entering a similar space but using different language to describe this space and ostensibly having a different goal through the same action.

A similar crossover has occurred when I talk with my sister, who is an artist, about creating something and the point where that 'something' comes alive. Now my sister doesn't share my interest, belief or use of magick, but as an artist her perspective puts her on the same page as myself.

Personally, I believe that growing up in New Zealand in a time when it was incredibly isolated and having little or no family history gave me a magickal edge of sorts.

It was easier to access a core animist centre that is aware of inherent life in everything, as I didn't have obvious cultural links through the land I was born in or a known genetic heritage that dictated my spirituality.

Despite the geographical distance from the UK, myself and my New Zealand peers at the time followed a similar tangent to Britain, in a slightly chaotic merging of currents and, a worshiping at the altar of radical countercultural creative expression as presented by William S. Burroughs, Austin Osman Spare, Genesis P-Orridge, the IOT (Illuminates of Thanateros), graphic novels and industrial music, although I only realised this in retrospect.

When I moved to England and explored various magickal traditions, I found performance and artistic process were inherent to all of them, be they a highly ritualised group like the OTO, the more freeform and eclectic approach of the IOT, or the folk and traditional practices. However my own background gave me a stripped-down approach with a praxis that necessarily included deconditioning and rearrangement of aspects of the self, both inner and outer, and whilst perhaps there were groups that I had a draw towards, and some I worked with, I always preferred to work solo. If I did a group working, go for a quick, exciting and combustible, short relationship. Then walk away.

Ten years ago or so, I was at a talk given by Jaz Coleman at Occulture in Brighton where he presented the idea that New Zealand was an entry point to Universe B: the qliphothic universe. He then played some music he composed and a film that represented this 'wormhole'.

Two people reacted strongly to the music: myself and performer Orryelle Defenestrate, who is from Australia. I think Jaz was perhaps spot on with his summation but the way he communicated his beliefs was what really carried the impact.

As I keep saying, words have the limitations of language, culture and conditioning. Art and performance have the potential to go beyond all those things, and as magick is about the indefinable, the limitless, it makes sense that the language that is used to convey it is a language that has the widest scope; a language that sees this reality as a gateway, not a box.

Magick is active transformation, a movement of energy allied with intent, so whether it is free flow or deliberate and choreographed, it is essentially a focusing that creates change.

The more people involved in this process, the greater its potential for both chaos and transformation.

Stripped to the core, magick and art are necessary bedfellows, and it is the artist/practitioners' choice how those bedfellows choose to lie together.

Dynamics of the Occulted Body

Alkistis Dimech

'Appearances are a sight of the unseen' – Anaxagoras

I am a dancer; my body is the material for my art, and movement is my practice. It is an obsession. Movement arises mysteriously, at the very source of life and before even a self forms. Butoh (which translates as 'dance steps') is unique amongst dance forms, perhaps most markedly in the way movement is discovered or evoked in the dancer, who is continuously engaged in pushing body and psyche into the *eremos*, the wilderness and borderlands, where one encounters oneself as a stranger, as enemy, ancestor, animal, as elemental force, as a shape dredged from the primal ocean. Butoh is engendered by the living body confronting death. As one of my teachers, the late, great Ko Murobushi wrote, '… the smell of the corpse makes life stand out, stand out desperately. The origin of Butoh is in the intensity of this stance …' (Murobushi, 'Hinagata' *Works 1972 – 2013*. Ko&Edge Co. 2014). We are born to this visceral and vital struggle; becoming aware that it is a dance, *the* dance, in time.

Counter to this experience of the closeness of death, and impossibility to move, is the impossibility *not* to move, the experience of the fullness of sensual being. The other element of my practice concerns Babalon. Without going into the detail of my magical and occult practice, which I have touched on elsewhere, this work is very much grounded in the retrieval of the body and its inherent potentials from the bonds that have been put on it. Babalon is naked, unconditioned power; female sexual response and the female orgasm evince this power in its inexhaustible variety, its unquenchable fire – although it is a force in which all participate and in which all are burned. It is a work that leads to an intimate knowledge of the occulted body; its subtle anatomy; and its role in sorcery, divination and the cultivation of sexual and erotic energy. It is a work which, like my practice of Butoh, utterly immerses one in the experience of the flesh, and through which one touches and comes to know 'the flesh of the world.' (Merleau-Ponty, *The Visible and the Invisible, Followed by Working Notes*. 1968).

The occulted body

First, what do I mean by the occulted body, and particularly its relation to consciousness and 'the unconscious'? In the first place, it is the body; a body that has been obscured or overwritten. But more specifically, I equate the occulted body with what is anatomically hidden, or in the dark; what the philosopher, phenomenologist and former dancer Maxine Sheets-Johnstone calls our 'bodily insides' (Sheets-Johnstone, *The Roots of Power*: 172); that is, what is accessible to us only through the 'dark' senses: touch, kinaesthesia, proprioception; or what lies below the threshold of sensory awareness, such as those processes associated with the autonomic nervous system. In Butoh, this body is often referred to as *nikutai* – the 'body of flesh' or 'body of desire' – which is the lived, individual body (as opposed to a generic and purely functional one) and is the vehicle for the manifestation of the interior landscape, and the realm of images.

The occulted body is possessed of its own selfhood, it has autonomy, it is autopoietic and conscious. It is a dynamic, living body. Kinetic processes cycle incessantly at every level of its organism, from the molecular and neural to the gestural, and at every level inhere it in its environment and interrelations. Furthermore, these movements are in no way mechanistic or motoric; they exhibit autonomy and coherence across the entire spectrum of being; what the bio-physicist Mae-Wan Ho described as 'organized heterogeneities, or dynamic structure on all scales.' (*The Rainbow and the Worm*: 21)

The occulted body is the source of the 'body consciousness' or 'ground consciousness' from which arises psyche, and a subject (or ego). Freud, in 'The Ego and the Id' acknowledged: 'The ego is first and foremost a bodily ego...'[1] but the psychoanalytic method he pioneered is rooted in discourse and not in the body. My practice reaffirms the authority of the body: it is first of all the body that communicates, revealing its inner life, its affectivity, its vulnerability as well as its strength. Discourse does not, and cannot, efface or replace the originary ground of existence. The body is the mother of language; our prelinguistic mother tongue, the primal voice of movement.

DYNAMIC GNOSIS

'For behold, I am Understanding, and Science dwelleth in me.'
– the Daughter of Fortitude

Movement is essential to tactility, proprioception and the kinaesthetic sense. An organism or body's incessant motion gives rise to its proprioceptive, kinaesthetic and tactile consciousness. As the foundation of the sensorium and affectivity, the moving body is fundamental to, and *generative* of, gnosis. Aristotle recognised how fundamental movement is to life; he calls it *koinē aisthēsis* (*De anima III*, 1, 425a27), that is, the *sensus communis* or common sense; the primary faculty of perception, as it unifies all the senses, and underpins an organism's self-awareness or apperception. Aristotle ascribes to the *koinē aisthēsis* the ability to discriminate or

---

1 And his footnote: 'The ego is ultimately derived from bodily sensations, chiefly from those springing from the surface of the body. It may thus be regarded as a mental projection of the surface of the body...'

judge, and as such we can link it to *under*standing: a deep instinctual preternatural understanding.

For me, to dance is to to initiate myself into the body's mysteries, again and again; to know myself in the process of becoming and to know the world in its becoming, through an intertwined corporeal consciousness. Here is the 'place of enquiry,' the repository of ancestral knowledge and accumulated individual experience.

PROTEAN BODY, PROTEAN VOICE

The human body and the human voice have a phenomenal capacity for mimesis. This capacity emerged from our primate ancestry, but with bipedality came an enhanced potential for mimetic expression. The upright body is freed to elaborate an ingenious protolanguage of gesture and movement. At the same time, vocal expression achieves a hitherto unheard power, subtlety and range, as the apparatus of breathing and eating are modified and mastered.

One can even see this shift in the eye, with the hand and the erect phallus, a primal symbol of power, mundane and magical. The eyes of primates do not speak, they are dark, obtuse; the human eye, by contrast, is agile, mercurial. The pupil flashes and darts in its milky orb; it has intent, it hungers and it eats, it misleads or blinds, it undresses and it intimates, giving glimpse of the interior. One can make an entire dance with the eyes alone, for, like bodies, they are highly expressive, communicating kinetically, and resonant with the hidden regions of soma and psyche.

Our enhanced mimetic faculty is the bedrock of human culture: it is the ground for iconicity, for analogical and symbolic thinking, and for the emergence of language. It is an ambivalent aptitude.

The evolution of an expansive, rich and fluid *lingua franca* composed of sound, sign, signal and gesture – elaborated in song, dance, play and ritual – enabled communication with peers, with neighbours and strangers, and with an entire ecology of spirits, ancestors, flora and fauna sharing a common habitat, 'a single social field' which is vibrantly animist in character. But a shared habitat is a place of conflict and survival, in which we – as predator and prey – occupy and exploit a distinctive niche. With mimesis came a refined potential for deception, for cunning. Mimicry is a critical skill for the hunter; it is predicated on a hypersensitive awareness to one's environs, the ability to read its signs, or listen to its utterances; and to the transmission of this art through imitation and reenactment. Vocal mimicry in particular was used lure prey. Almost universally animals cannot detect the intent behind a signal, they cannot fake; they do not participate in the 'lie', knowingly, subtly, as humans do. Exceptions are rare and striking: corvids, parrots and cephalopods act mimetically, and with a recognition of deception. Unsurprisingly, we regard them, warily or admiringly, as supernatural.

Both the human voice and the human body are protean in their transformative potentials. This archaic protean quality is what draws me, as a dancer and a magician, to ceaselessly explore the body's mystery and power. It is a quality that manifests most remarkably in the body's fascia, a coherent web of tensile strength that constantly renews and transforms itself in response to movement. I consider the fascia, the connective tissue, to be the physiological substrate of consciousness. The dense, penumbral form of the occulted body corresponds to the 'unconscious,' and finds in the fascial web its genetrix and matrix.

The fascia is the largest organ in the body, a web of connective tissue that structures, binds and supports. It is present throughout the body, interpenetrating and surrounding muscles, bones, nerves and blood vessels; in fact, all the cells in a body are interconnected through the connective tissue. Fascia can be grouped into three main types: superficial, associated with the skin; deep, associated with the muscles, bones, nerves and blood vessels; and visceral, comprising all tissues and membranes covering the organs and lining the cavities within the body. The deep fascia is richly innervated with sensory receptors that convey the presence of pain, changes in movement, pressure and vibration, in the chemical environment and in temperature. It forms the bones, supplies the body with blood from the marrow, and conducts nutrients and energy throughout the body; it is essential to healing and regeneration. Intrinsically connected with movement, it is the medium through which our inner environment interacts with the outer; it is, thus, the organ of knowledge *par excellence*. The complex functions and phenomenal properties of connective tissue, indeed the body as a whole, is due to its liquid crystalline composition, which underlies the electromagnetic body and its subtle anatomy.

The liquid crystalline structure of the living body (which had been predicted by Joseph Needham as early as 1935) was confirmed through the research of Dr Mae-Wan Ho. Her fascinating enquiry into the quantum biophysics of living organisms is documented in *The Rainbow and the Worm*, and in the many papers which she has written (www.i-sis.org.uk). I will quote from one, to précis the significance of liquid crystallinity to an animate body and its corporeal consciousness:

> There is a dynamic, liquid crystalline continuum of connective tissues and extracellular matrix linking directly into the equally liquid crystalline cytoplasm in the interior of every single cell in the body (see Ho, 1997; Ho, 1998; Ho and Knight, 1998, and references therein). Liquid crystallinity gives organisms their characteristic flexibility, exquisite sensitivity and responsiveness, thus optimizing the rapid, noiseless intercommunication that enables the organism to function as a coherent, coordinated whole. In addition, the liquid crystalline continuum provides subtle electrical interconnections which are sensitive to changes in pressure, pH and other physico-chemical conditions; in other words, it is also able to register 'tissue memory.' Thus, the liquid crystalline continuum possesses all the qualities of a 'body consciousness' that may indeed be sensitive to all forms of subtle energy medicines including acupuncture. (Dr. Mae-

Wan Ho, 'Coherent Energy, Liquid Crystallinity and Acupuncture.'
Presented to British Acupuncture Society, 2 October, 1999)

Whilst the implications of her research have still to be played out – in main-stream science, in social organisation, in the structure of politics, and in the occult – for me, this confirmation of the body's essential fluidity, its unified dynamic coherence, has immediate import. It affirms the fundamentally *animate* nature of the living body; it reveals a unified, coherent and dynamic matrix which is simultaneously the source, the medium and the field of physical form, and of psyche, that convulsive zone inhabited by a primordia of atavisms, archetypes and eidola.

Every living being is also a fossil. Within it, all the way down to the microscopic structure of its proteins, it bears the traces if not the stigmata of its ancestry. (Jacques Monod, *Chance and Necessity: Essay on the Natural Philosophy of Modern Biology*, 1970.)

I call the body 'the place of enquiry' – in reference to the grave and divination – for the body limns and enfolds this occult world as the skin limns and enfolds the sensate. The matrix of connective tissue is the repository of our individual and ancestral memory (cf. Freud's notion of an 'archaic heritage' and Jung's description of archetypes as 'biological instinctual constellations.'). It is equally attuned to motion and emotion, which it registers and retains, submerged in and holographically distributed throughout the liquid crystalline continuum. This body memory, which is always oriented to the future – that is, to survival and evolution – is engaged directly through the dynamics of the living body.

REVELATION OF THE OCCULTED BODY

Dance is an incessant resurrection and dissolution of forms; a 'perpetual revelation of force,' as consciousness unfurls itself, like the petals of a rose, awakening in the sensorium of our common humanity. The occulted body is exposed in the quality and affect of movement, in the timbre or 'grain' of the voice; and in its wake latent images, dreams and visions surface from their visceral dwellings.

It is with this body and voice that I work, in dance, as in my occult practice. It is important to work from the ground up, with breath and its connection to earth and body through the feet. Preliminary to beginning work, as part of my warm up routine, I practice exercises which I call collectively 'choral techniques.' The term derives from the work of Anca Manolescu and is discussed by Nicoletta Isar in her work on chorography and Byzantine liturgical dance; it references Plato's concept of the *chôra* (alternatively, *khôra*), the third nature that is the mother and receptacle of being. Mirroring the cosmogonic chôra, there are in the human body its likenesses, fulfilling the same functions and operating in the same way. Plato equates the bodily chôra with the liver, which has an occult connection with vision, divination and fate; but, I suggest, we should understand the fascia as the primary choraic organ (genetrix and matrix), holding form and giving space as it does; and, above all, in its absolute affinity with motion.

The body will autonomously shake or tremble to release trauma, as it does in orgasm, and in the spontaneous movement of sexual energy through the body. Movements that rhythmically shake the body – trembling, pulsating, vibrating, undulating – such as the water body techniques of Noguchi gymnastics – exert a profound and direct influence on the connective tissue and the ground conscious-ness, having an energising and regenerating effect, as well as bringing the body-mind to an exquisitely sensitive and receptive state. This is at the same time a state of heightened creativity, volatile and generative. Tensions and associated habitual patterns and mental fixations are (progressively) loosened; the body is physically tempered; and the body-mind entranced…

These techniques produce a cleansing, or a polishing, of the dark mirror of the body, from which those visions arise that are 'a sight of the unseen.' This is critical for my dance method, and for magical practices such as divination, skrying and the techniques of active imagination. The body is prepared, it is receptive to images: those I give it to stimulate movement, as in butoh-fu, or the dance score; and those that issue from the unconsciousness, or the 'other,' the power or intelligence with which I am working.

Such choral techniques also have a separating or discriminating effect, as in threshing, an image that Plato employs in his elucidation of the mysterious chôra; what is unnecessary is discarded, the essential is retained. The threshing floor is a key image for me – in my expression of butoh (sabbatic dance) and in the aims and methods of my magical practice – situating both explicitly in an eschatological, transforming and revelatory context. It will be the subject of a forthcoming presen-tation, on the witches' dance.

> 'The daughter of Babylon is like a threshing floor. It is time to thresh her: yet a little while and the time of her harvest will come.' (Jeremiah 51:33)

SELECT BIBLIOGRAPHY

—᠊᠊— Becker, Robert O. & Gary Selden. *The Body Electric; Electromagnetism and the Foundation of Life.* NY: Morrow. 1985

—᠊᠊— Ho, Mae-Wan. *The Rainbow and the Worm.* World Scientific Publishing Company. 1998

—᠊᠊— Isar, Nicoletta. 'Chôra: Creation and Pathology; An Inquiry into the Origins of Illness and Human Response.' *Europe's Journal of Psychology* 2/2009: 96–109

—᠊᠊— Merleau-Ponty, Maurice, and Claude Lefort. *The Visible and the Invisible; Followed by Working Notes.* Northwestern University Press. 1968

—᠊᠊— Schultz, R. Louis & Rosemary Feitis. *The Endless Web: Fascial Anatomy and*

Physical Reality. North Atlantic Books. 1996
—⁓— Sheets-Johnstone, Maxine. *The Roots of Power: Animate Form and Gendered Bodies.* Open Court. 1999
_____ *The Primacy of Movement.* John Benjamins Publishing Company (2nd edition). 2011

Cut-up as Egregore, Oracle and Flirtation Device

Fred Yee

Vanessa's Box

During a going away party for our friend Sammy Crawford, Vanessa Sinclair pulled out a box filled with cut-up writings of her favorite authors. The activity of the evening was to make a William Burroughs/Brion Gysin inspired word cut-up. Nine of us created the cut-up, cutting and pasting words onto a sheet of paper with the kind of childhood enthusiasm that comes from using glue sticks and invisible tape. Once the words were assembled, Vanessa brought out her laptop and instructed us to start speaking the phrases in no particular order. She pressed "record" and off we went. The resulting effect was a kind of rolling mantra filled with overlapping words, pregnant pauses, self-conscious fumbles and car-crash word making. If you are used to employing accidents in art-making you will recognize the random act has a beauty that can't be recreated. It needs only be recognized. I recognized something else: the entire enterprise was loaded magically. Not a surprise as nearly every participant was a practitioner of magic.

If a friend creates a cut-up and presents it to me I usually have the same reaction as if that same person were to tell me their dream. They would ask "Don't you find it utterly fascinating?" The answer is that it is of utmost importance to the person to who received it and largely meaningless to anyone else. However the magician in me saw the possibilities. I started thinking of ways to turn this process into an activity in the sphere of action.

My practice

I should discuss my own practice to place these experiments in some sort of context. I have been practicing meditation at the time of this writing for seventeen years. For the first ten years the practice was formless and nameless within a non-dualistic, Taoist and animist sensibility. I am Chinese and liken my parents' Taoist influences as similar to one who was raised Catholic and is no longer observant but still drawn to the ritualistic aspects of the religion. For me, the ancestors were always in the background and there was nothing about Taoism that was particularly at odds in my esoteric pursuits.

In 2014, I stumbled upon the occult scene in Brooklyn and it inspired me to teach and put my work into the world, which had been up to that point a personal practice. In the two years since, I have formed a consistent and intimate group of students who meet regularly for meditation. These occult experiments are happening within that context – among people I have known and worked with for approximately a year, who themselves are practitioners of different magical paths.

FLIRTATION DEVICE

I had attended Vanessa Sinclair and Katelan Foisy's talks on cut-ups at the Morbid Anatomy Museum. A curious result of Katelan's cut-ups was that she actually ended up meeting the authors of the words she used and formed friendships with them. Granted, she is an incredible networker. Still, the idea that a cut-up can serve as an active bridge to the person in the world was a fascinating idea.

It just happened that at the after party I met a charming writer with whom I struck up a conversation. Afterwards, I asked if I could read samples of his writings. I asked if it was OK if I made cut-ups of his work. He agreed. I used Photoshop to create a series of cut-ups from his words. The process was a lot of fun, and in a short burst I created six or seven of them.

I recognized that something was happening when you cut in and out of someone's writing. You recreate their voice in your own consciousness, at least a part of it. There is an individual tenor, rhythm, and a shape to everyone's speech. It's like a signature. I was forming a connection with this writer. I raised my courage and casually asked if he would go out for dinner. We met on several occasions and ended up having a fleeting romance. Perhaps I could just be a really good networker, too.

CUT-UP AS EGREGORE

At the same party that Vanessa introduced me to her cut-up box. My friend Derek Elmore had brought his sketchbook and encouraged folks to create automatic drawings. My response to the activity was tepid. I felt the activity was a solitary one not particularly conducive in a group setting.

But this activity inspired me. I played with a variation on the surrealist Exquisite Corpse. I wanted to add a level of abstraction to the image. So I took Austin Osman Spare's sigil making technique of taking a written intention and reducing those words down into a graphic symbol. The difference here is that I would be using drawings instead of words.

The first iteration of this experiment took place in my meditation class. Participants brought sketchpad and pen. I laid out a grid of the index cards. Each card was labeled with the X and Y axis position. The cards were shuffled and an equal number of cards were given out to each guest.

A-1	A-2	A-3	A-4	A-5	A-6	A-7
B-1	B-2	B-3	B-4	B-5	B-6	B-7
C-1	C-2	C-3	C-4	C-5	C-6	C-7
D-1	D-2	D-3	D-4	D-5	D6	D-7
E-1	E-2	E-3	E-4	E-5	E-6	E-7
F-1	F-2	F-3	F-4	F-5	F-6	F-7
G-1	G-2	G-3	G-4	G-5	G-6	G-7

Cut-up drawing grid

Participants are asked a series of questions like "Pick an animal you have never seen", "Draw a part of the human anatomy that you find most compelling", "Draw something you saw in a childhood friend's home that puzzled you." Each of these questions correlated with an X or Y axis position. These drawings are visually combined depending on whatever cards were issued to each of the participants randomly. The resulting image was drawn on the cards and returned to me. I reassembled the cards back into its original order on the floor.

The result was anti-climactic. The images did not visually congeal into anything particularly meaningful. Though all the images themselves had a very odd quality to them. That night I took the index cards home, wanting to properly transcribe the results. I did a meditation before I went to bed and noticed there were an awful lot of spirits whizzing about. I did not get much sleep that night. In the morning I decided to take action and burn the cards. Upon doing that, the anxious energy dissipated. I have been relayed stories of folks keeping remnants of active magical rituals in one's home, often leading to tragic consequences. So I relay this warning to you. Don't keep them.

Later that week I decided to look at the images once more, when whatever spirit activity happened previously was not present. I brought all the imagery into Photoshop. The problem with the imagery was one of scale and density. Some images were small, others large, some were drawn delicately, others forcefully. I needed to equalize all the components into a seamless image. I combined all the images and stripped out their backgrounds. I scaled up the images so they were readable, allowing them to overlap

What I noticed was each of these things had a head and most had a torso. I ended up with five very strange looking entities. There were five participants in the class. I had an eerie feeling these chimeric spirits were presenting themselves to us. I sent the final image to all the participants and asked them "If each of these figures somehow represented a person in class who would they be?" There was zero consensus on who was who but nearly everyone thought the creepy clown thing represented Derek.

Cut-up drawing

CUT-UP AS ORACLE

I decided the next iteration would use words. Not someone else's but our own. The idea was the same: to take a random sampling of information, combine it by random process and see if any coherent messages arise. The advantage here is that this process lends itself to oracle making. It is an oracle empowered by the group itself and not the skill of an individual seer. I had a birthday coming up and it seemed an appropriate opportunity to do the deed.

When I was a kid I used to play Mad Libs, which were stories that had various parts of speech blanked out. Participants would supply these words without foreknowledge of the story and the resulting mismatch was read. The juxtapositions were to my young mind hilarious. In retrospect, it is a wonderful introduction to cut-ups, a method of subverting meaning. It is that sense of subversive play I wanted to inject into this process.

My birthday party had arrived and the proper ritual tools were present: Grappa, music by Coil, bagged chips of many varieties. When a guest arrived I gave them a "query card" which was numbered. I told them to write down a question that needed answering in their life.

We started the experiment proper. I gave out an equal number of shuffled cards and pens. As in the previous experiment I prepared a series of instructions that correlated to the X and Y axis positions. Instructions went along the lines of "Write down a word or phrase that has been in your head all week," "You recognize this relationship in every situation you are in," "Open up Facebook and write down the current status update."

Everyone wrote down their answers and returned the cards to me. Again I reassembled the cards back to their original order. One at a time folks read their question aloud. The query card had a number on it; that number corresponded to a row, and that row was their answer. The results were impressive to me and to my guests. Each reply seemed to respond to the questions asked. There was more signal than noise.

Folks who have worked in mediumship may recognize instances when the message delivered did not answer the question asked. Which is to say the answer that was given to the question that actually needed to be asked.

One friend was asking about career but several of the answers addressed romantic relationships specifically. The last answer seemed to refute the original assertion "Nothing to Evaluate."

1) Will all of my ambitions manifest?

physical fantasies	mine in agreeing to this	Relaxing at home last night playing computer games with my Cat	Nothing	Sad Alone	Succubus	dutch music box

2) Will it ll work out the way I will?

Goetia	Bastard	Cafe	"Commonality"	In my home today	Fae	Contradiction

3) How do I take back, regain, strengthen & stay in my power?

Find a place to hide	Man	Johnny Marr	Met attractive person at the Strand	"Bless Pat"	"Protect the Weak"	Authoritarian

4) Where am I supposed to be?

Belly Laugh Time	Fame	Completing the Icons	I was given a free ticket to a film screening	People who try and get to know someone but have ulterior motives	Action without Forethought	See Me

5) How will I be able to afford my long-delayed first trip to Europe which I had planned to take this year before losing my job?

So this isn't concerning at all	The Internet	First time eating oatmeal all to the soundtrack of Marilyn Manson	Doubt Confidence Doubt Want	You're Better Than That We All Are	power-seeking	Black Person

6) What do I need to know about this new potential romance?

"1989"	Nut Job	Wanting to Connect	I was serenaded with poetry	Expert/Pupil	Valuing the "Personhood" of a corporation over the environment or the struggles of the individual	A printing I received for Christmas

7) What field should I pursue to work in?

A man woman romantically involved who were taught to expect far different things from a romance partner/heterosexual relationship than the other gender	Child	The obsessional-hysteric dynamism	Dreaming of my Mother Talking of her ex & telling me he is a nice guy	Walking in the Snow	Antietam Battlefield on X-mas Day	Nothing to Evaluate

Another friend made an inquiry of romance and received several obvious responses. The information included someone's age, a possible critique of that individual's mental health "Nut Job" and a possible form of the relationship "Expert/Pupil."

One friend who asked about regaining one's personal power also received very direct responses. "Find a place to hide," which sounded sensible. The last two answers could be taken together "Protect the Weak" from "Authoritarian(ism)." This is relevant as the friend's occupation is social work.

That night I took the index cards home and I experienced the same flurry of spirit activity as with the previous experiment. Again, I burned the oracle cards in the morning and again the anxious energy dissipated.

CONCLUSIONS

I had planned to do a further experiment involving the creation of a group collage but I realized not everyone would be willing to see their work burned before their very eyes, which I am viewing as a necessary step. I decided to put any future cut-up experiments on hold until after the *Psychoanalysis, Art and the Occult* conference in London. There was a massive amount of momentum going on with that event, and I did not know how our experiments would interact with it

I have come to view the group experiments as a form of evocation. It was not simply the relaying of information. It was the summoning of forces for a specific action. Even with the drawing cut-up I felt each participant was likely articulating an implicit desire non-verbally and the universe responded in kind. I have always been aware of the line where oracle becomes operative magic. Where one stops seeing and one starts doing.

Over the last couple of years, I have attended private and public rituals of all sorts. Always at these events I ask the question, "What makes a ritual effective?" I suspect what makes a ritual work is the involvement of the individuals in the act. They need to be invested into the action. They need to be engaged. There are no lurkers in magic. You add or you take away from the proceeding. If you have an audience for ritual you are not doing ritual, you are doing theater. I make it clear to folks who come to my class: I'm not here to provide you passive entertainment for you to consume. What you put into the box is what you get out.

Androgyny, biology and latent memory in the work of Austin Osman Spare

Robert Ansell

I'd like to begin by drawing upon something that Charlotte Rodgers mentioned here yesterday, which was the tension that seems to exist if you are a practitioner; between yourself and what Peter Grey referred to as the 'monoculture'. What interests me is why we, as a community, seem to have an existential crisis about this; our relationship with the wider culture? After all, there are plenty of other minority groups that don't wring their hands, as they exist quite happily, but for some reason we take this tension quite personally. When I consider this, the tension seems to stem from ideas of authenticity, of validation, and also of intimacy. Because the reason that we're here, I think, is that we have questions that we need answered. Sometimes these are questions that have been born from personal experience. Sometimes there is a crisis in life that prompts us to make us challenge the way we think about the world. I'd like to share with you the reason that I'm here. My very first memory – I was probably about two years old – I can remember lying in my cot, and suddenly becoming aware that if I made a particular noise in my head (a sort of metal jangling sound) that this strange, turtle-like man would appear. He would wander down the corridor of the house, lean over the cot, reach into my stomach and I would begin a dialogue with him. He would ask me what kind of animal I would like to be and I could choose. Then I would have this erotic sensation that would sweep over me. So, these personal experiences – the things that are within us – perhaps we have difficulty sharing them with the world because of the way that we are judged. And so it's difficult, perhaps, to be entirely ourselves.

What I'm going to talk to you about today is how an artist a hundred years ago approached this problem: Austin Osman Spare.

This is a picture of Spare taken in his Wynne Road studio in the 1950s by Bert Hardy. It's chaotic, as you can see. He was living in extremely reduced circumstances; he'd had a life of great hardship. He came here, living with a friend of his from the early days, Ada Pain. He was bombed during the war – he lost his studio, he lost everything – and he ended up living in her basement creating works of art; pastels on paper mostly. This is quite a well-known image of Spare, actually, and this is the Spare of Kenneth Grant. For those of you don't know, Kenneth Grant was fresh from meeting Crowley, he was an occultist, encountered Spare, and the two men immediately bonded. They had a shared love of art (Kenneth was

keen on Surrealism, which Spare wasn't so happy about), but also a great similarity of attitude towards the world. Spare respected Grant and after Spare's death Grant inherited all Spare's manuscripts and papers; as his amanuensis, he had the authority that goes with that. Twenty years later, Grant wrote an account of Spare, *Images and Oracles of Austin Osman Spare*. Faced with the task of trying to explain how this man produced a body of work (probably 2,500 to 3000 images through the course of his life) and yet made absolutely no money whatsoever; well, how do you present that in a way that which makes it work, which makes it... *sexy*?

Well, Grant framed Spare as a romantic anti-hero. This was a guy who lived in south London; he was fucking barmaids, doing a school of art, betting on the horses, and he lived in studio above Woolworths on the Walworth Road; it's an extraordinary combination. Now, that reading of Spare has been enormously influential, because it's mythic, and its heroic. It's not my intent at all to dismiss that; instead I'd like to add another layer to that, but I'd like to talk about a different man.

This is Spare fifty years earlier, aged 17. His whole life is before him. In those days he was living with his parents in Kennington, he had a small studio in the attic, and used to beaver away making extraordinary works. But, a very early work he produced was accepted and hung at the Royal Academy Summer Show in 1904, and almost overnight, Spare became a national celebrity; 'the youngest ever exhibitor at the Royal Academy' they said (not quite true, but that's what they were saying at the time). Suddenly, there were journalists camped at his door, he was besieged, and as a very shy boy this was an overwhelming experience. He didn't really know how to cope with it; he certainly didn't want to be interviewed, and the press, in the way that they do when faced with a vacuum of information, started to make things up. Spare was going to be the 'greatest portraitist of his age', he was going to be President of the Royal Academy, *etc.*

Spare wasn't interested in any of that; he was interested in this:

This is a drawing from 1903, a strange biomorphic mass. What is it? Its partly dead, partly alive; it's a strange creature of sorts; nothing certainly recognisable. Fortunately for us, Spare has titled it: 'KIA Sat.' What is that? Well, KIA was a term that Spare later used to define the absolute. I suppose the easiest way of considering it in the lens of Taoism. KIA is Tao if you like; certainly in its maternal, creative, aspect. And Spare saw this expressed through living things; through the cycle of birth and death, *etc.* This is his earliest expression of it. It certainly wasn't what journalists wanted to see; they wanted him to be conventional and he felt like he had to issue some kind of manifesto. And he did, with his book, *Earth Inferno.* Now as you can imagine from the title, this draws quite heavily from Dante's *Inferno,* but Spare sort of inverted it. Because for him, the world that he was living in was absolute hell. Why was it hell? Because it didn't allow him to be the person he wanted to be. This is a little portrait of himself, in the book, and behind him there is a woman. He says:

> Strange images of myself did I create.
> As I gazed into the seeming pit of others.
> Losing myself in thoughtfulness
> Of my unreal self, as humanity saw me.[1]

---

1 *Earth Inferno* (London: Cooperative Printing Society, 1905) p.12.

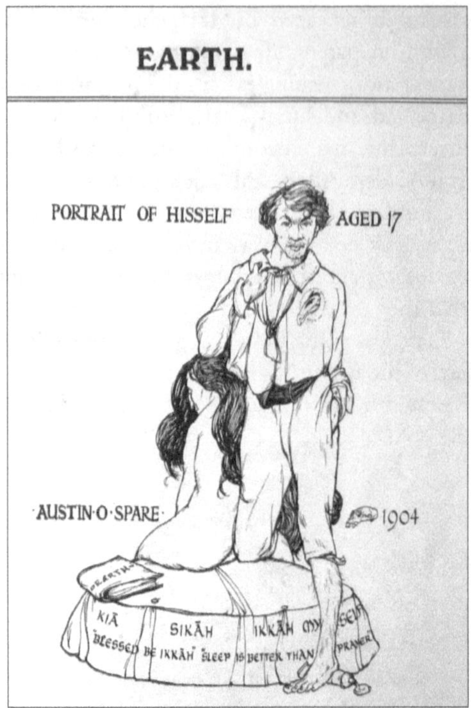

Note the way he's standing in front of this woman, who has her back to us. That's important.

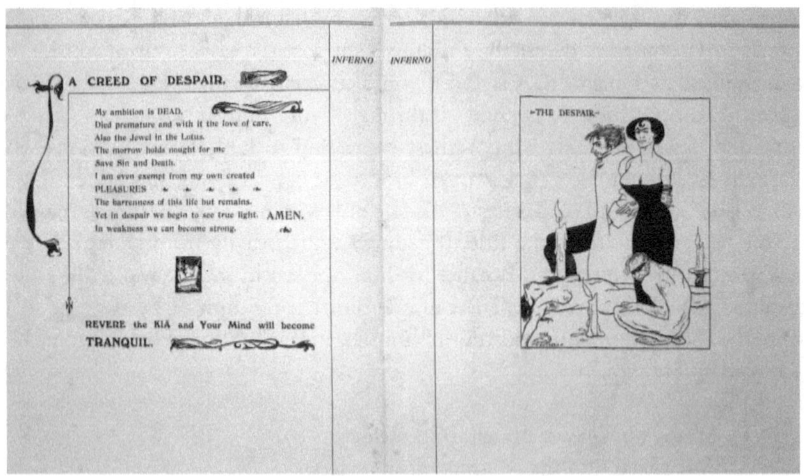

Here is another very important image; 'A Creed of Despair'.

My ambition is DEAD.
Died premature and with it the love of care.
...
I am exempt even from my own created
PLEASURES
The barrenness of this world but remains.
Yet in despair we begin to see true light. AMEN.[2]

Now, I think this line is very important, because it introduces the word 'amen.' And Spare says, 'Yet in despair we begin to see true light,' and the illustration opposite is called 'The Despair.' What we have here is a self-portrait of Spare wearing an overcoat and turned in profile to us, and next to him appears to be *another* self-portrait, but as a woman. Keep in mind this is a 17-year-old boy in 1905 who was depicting himself as a woman in a published work. Let me go back to that line: 'Yet in despair we begin to see true light. AMEN.' Well, Amen was of course an Egyptian God – the hidden God – and the maker of things. Spare was very familiar with Egyptology; with Budge's works, certainly.

SYNOPSIS OF INFERNO.

In the synopsis for *Earth Inferno*, which he gives us, you can see it's a great cycle. In the centre there is the KIA, which has evolved and become the head of a vulture. In the Egyptian pantheon the consort of Amen was Mut, who was seen sometimes as a vulture; it's a 'mother' if you like. But what I want to draw your attention here

---

2 Ibid, p.18.

are these strange single-celled creatures, these amoebae, because they are, I think, going to be quite important.

So the same year, 1905, Spare began to develop this idea. This is a manuscript called 'The Focus of Life: The Papyrus of Amen-AOS,' and you can see here again, this strange vulture-like creature rising up, tethered by a sorcerer (some chance, I think).

And this manuscript is full of the most extraordinary drawings of living things, bursting forth; all kinds of creatures, strange hybrids. Sometimes you can see the line is actually so frenzied he is not drawing anything specific at all, it's just the exuberance of expression of life.

At the end, there's a self-portrait, and we can see this halo around him, and above it says, 'The Ascension of AMEN-AOS.' And we see the KIA bird again; the vulture-head rising up, while Spare discards the mask of conventionality.

A few years later, he produced *A Book of Satyrs*. *A Book of Satyrs* is a series of Hogarthian critiques of modern society; it's quite political, but there is one image in particular that I wanted to show you, this one.

This is the artist – a more mature artist if you like – and you can see him staring intently at us while behind him is this vast, very masculinised woman. It's called the 'General Allegory.' Beside them both are masks hanging down – obviously as an ordinary individual, he has to integrate more with society he must have learnt many different personas – the many different ways of integrating. Now this was published in 1907 and it was in 1907 Spare had a show at the Bruton Gallery. At the Bruton gallery he met someone called Aleister Crowley. Now Crowley was quite taken by Spare – he was a young good-looking man with a huge talent – so he said, 'You should join my new order, the *Argentum Astrum*, it's going to be great...' So Spare signed up to that, and he signed up with this magical name: 'YIHOVEAUM.' Now I believe this to be a portmanteau of Yihovah + Aum. Why? Because Blavatsky, with whom Spare was undoubtedly familiar says, '...the name YHVH expresses a He and a She...' and 'Aum is the original of Amen....'[3] So, this is a hidden He and She, if you like.

Spare didn't do too well in the *Argentum Astrum*, he never passed beyond the grade of probationer. Crowley was to later write on his probationer form, 'An Artist, can't understand organisation or would have passed.' But, I believe the collaboration did bear fruit; in the book, *The Book of Pleasure*. Spare's relationship with Crowley was quite complicated because Crowley was quite rigorous in the way that he approached things; there was a sort of certain order, and Spare felt, I think, that he needed to express himself in a different way (to show that he could do it) and *The Book of Pleasure* is the result of that. *The Book of Pleasure* is an extension of Spare's early ideas, articulated in a new way, broadened and developed. But, one of the distinctive things about it is a series of extraordinary androgynous drawings.

In *The Book of Pleasure* Spare introduces us to some new ideas; central to these is still the KIA, but he introduces something called 'The New Sexuality'. He defines this as, 'the ancestral sex principle'. He says, 'Time has not changed it, hence I call it new.' He also introduces something called the 'Neither-Neither I'. I believe this is drawn from 'Neti-Neti,' which he got from the *Upanishads* – 'not this, not this' – and I think the best way to consider this is a sense of negated self. And he also introduces something called 'Self-Love'. Now, Phil Baker's biography dismisses this as a sort of narcissism. I think that's quite a shallow reading, actually, as I hope to show you in a moment. But, relative to this particular conference is Spare's introduction of the subconsciousness. Spare, throughout his entire life, was extremely quick to draw upon new things, and to draw them into his work, to incorporate it, and to make it relevant. That's a very sorcerous attitude; you use what's available, make it work for you. But he says something very interesting about the subconscious. 'Know the subconsciousness to be an epitome of all experience and wisdom, past incarnations as men, animals, birds, vegetable life, etc, etc [...] the last is the Almighty Simplicity.' He then also says, 'if we succeed in awakening

---

3 Helena Blavatsky, *The Secret Doctrine* (London: Theosophical Publishing Society, 1897) vol.1 p. 678 and vol.3 pp.450-1.

them, we shall gain their properties and our accomplishment will correspond.'[4] *The Book of Pleasure* was not a success. Spare thought it might go to a second or third edition, he thought it would be launching him on the world's stage, etc. It was simply too dense and complicated for most people. But also the following year after its publication (in 1913) the First World War started, and Spare discovered that his grotesque style was being trumped by the grotesque war that was happening. Suddenly, he was conscripted to the RAMC; he served briefly as a war artist, in a somewhat dishevelled way. The war was an enormously damaging experience for him; he lost his wife, the marriage dissolved, she sold his collection of books and tribal art while he was serving, and he emerges from the war with absolutely nothing. He ended up staying at a friend's apartment near the British Museum.

Now you would think, emerging from this very difficult experience, where he is living in very reduced circumstances, you would think, the first thing he would say would be, 'okay, I better get back on my feet, get employment'. But *no*, he returns to the idea that he had in 1905, *The Focus of Life*. He writes to a friend, Frederick Carter, and says, 'I want to do a book. Would you like to be involved?'[7] Carter did get involved; he edited the book and produced what is probably the most professionally produced book of Spare's entire career. *The Focus of Life* has

---

4 Austin Osman Spare, *The Book of Pleasure: The Psychology of Ecstasy* (London: Cooperative Printing Society, 1913), p.29.

a strange dream-like narrative and it's full of these extraordinarily delicate pencil drawings, but it's a very difficult book to read simply because it's so obscure. But quite recently, there was an extraordinary... Well, it's very rare in my life (having been involved with Spare's work for over 30 years) that the hairs on the back of my neck stand on end. But when I saw this folio for the first time, that's exactly what happened. It's the sort of thing that you see, and you think, 'I never thought I'd see anything like this.' The folio of original preparatory drawings for *The Focus of Life* was discovered, and since the early 1930s it had been (if you can believe it) in the collection of the novelist E.M. Forster.[5] It's my sentiment that Spare knew Forster, and sold it to him direct, because the folio contains things that could not be sold on the open market. I'll just draw your attention to that round, circular being there for a moment.[6] Here, Spare says, 'AOS renouncing the past sexuality.' It's a very clear statement of intent. Now you see here, 'The Focus of Life: The Mutterings of Aāos,' I think 'Aāos' is actually 'Amen-Aos' and Spare has hidden the word Amen, he's truncated it. Note again that strange round circular being, and this time, this

5 Published as Austin Osman Spare, *The Focus of Life (Redux)* (London: Fulgur Limited, 2012).
6 Cf. the round androgynous beings in Plato, *Symposium in The Dialogues of Plato*, translated by B. Jowett, (Oxford: Clarendon Press, 1871) p.509.

vast cloak seems like a cosmic womb. This preparatory folio is full of the most extraordinary, exquisite drawings, but there is one particular suite of drawings that I think are essential to our understanding of Spare's entire ontology.

Now in *The Focus of Life* there is one passage which is buried in the book, and in it, Spare says, 'I assert this self-love to be a most secret ritual hidden by blasphemous ideographs; and he who calls, pronouncing the word fearlessly, the entire creation of women shall rush into him.'[7] Why? What is he seeking to do here? In *The Book of Pleasure* there is a text:

> A microbe has the power to destroy the world (and certainly would if it took an interest in us). If you were to dismember its limb, the mutilated part would regrow, etc. So by evoking and becoming obsessed or illuminated by these existences, we gain their magical properties, or the knowledge of their attainment.[8]

---

7 Austin Osman Spare, *The Focus of Life: The Mutterings of Aāos,* (London: Morland Press, 1921) p.22.
8 Austin Osman Spare, *The Book of Pleasure: The Psychology of Ecstasy* (London: Cooperative Printing Society, 1913), p.47.

In that preparatory folio there was a drawing, *Aāos destroying the cosmos*. And the actual frontispiece to the published book, *The Focus of Life* is very similar. Here we see Spare with the logos – the book – over his genitals. He said to his great friend, Frank Letchford, that when he posed for this photograph, the flash was so intense that it singed his genital hair. I think this is referencing Dürer's *The Resurrection of Christ*. The drawing is called *The New Dawn*. And again, you see the woman behind him, you can see this great menagerie of animal forms and life, etc., and there's an alchemical element to this too.

In conclusion, what is Spare trying to do? I think what we're looking at here is an ontological ground zero; we are looking at a gender reboot. I think what he's hoping to do, is by assimilating and becoming this androgynous being, he is taking himself closer and closer to the memory of the first cell – the 'almighty simplicity.' It is an extraordinary notion that everyone in this room shares one thing; an unbroken chain of life between us and the first cell that existed on this earth. Spare was hoping, if he could trace those steps, to go back and to assimilate the properties of that single cell, that all its accomplishments, the entirety of life on earth – all the energy that goes to inform that – would be his to command. What I believe he hoped to do was to express this through his art; to make art that would change the world, to create a completely new culture.

Double, Double, Toil and Trouble; Psychoanalysis Burn and Surrealism Bubble

Dr. Ray O Neill

"Because it is my name! Because I cannot have another in my life!
Because I lie and sign myself to lies! Because I am not worth the dust
on the feet of them that hang! How may I live without my name? I
have given you my soul; leave me my name!"

Within Arthur Miller's *The Crucible* the occult, hysteria, madness and sexuality are mobilised to this frenetic climax in Act IV where John Proctor, having already acknowledged himself as an adulterer and perjured himself in confessing to witchcraft, his reputation now ruined and soul lost, is unable to sign the confession as there is one thing he wishes to salvage/save: his name.

The most common answer to the basic existential question 'Who am I?' is with a name. I may be introduced to you in a variety of ways, but ultimately I am presented and presenting as Ray; this is who I am because it is my name.

But this is not *my* name. It is my parents' name for me, and to be fair they originally christened me Raymond, after my father's second name. Our names are never our own, they come with legacies, desires, significations and ghosts.

My brief time working in Zimbabwe last month soon shattered any previous witness of deprivation and poverty, but when I had heard that a very starved, ill, heavily pregnant woman had given birth to a boy she had named in Shona "Hard Life", I was shocked and disturbed though throughout my time, I was meeting people who carried either English or Shona names that were 'Blessing'; 'Fortune'; 'Last One'; 'Faith'. There was even a mother who named her daughter 'Apology', I did not ask why.

Something is signified in names, and though modern Western cultures may be inclining towards a naming that mirrors trends and celebrity personae, or the children of such couplings; is there not still desire within such parents that their children, or themselves, will share in the glamour of a Paris, a North West, or a Chardonnay? Shona namings do not seem so strange against Gaelic Irish language names, such as Brónach literally meaning sadness or grief; Saoirse meaning freedom or liberty; or Gráinne, relating to either love, Grá, or to Gránna, meaning ugly. Considering the name Cian is a Gaelic word for longing and melancholy, caoineadh, from which the English word keening evolves, suddenly 'Hard Life' seems not so odd.

The name we are – that primary signifier through which we identify – comes with other desires and significations that as with all language, we are born into and immersed in throughout our lives. We are named after someone or something, and with those someones and somethings comes something more, something both seen and unseen, familiar and unknown, an occultist legacy, an unheimlich naming, a homo-doubling.

I am thinking of a client I will name Joseph, who suffered from an anxious depression which was intensified for him as, within our cause and effect culture, he had never understood 'why' since he had had no 'trauma' in his life. Only in the course of his analysis did he mention his being named Joseph, after a younger brother of his mother's who had died before he was born. Subsequent questioning of his mother only produced a limited reluctant story that this beloved twenty-four-year-old brother had drowned in a bath at home while his mother was pregnant. This possible suicide and Uncle Joseph's struggles with his own life were silenced/repressed within the family but understanding something of the ghosts he inherited in his name allowed Joseph to speak differently of his depression, of it not being *only* his, that in analytically responding to it, he was absolved from the weight of its full responsibility.

I think of a clinical case file of a man I will call Eoghan Murphy who had been incarcerated most his life in a rural Irish psychiatric institution for schizophrenia, and multiple personalities. But when a psychiatrist who was psychoanalytically informed began working with him, he noted that his suffering centred more around not knowing which he was, rather than who he was. Further conversations revealed that Eoghan was the youngest of nine brothers all of whom had died either in birth or in very early infancy, and all of whom had been called Eoghan Murphy. Such had been the father's desire, determination, to have a son who carried his name, that this Eoghan carried the burden of eight lost lives/desires/anxieties. Eoghan means 'noble born'.

Similarly in Eugene O Neill's autobiographical *Long Day's Journey Into Night* the protagonist Edmund, Eugene's counterpart, is named after Eugene's older brother who had died in infancy and whose death catalyses the family traumas, resentments, griefs and fears around which the play lingers. And in the play when the dead baby is spoken of, this dead brother that Eugene was born to replace, is rechristened by the playwright as 'Eugene', the anglicisation of Eoghan, the noble born.

All names and namings carry ghosts of the past and present desires. For each of our namings there is a *Doppelganger*, a homo-double from whom that name has been stolen/inherited/pushed; be it an actual person or a desired personal identity of which my Rayness can only ever be but an echo, a copy, a reproduction.

WHEN DALÍ MET FREUD

1922's first Spanish translation of *The Interpretation of Dreams* kindled Salvador Dalí into a fanatical Freudian enthusiast. Reading of Freud's flee from the Nazis,

Dalí, who had thrice already attempted to see Freud, wrote to Zweig who arranged the meeting on July 19th 1938, describing Dalí to Freud as "the only painter of genius in our epoch ... he is the most faithful and most grateful disciple of your ideas among the artists". (Brown, 2012: 295)

Dalí defined this meeting as one of his life's most important experiences, forcing him to reconsider his whole view of surrealism. The painting he presented, *Metamorphosis of Narcissus*, signifies something Dalí wanted to communicate to Freud about Freud, about psychoanalysis, and most importantly perhaps, about Dalí's desire vis-à-vis Freud himself. Dalí was of course aware, not only of the metamorphosis of Narcissus by psychoanalytic discourse, but how psychoanalysis metamorphosed discourse around sexuality, desire, libido and paranoia. For Dalí, psychoanalysis's recognition of the 'double' was critical not only for his art, but for his inherently doubled self.

DALÍ AND FREUD'S PARANOIA

> Paranoid phenomena are well-known images with a double figuration – the figuration can be multiplied theoretically and practically everything hinges on the paranoid capacity of the author. Different spectators see different images in the same painting; the realisation is scrupulously realistic. (Dalí quoted in Bosquet, 2003: 62)

Dalí acknowledged surrealism as the only "adequate outlet for activity" criticising surrealist practices such as automatic writing, as "genuinely passive", advocating his more active "paranoiac-critical method of interpretation" (Dalí, 1998: 95), fashioned after the paranoid patient's unwavering personal system of interpreting reality which structures them alone uniquely. Dalí recognised paranoia as an alternative parallel mental processing, closer to its original ancient Greek meaning, of 'beside mind'.

Dalí and Freud both reject psychiatry's definition/dismissal of paranoia as 'madness', 'irrational', and thus socially unacceptable. In his Schreber Case, Freud discoursed paranoia as the unconscious structuring the interpretation of perceived objects through projecting onto the external world unconscious undesirable phantasies. In analysing Schreber's own language, Freud argues that paranoia is not an illness *as such*, but actually an "attempt at recovery", a parallel thinking, evidencing an attempt by the paranoid ego to re-connect to reality through its integration with a fictional world. (SE XII, 209).

Freud's psychoanalytic theorisations on homosexuality consistently located narcissism in its primary roots but in his last major contribution to this subject, 1922's 'Some Neurotic Mechanisms in Jealousy, Paranoia, and Homosexuality' Freud elaborates: "I never regarded this analysis of the origin of homosexuality as complete, and I now point to a new mechanism leading to homosexual object-choice" (SE XVIII: 231) which was the operation of paranoia in neurotic homosexuality, a form of homo-sexuality that need not be exclusive, as later heterosexual objects are still quite possible.

This theory differs significantly from his other homo-sexual theories in involving neither identification with the mother nor a fear of female genitals caused by castration anxiety. It begins with an intense love for the mother, leading to jealousy of "great intensity" towards rivals, brothers and the father that mobilises hostility and death wishes towards them. But these "impulses yielded to repression and underwent transformation" into "the first homosexual love objects". (231) Freud sees such defence "reaction formations" as the inverse of the process by which passive homosexual love is transformed into persecutory or delusional paranoia. In this latter case, explored in Schreber's case, the unbearable homosexual impulse, "I love him", is transformed by negation into "I hate him", and then rationalised through projection into "He hates me", so that paranoia keeps the subject from becoming homosexual.

METAMORPHOSIS OF NARCISSUS

The *Metamorphosis of Narcissus* doubles not only the figure of Narcissus on the left looking at this reflection in the body of water with the image of the outreaching hand holding an egg from which a narcissus flower is emerging; but Dalí's very canvas was also doubled with a poem written to accompany his painting. (Dalí, 1937) Like mirroring like; language augmenting art; signifiers doubling the image, this was the first work Dalí ascribed as being painted in his paranoid, critical interpretive methodology.

Dalí's accompanying poem explicitly calls the group of people in the mid-space between the dual Narcissus forms as 'the heterosexuals'. The Narcissus figure is significantly described as "Far from the heterosexual group"; marginalised, excluded, separate, different? Why would/did Dalí choose this signifier 'heterosexual' to designate this group drawn in opposition to Narcissus?

In the doubling poem, Dalí describes the body of water where Narcissus leans as "the obscure mirror of the lake" in which his own body "fixes itself, frozen, in the silvered and hypnotic curve of his desire". It is within this mirrored, obscured desire that "Narcissus loses his being in the cosmic vertigo in the deepest depths … of his own image." Within this mirroring "The body of Narcissus flows out and loses itself in the abyss of his reflection" and Dalí warns "Narcissus, you are losing your body, carried away and confounded by the millenary reflection of your disappearance your body stricken dead, your white body, swallowed up." (1937)

This notion is of Narcissus's mirroring as a location where the body is seen and lost, where the price of confronting desire is loss; the mirror as a place where we find ourselves only to be metamorphosed into a being, alienated, lost, dead, swallowed up. All of this doubling prefigures some of the dynamics and movements of Lacan's Mirror Stage, the original version of which was delivered at Marienbad in 1936, the very year Dalí began this painting.

1936: The Year It All Began – And Ended

> You're well aware that the profound structure of my personality
> is binary: I'm double-headed and twofold. There are two Dalí's.
> (Bosquet, 2003: 15)

1936 was also the year when Lorca, Dalí's great 'friend', fellow artist and love was assassinated by right wing nationalists. They had met at the *Residencia de Estudiantes*, where theirs was an intense passionate relationship, construed by Dalí as:

> He was homosexual, as everyone knows, and madly in love with me.
> He tried to screw me twice .... I was extremely annoyed, because I
> wasn't homosexual, and I wasn't interested in giving in. Besides, it
> hurts. So nothing came of it. But I felt awfully flattered vis-à-vis
> the prestige. Deep down, I felt that he was a great poet and that I
> did owe him a tiny bit of the Divine Dalí's asshole. He eventually
> bagged a young girl, and she replaced me in the sacrifice. Failing to
> get me to put my ass at his disposal, he swore that the girl's sacrifice
> was matched by his own: it was the first time he had ever slept with
> a woman. (19-20)

Soon after they became estranged; the fear and discomfort around their feelings for one another with which both struggled with differently, undoubtedly contributing. Dalí was "obsessed by Lorca, but troubled by this obsession" (166). Dalí refers to both himself and Lorca as St. Sebastians throughout his letters, and in one such letter remarks, "Didn't you ever think how strange it is that his ass doesn't have a single wound?" before finishing with his usual, "I love you very much". (62)

Whatever the 'nature' of their relationship, Dalí's 1969 comments interestingly identify Lorca as homosexual, while refuting his own desire, though significantly using the past, not the present tense: "because I wasn't homosexual". He arrogantly is flattered by Lorca's attention, but ominously again associates this/his/homosexual desire with anal sex, but with Lorca as penetrator, himself as recipient: "He tried to screw me twice .... I did owe him a tiny bit of the Divine Dalí's asshole. Failing to get me to put my ass at his disposal". (Bosquet, 2003: 19) However their sexuality was or was not enacted, Dalí significantly perceives his own desire vis-à-vis Lorca's as a "giving in" and seems to have an awareness that this desire demands painful "sacrifice" whether involving anal sex or not: "Besides, it hurts."

Dalí references an event when Lorca "bagged a young girl, and she replaced me in the sacrifice". (20) Dalí himself participated by being present and voyeuristically watching Lorca's first sexual act with a woman. Dalí views the object of his desire sacrifice himself to the heterosexuals. Again there is a doubling, both participating, one actively, the other narcissistically; both bound in the desire of the Other.

Another defining *homo* relationship of Dalí's was his relationship to his own older brother, also named Salvador who had died of gastroenteritis two months before he turned two, and nine months before Dalí was born. In other words, Dalí was conceived in his parents' grief at the loss of their first born son. His brother's loss was in his own conception; his brother's name, memory and identity, waited for him at this birth; given his dead brother's name, clothes to wear and toys to play with.

When he was five, Dalí was brought to his brother's grave to be told by his parents he was his brother's reincarnation, something Dalí came to believe, and incorporate, saying of his brother, "(we) resembled each other like two drops of water, but we had different reflections (he) was probably a first version of myself but conceived too much in the absolute." (Dalí, 1993, 3) This was written in 1942, after his *Metamorphosis of Narcissus*, evoking his brother in water, in reflections, in the mirror.

The mirror image/identity of Dalí's long-dead brother repeatedly reappeared embedded throughout his work, most ominously in 1963's *Portrait of My Dead Brother*. Painted when he was 59, the image is clearly not of a two-year-old but a much older boy, whose hair morphs into a crow, a harbinger of death. Dalí continually spoke of his challenge in establishing his own identity to free himself from his parents' inevitable and persistent comparisons with the deceased and thus idealised sibling.

Dalí continually asserted his parents' desire for him to be a replacement for his dead brother; a spectre which affected and indeed threatened him, compelling him to cultivate his eccentric behaviour, his "dandyism" in order to establish, indeed prove that he was different from the first, perhaps better-loved version of Salvador Dalí. The group of lance bearing conquistadors in the bottom right of the painting could evoke Dalí's desire to dispel and vanquish his brother's enduring memory that continued to overshadow him. Dalí said of this double/twin/brother:

> Every day, I kill the image of my poor brother, with my hands, with kicks, and with dandyism. Today, I made him take flowers to the cemetery. He is my dark God, for he and I are Pollux and Castor; I am Pollux, the immortal twin, and he is the mortal one. I assassinate him regularly for the "Divine Dalí" cannot have anything in common with this former terrestrial being. (17-18)

The double, the mirror, is a threat. Dalí maintains himself in being/performing/ becoming highly unique, an original, and part of maintaining him-self and 'killing' his brother is performed/lived through dandyism, which culturally has its own discursive alignments with sameness, homo-sexuality and narcissism.

In the lower left of Dalí's painting is a variation of Millet's famous *The Angelus*, which long obsessed Dalí, from his childhood daydreaming in primary school, where *The Angelus* hung on the wall, and staring at it he would invent stories about the couple. A fantasy continually repeated throughout his oeuvre as an adult artist.

Dalí believed Millet had originally painted the couple bowing over the coffin of their dead child rather than, as they are in the finished version, praying over a basket of potato crop. Although a very unpopular view, at Dalí's insistence, the Louvre x-rayed the painting, to indeed reveal a small coffin over-painted by the basket.

THE DOUBLE AND THE PARANOIAC CRITICAL METHOD

> [t]he attainment of … a double image has been made possible thanks to the violence of the paranoiac thought which has made use, with cunning and skill, of the required pretexts, coincidences, and so on, taking advantage of them so as to reveal the second image, which, in this case, supersedes the obsessive idea. (Dalí, 1998: 224)

Dalí's 1930 essay "The Rotting Donkey" outlined his paranoiac-critical method of interpretation, arguing "Paranoia makes use of the external world in order to set off its obsessive idea", utilising it "to control an imaginative construction", an alternative/ double/other 'knowledge'. Interpreted thus, Dalí presents his famous double/ multiple-image technique as equivalent to the formations of a paranoid delirium, a continuation on from Freud's theoretical considerations of the manifestations and delusions of a paranoid delirium functioning as a "protective fiction" (Masson, 1985: 250).

The image Dalí offers to demonstrate and frame this paranoiac double was his *Invisible Sleeping Woman, Horse, Lion*; a woman which is unconsciously associated with and accommodates the image of a lion, which in turn is unconsciously associated with and accommodates the image of a horse. Together, contradictory things are seen: multiple and parallel realities, each legitimate, a logical alternative, another possibility, deconstructing the concept of one, or indeed any reality. This Dalí related to the paranoid employment of the reality of the external world "as illustration or proof" of the obsessive idea, "with the disturbing characteristic of verifying the reality of this idea for others" (223).

> Paranoid phenomena are well-known images with a double figuration – the figuration can be multiplied theoretically and practically everything hinges on the paranoid capacity of the author. Paranoid-critical activity thus reveals new and objective "meanings" of the irrational; it tangibly makes the very world of delirium pass to the level of reality. (Bosquet, 2003: 62)

Dalí identified *Metamorphosis of Narcissus* as "the first poem and the first painting obtained entirely through the integral application of the paranoiac-critical method". A discursive circle of narcissism, doubling, homo/heterosexuals and paranoia inform a painting conceived in the year Dalí's beloved dies, by an artist conceived in the wake of his brother's death, bearing his name, his likeness, this homo hommo, as Lacan delivers his theory of the mirror stage at Marienbad.

WHEN LACAN MET DALÍ

> (When) Rouméguère read me his thesis. For the first time in my life, amid incomparable thrills, I felt the absolute truth: a psychoanalytical thesis revealed the sensational conflict at the basis of my tragic structure: the ineluctable presence, deep within me, of my dead brother, whom my parents had been so fond of that when I was born they gave me his name, Salvador. My shock at this doctor's disclosure was a violent revelation. I now understood the terror besetting me every time I stepped into my parents' bedroom and saw the photo of my deceased brother: a lovely child all decked out in lace. The photo was touched up regularly, so that I, by way of contrast, spent all night picturing my ideal brother in a state of total putrefaction. I managed to drop off to sleep only at the thought of my own death and by accepting the idea of lying at rest inside the coffin. An experience of the viscera justified the mental structure of my being. (Bosquet, 2003: 18)

This thesis of Rouméguère's Dali refers to was not the first psychoanalytically informed thesis to impact on Dali, nor indeed to have settled a question from him, especially around the doubling from a predeceased sibling from whom one has inherited their name, but more treacherously their legacy, their fantasy, their identity.

It could be argued that before Lacan was a psychoanalyst he was a surrealist, being friendly with Breton, Duchamp, Picasso, Masson. Lacan was a long time collector of art and borrowed from the visual arts to explain his theories. In his twenties, training as a psychiatrist and researching his doctorate, Lacan also found time to write for the surrealist *Minotaure* magazine. It was here his writings were to meet Dalí's.

In 1932, Lacan had just translated the earlier mentioned Freud's 1922 paper, 'Some Neurotic Mechanisms in Jealousy, Paranoia, and Homosexuality' for *Revue Française de Psychanalyse*, referring to this paper throughout his 1933 doctoral thesis 'On Paranoid Psychosis and Its Relation to Personality', which Dalí cited later in 1933 in *Minotaure's* first issue as "Jacques Lacan's admirable thesis" praising his identification of "the paranoiac mechanism as the force and power acting at the very root of the phenomenon of personality." (Toboul, 2005: 37) Lacan took pride in Dalí's words; *Écrits* description of his doctorate as merely an introduction to "paranoiac knowledge" (Lacan, 2006: 65), references Dalí's own 'paranoiac-critical method'.

Lacan's Case of Aimée

From the outset of his publishing career, Lacan evidenced an interest in paranoid psychosis. It was encountering Marguerite Pantaine, a thirty-eight-year-old woman, which enabled him to demonstrate his views on paranoia, specifically the paranoia of self-punishment. (Roudinesco, 1997: 34) Another likely motive for his choice was the great public interest in Marguerite's knife attack against the famous actress Huguette Duflos which took place outside a Parisian theatre in April 1931.

> Journalists, writers, actresses such as Sarah Bernhardt were all some-how involved. She herself was being plagiarised. 'Ces personnages l'ont plagiée, ont copié ses romans non publiés et son journal intime.' (These people have plagiarised it, have copied the novel that she did not publish, and her intimate diaries.) (Cox-Cameron, 2000: 28)

This widespread sensation was not lost on the surrealists, especially as Marguerite "unreasonably" accused the actress of persecution and spreading scandalous rumours about her; "these crimes frequently, though not always, contain elements of the late nineteenth-century obsession with the *Doppelganger* or psychic double". (25)

Lacan utilised Freudian paranoia theories to address Marguerite's case whom he renamed Aimée, after the heroine of one of her novels, diagnosing her sufferings as a "delirium of interpretation" arguing paranoiacs' "psychical functions of representation" (Lacan, 1975: 291) not as 'false' meanings but 'personal' meanings.

In paranoid delirium/discourse Lacan diagnosed a key conceptual structure "indicating a principle of *iterative identification*" (296) evidenced in Aimée's case in her repeated identifications with successful women, who ultimately become her persecutors. In terms of Lacan's psychoanalytic reading, Aimée's identifications were identifications with her ego-ideal, the ideal the ego aspires to. For what lies at the heart of paranoia of self-punishment, the object of Lacan's thesis, as well as of the paranoid delirium/discourse that it generates, was the fact that the paranoid patient engaged in attacking her doubles, her mirror-images, the women she identified with, *realising*, in a way, her wish to punish herself.

Lacan's thesis analysed the distinctive character of Aimée's female persecutors (her older sister, her female friends, the attacked), as "purely symbolic significance" (252) within Aimée's "personal signification" (296), interpreting these persecutory women as "the double, triple and successive 'printings' of a *prototype*" (253).

The Double Narcissistic Paranoid Mirror

Lacan's thesis hinged on his recognition of the importance of doubling effects.

The gravitational pull of Aimée's story, told in two different places

> in Lacan's thesis, drew Lacan strongly towards the insights which fuelled the Mirror Stage and the Dalínian *connaissance paranoïaque* which marked his thinking in the thirties and forties. (Cox-Cameron, 2000: 10)

Dalí, like Marguerite/Aimée, is born into a mould, a desire, a name of a deceased older sibling "whose ghost was there at the start to welcome me" (Davies, 1998: 12). Dalí's paranoiac critical interpretative approach exemplifies the madness which threatens those 'born double', all born into the homo desire of a same-named personage, which binds us all consciously or unconsciously within such homo desire. In our names, we are all born into a doubling of whatever this name signifies, passes on, bequests; we all suffer a paranoid knowledge that our names, who we are, is not ours; that our names, this primary identification of our selves, indicates desires that are not ours but homo – bound to a similar other, our nominal Doppelganger? And *"Wo es war, Soll ich werden"* (Freud, SE XXII: 80); Where it was, I am to become.

In Freud's 'On Narcissism' the ego is divided with one part set against the other as judge and critic. The ego carries within itself its own ideal, a homo-perfection, which Freud names as ideal ego or ego-ideal. "What he projects before him as his ideal is the substitute for the lost narcissism of his childhood in which he was his own ideal." (SE XIV: 94) And this homo-ideal can be equally loved or hated, desired or feared, evidenced in Lacan's doctoral thesis where "the same image which represents [Aimée's] ideal is also the object of her hatred." (Lacan, 1975: 253) Such a foundational, if indeed ambiguous relationship to an ego ideal image is precisely what in/forms Lacan's devising of his 'Mirror Stage' theories.

Despite our contemporary hyper-narcissistic culture, where everyone is selfied, I mean selfishly enthralled to their image, the Doppelganger continues to be portrayed as an ominous threat, an intrusive menace; the anxiety provoking Mr. Hyde Shadow, the Dostoyevskian double seeking to usurp one's life. The Doppelganger must be fought, killed or else one must die. Why if we want to love ourselves so facebookly do we fear, dread this encounter with the original of our selves?

In Scandinavian folklore the *Vardøger* is a spirit predecessor, where a spirit with the subject's appearance precedes them in a location or activity, resulting in witnesses believing they've seen or heard the actual person before the person physically arrives. The *Vardøger* is a harbinger of luck, fortune and foresight.

But in matters of desire, a desire for same is still feared and repressed within our culture. Anything homo is to be feared, belittled, marginalised, seen as a threat. And Is Not the Doppelganger Our Ultimate Homo? A Double in image or in name with whom we can encounter something truly unheimlich about ourselves; something that is strangely familiar, and yet unsettling, evocative, provocative, something to which we are simultaneously attracted to, yet repulsed by. Any discourse, be it psychoanalysis, art or the occult, that encourages an authentic, non narcissistic, encounter with the depths of ourselves is to be encouraged; but only through practitioners that do not seek mirrors of themselves, their theories, or their desires, but can act as mediums, witnesses for the client's truest encounter, which is never with the practitioner but with themselves: the truth of their own experiences.

BIBLIOGRAPHY

—⚭— Bosquet, Alain. (2003) *Conversations with Dali* Ubu Classics Available on http://www.ubu.com/historical/dali/dali_conversations.pdf Accessed 25/4/2015.

—⚭— Brown, Craig. (2012) *Hello, Goodbye, Hello: A Circle of 101 Remarkable Meetings* New York, Simon & Schuster.

—⚭— Cox-Cameron, Olga. (2000) 'Lacan's Doctoral Thesis: Turbulent Preface or Founding Legend?' *Psychoanalytische Perspectieven*, 2000, nr. 41/42.

—⚭— Dalí, Salvador. (1938) 'The Metamorphosis of Narcissus' (poem) Full Text available at http://www.tate.org.uk/art/artworks/dali-metamorphosis-of-narcissus-t02343/text-catalogue-entry. Accessed 5/5/2015.

—⚭— Dalí, Salvador. (1993) *The Secret Life of Salvador Dalí* Dover Press Reprint of the Dial Press, New York, 1942 edition.

—⚭— Dalí, Salvador. (1998) *The Collected Writings of Salvador Dalí* Haim Finkelstein (editor). Cambridge, Cambridge University Press.

—⚭— Davies, Betty. (1998) *Shadows in the Sun: The Experiences of Sibling Bereavement in Childhood* New York, Psychology Press.

—⚭— Freud, Sigmund. (1911) 'Case History of Schreber' *The Standard Edition of the Complete Works of Sigmund Freud* Volume XII, trans. James Strachey. London: Vintage, (2001)

—⚭— Freud, Sigmund. (1914) 'On Narcissism: An Introduction' *The Standard Edition of the Complete Works of Sigmund Freud* Volume XIV, trans. James Strachey. London: Vintage, (2001)

—⚭— Freud, Sigmund. (1920) 'The Psychogenesis of a Case of Homosexuality in a Woman' *The Standard Edition of the Complete Works of Sigmund Freud* Volume XVIII, trans. James Strachey. London: Vintage, (2001)

—⚭— Freud, Sigmund. (1933) 'The Dissection of the Psychical Personality' *The Standard Edition of the Complete Works of Sigmund Freud* Volume XXII, trans. James Strachey. London: Vintage, (2001)

—⚭— Lacan, Jacques. (1933 [1975]) *De la psychose paranoïaque dans ses rapports avec la personnalité, suivi de Premiers écrits sur la paranoïa*, Paris, du Seuil.

—⚭— Lacan, Jacques. (2006) *Écrits*. The First Complete Edition in English, trans. B. Fink, New York: Norton & Co.

—⚭— Masson, Jeffrey Moussaieff. (1985) *The Complete Letters of Sigmund Freud to Wilhelm Fliess 1887-1904* Cambridge, Harvard University Press.

—⚭— Roudinesco, Elisabeth. (1997) *Jacques Lacan* Barbara Bray (trans) New York, Columbia University Press.

—⚭— Toboul, Bernard. (2005) *International Dictionary of Psychoanalysis.* Editor: Alain de Mijolla. Volume 1. Detroit, Macmillan Reference.

Dreams and the Neither-Neither

Derek M Elmore

After the publication of *The Book of Pleasure (Self-Love): The Psychology of Ecstasy* (1913), Austin Osman Spare wrote to a friend, exclaiming that Sigmund Freud had written him a letter describing his work as "one of the most significant revelations of subconscious mechanisms that had appeared in modern times."[1] This dissertation will try to uncover whether the epiphanies relating to the subconscious discovered by Spare during deep intellectual thought and trance states, such as the Death Posture and during periods of Automatic Drawing, can be used to justify the comparisons set by Spare to the findings by Dr. Sigmund Freud. Where do these two disparate tangents in history meet, if at all?

I will examine this question through the lens of six concepts, of which both Spare and Freud have had their individual opinions. For Freud, I will look at these concepts through his best-known works, such as *The Interpretation of Dreams* (1900), *A General Introduction to Psychoanalysis* (1917), and *Civilization and Its Discontents* (1929). As for Spare, again I will use three of his most notable writings, *The Book of Pleasure (Self – Love): The Psychology of Ecstasy* (1913), *The Focus of Life* (1921) and *The Zoëtic Grimoire of Zos* (Published posthumously).

The categories of my analysis are the following: Love, Sex, Obsession, Unconscious, Dreams and Death. The ordering intends to follow a path from the known physical into the unconscious form, steadily delving deeper into the collective unconscious of both thinkers. It begins with love and concludes with concepts much further in the abstract, such as the unconscious and death, as these concepts (Where do memory and dreams reside? Where does our consciousness go when we die?) will continue to be a mystery.

Love

> How many mothers who to-day love their children tenderly, perhaps
> too tenderly, received them unwillingly, and at the time wished that
> the life within them would not develop further; indeed, translated
> this wish into various actions, happily harmless. The later death-
> wish against some loved one, which seems so strange, also has its
> origin in early phases of the relationship to that person. (Sigmund
> Freud, *A General Introduction to Psychoanalysis*, p 176-177. 1917)

---

1 Quoted in Baker, Phil: *Austin Osman Spare: The Life and Legend of London's Lost Artist*, p 106.

Are not the animals we see in circuses trained by torture? And do not the animals reared in love, slay their master? The wise embraces and nourishes all things, but does not act as master. Only when passions are ruled by foreign environment are they dangers. Control is by leaving things to work out their own salvation – directly we interfere we become identified with and subject to their desire. When the Ego sees self-love – there is peace it becomes the seer. (Austin Osman Spare, *Book of Pleasure (Self – Love): The Psychology of Ecstasy*, p 23. 1913)

Analysis: There is a thread connecting these diverse thoughts on love. Where Freud acknowledges that love eventually occurs even when the object of that love is not always planned, and in fact the proprietor of that love may prefer that that life not continue on upon the initial discovery of the new individual, Spare comes from the direction of the animal and master relationship, specifically in the context of a circus. That often animals, albeit raised with tenderness and care, will still abide primal instincts and kill their owners, whereas animals trained in torture at the circus may appear safe and abiding to their trainers, at least from the perspective of the audience – although this is an illusion provided by the spectacle. Menace still being present, despite the docile appearance of any of the otherwise dangerous animals. Spare argues that if we let the natural order occur we can become an object of desire, whether it be to love or kill, unless one's ego identifies the other individual as already having a sense of self-love, the relationship can continue in peace, and hopefully, mutual love.

SEX

Among the instinctive forces thus utilized, the sexual impulses play a significant role. They are thereby sublimated, i.e., they are diverted from their sexual goals and directed to ends socially higher and no longer sexual. But this result is unstable. The sexual instincts are poorly tamed. Each individual who wishes to ally himself with the achievements of civilization is exposed to the danger of having his sexual instincts rebel against this sublimation. Society can conceive of no more serious menace to its civilization than would arise through the satisfying of the sexual instincts by their redirection toward their original goals. (Sigmund Freud, *General Introduction to Psychoanalysis*, p 17)

There is only one sense, – the sexual. There is only one desire,-procreation. I am the cause – thou the effect. I am all that I conceive. Not for all time but at some time. 'I multiply I' is creation: The sexual infinity. (Austin Osman Spare, *The Focus of Life*, p 3. 1921)

Analysis: While Freud argues that instinctively the desire for sex is automatically "sublimated", the desire pushed down into the subconscious and redirected towards another goal, or at least thinly veiled – though not recognized in the conscious mind – the desire is still sexual at the heart of any given need or desire. Spare instead dispels this automatically with the revelation that there is only one "sense", that being sex. Spare defies Freud by saying that there is no "desire" and no sublimation. Sex IS desire and he then relates it to evolution. Life begets life. All of life is sexual. The sex is desire itself, which begets infinite creation.

OBSESSION

> In our study of the neuroses, in which we have found invaluable clues towards an understanding of normal people, we find some very contradictory states of affairs in this respect. In one of these maladies, the obsessional neurosis, the sense of guilt makes itself loudly heard in consciousness; it dominates the clinical picture as well as the patient's life and lets hardly anything else appear alongside of it. But in most of the other types and forms of neurosis it remains completely unconscious, without its effect being any less great, however. Our patients do not believe us when we ascribe an unconscious sense of guilt to them; in order to become even moderately intelligible to them, we have to explain that the sense of guilt expresses itself in an unconscious seeking for punishment. (Sigmund Freud, *Civilization and its Discontents*, p 35. 1929)

MAGICAL obsession is that state when the mind is illuminated by sub-conscious activity evoked voluntarily by formula at our own time, etc., for inspiration. It is the condition of Genius.

Other obsession is the "blind leading the blind," caused by quietism, known as mediumism, an opening out of the Ego to (what is called) any external influence, elementals, or disembodied energy. A transmutated consciousness that is a resistance to "true" sub-conscious activity, it being a voluntary insanity, a somnambulation of the Ego with "no form" or control to guide it: hence its emanations are stupid in suggestion, or memories of childhood.

Obsession known as or related to insanity is an experience that is dissociated from the personality (Ego) through some sort of rejection. It is sub-crystalline, and cannot become permanently attached to the sub-consciousness, not having exhausted or completed itself by realisation. Depending on its degree of intensity and resistance shown at some time or another, the Ego has or has not knowledge of the obsession; always is its expression autonomous, divorced from personal control, power of direction and timing.

Concentration determines dissociation. Enthusiasm for one object seeking completion by identification, sacrifices all else, or deliberately forgets. Its separation from the Ego (it becoming equal, or more in bulk than the rest of the consciousness, causes subdivision or "double personality"), is caused by its own intensity or by shock of resistance determined by some incompatibility of the desired or desire. (Austin Osman Spare, *The Book of Pleasure*, p 28)

Analysis: Freud gives us two types of obsession while Spare gives us three. Stating what forms of obsession he has observed, Freud offers us two contradictory types: An "Obsessional Neurosis" wherein a sense of guilt causes a person's conscious mind to become overwhelmed with the thought of the cause of said guilt and then gives us the concept of "the unconscious sense of guilt", in which patients have the unconscious desire for self punishment, and a sense of disbelief towards Freud and other psychoanalysts describing this peculiar ailment to these patients.

Spare begins with "magical obsession", defining it as a sub-conscious activity activated by voluntary stimulus when used to find inspiration, and further defines it as genius. Secondly he gives us a form he defines as "blind leading the blind" where the ego becomes attached to some kind of external influence, such as an elemental or disembodied spirit, describing it further as a "transmutated consciousness" – easily in a realm psychoanalysis has yet feared to tread. Spare calls it a "voluntary insanity" as akin to a dream-state and relates it to memories of childhood. Spare lastly defines another form as relating to insanity; when one is disconnected from the ego, having no means to connect to the sub-conscious and he or she is divorced from the voluntary control of it, the person sacrifices everything or deliberately forgets, and in turn this causes a split in personality. Spare seemingly appears to diagnose split-personality (Dissociative Identity) disorder.

Unconscious

Consciousness actually means for us the distinguishing characteristic of the psychic life, and psychology is the science of the content of consciousness. Indeed, so obvious does this identification seem to us that we consider its slightest contradiction obvious nonsense, and yet psychoanalysis cannot avoid raising this contradiction; it cannot accept the identity of the conscious with the psychic. Its definition of the psychic affirms that they are processes of the nature of feeling, thinking, willing; and it must assert that there is such a thing as unconscious thinking and unconscious willing. But with this assertion psychoanalysis has alienated, to start with, the sympathy of all friends of sober science, and has laid itself open to the suspicion of being a fantastic mystery study which would build in darkness and fish in murky waters. You, however, ladies and gentlemen, natural-

ly cannot as yet understand what justification I have for stigmatiz-
ing as a prejudice so abstract a phrase as this one, that "the psychic
is consciousness." You cannot know what evaluation can have led
to the denial of the unconscious, if such a thing really exists, and
what advantage may have resulted from this denial. It sounds like
a mere argument over words whether one shall say that the psychic
coincides with the conscious or whether one shall extend it beyond
that, and yet I can assure you that by the acceptance of unconscious
processes you have paved the way for a decisively new orientation in
the world and in science. (Sigmund Freud, *A General Introduction to
Psychoanalysis*, p 16)

In that state which is not, there is no consciousness in any sense
that thou art "that" (Kia), which is superb, beyond the range of definition: there is no temptation of freedom, "it" was not the cause
of evolution. Hence "it" is beyond time, consciousness or unconsciousness, everything or nothingness, etc.; this I know through the
"Neither-Neither" which is automatically beyond every conception,
ever free in every sense. Perhaps "it" may not be obscure by continual afterthought and vaguely felt through the hand of innocence- but
whoever understands such simple meanings? "It" is never perceived,
(Austin Osman Spare, *The Book of Pleasure*, Pg. 19)

Analysis: Freud begins his definition of the unconscious by defining consciousness,
which he describes as "the distinguishing characteristic of the psychic life" further-
ing that psychology is "the science of the content of consciousness", and that this
definition asserts that there must be things underneath the known thoughts and
feelings, therefore; unconscious thoughts and feelings within the psyche which the
science of psychology can interpret.

On the other hand, Austin Spare negates all such definitions aside from linking,
or negating all together the unconscious in favor of his own concepts of the Kia
and Neither -Neither, the Kia being a conception of a universal mind in which the
living and the dead of all creatures are eternally linked (its philosophical relatives
would be the Tao of Taoism and the Clear Light of The Void in Tibetan Buddhism).
The Neither-Neither is an intermediary space, something that is neither one thing
nor another. Essentially linking all known physical and metaphysical phenomena to
the infinite, that which is "beyond every conception". That is Spare's unconscious.

DREAMS

If I were asked what is the theoretical value of the study of dreams, I
should reply that it lies in the additions to psychological knowledge
and the beginnings of an understanding of the neuroses which we

thereby obtain. Who can foresee the importance a thorough knowledge of the structure and functions of the psychic apparatus may attain, when even our present state of knowledge permits of successful therapeutic intervention in the curable forms of psychoneuroses? But, it may be asked, what of the practical value of this study in regard to a knowledge of the psyche and discovery of the hidden peculiarities of individual character? Have not the unconscious impulses revealed by dreams the value of real forces in the psychic life? Is the ethical significance of the suppressed wishes to be lightly disregarded, since, just as they now create dreams, they may some day create other things? (Sigmund Freud, *The Interpretation of Dreams*, p 192. 1900)

The deliberate transference of a desire by symbols and sigils with their meanings to the subconsciousness, thus sublating them from the conscious, is a magical act. It works on the thesis that the subconscious is all knowing, all memory, and, being universal, can tap any source of knowledge. The veriest moron, even, may have dreams as wonderful as those of a genius, whatever their difference of level. Dreams are a mental conation, unrecognized as perfect artistry. They prove the creative power of the subconsciousness. Our own degree of ability as a personal equation derives from it, for, genius or not, all difficulties are of expressing adequately our own ethos of inherent ability. (Austin Osman Spare, *The Zoëtic Grimoire of Zos*, p 12)

Analysis: We get a definition based on the theoretical value of dreams from Freud; using the comprehension of the different types of neuroses by way of the "psychic apparatus" and the study of said apparatus, followed by a "therapeutic intervention" through the science of psychoanalysis, a very clinical definition as fitting Dr. Freud. He concludes that it is in the peculiarities of the dream-state that the unconscious impulses of an individual are revealed.

Dreams as interpreted by Austin Osman Spare are on a different trajectory altogether and very much suited to his peculiar visionary temperament. He cites dreams as "perfect artisty" and that an incompetent person or moron can have the same potent dreams as that of a genius. To Spare, dreams are the communicative processes through which the unconscious sends symbols and sigils relevant to any particular desire the individual may have. Transferring their particular meanings from the conscious to the subconscious and by this process it is therefore defined as a magical process. Not at all surprising from a master magus and conduit for the mysteries of the unconscious.

DEATH

Yet there still remained in me a kind of conviction, for which as yet there were no grounds, that the instincts could not all be of the same nature. I made the next step in Beyond the Pleasure Principle (1920), when the repetition-compulsion and the conservative character of instinctual life first struck me. On the basis of speculations concerning the origin of life and of biological parallels, I drew the conclusion that, beside the instinct preserving the organic substance and binding it into ever larger units, there must exist another in antithesis to this, which would seek to dissolve these units and reinstate their antecedent inorganic state. That is to say, a death instinct as well as Eros; the phenomena of life would then be explicable from the interplay of the two and their counteracting effects on each other. It was not easy, however, to demonstrate the working of this hypothetical death instinct. The manifestations of Eros were conspicuous and audible enough; one might assume that the death instinct worked silently within the organism towards its disintegration, but that, of course, was no proof. The idea that part of the instinct became directed towards the outer world and then showed itself as an instinct of aggression and destruction carried us a step further. The instinct would thus itself have been pressed into the service of Eros, in that the organism would be destroying something animate or inanimate outside itself instead of itself. Conversely, any cessation of this flow outwards must have the effect of intensifying the self-destruction which in any case would always be going on within. From this example one could then surmise that the two kinds of instincts seldom perhaps never appear in isolation, but always mingle with each other in different, very varying proportions, and so make themselves unrecognizable to us. Sadism, long since known to us as a component-instinct of sexuality, would represent a particularly strong admixture of the instinct of destruction into the love impulse; while its counterpart, masochism, would be an alliance between sexuality and the destruction at work within the self, in consequence of which the otherwise imperceptible destructive trend became directly evident and palpable. (Sigmund Freud, *Civilization and Its Discontents*, p 28)

Sleep has many depths and death is but a reparative becoming, for we are of eternity in time. Therefore, be willing to pay in the giving and taking without argument, and for him who cheats there is ultimate repayment, for where the morality of exchange ends, business would begin. Sin, however disguised or legalized is sin against self as much as against others. Thus emanates our great inferiority, the down-stepping to the point at which the predator must repay and incarnate as...? – as he deserves. (Austin Osman Spare, *The Zoëtic Grimoire of Zos*, p 13)

Analysis: Freud gives us a complex definition of the Death Instinct, being the antithesis of the Eros Instinct; in the innate urge to preserve "the organic substance and binding it into ever larger units" the opposite would therefore be, something that seeks to "resolve the inorganic state". He tells us that part of this instinct gets directed to the world around us while manifesting as an instinct of aggression, and seeks to destroy things outside of itself, any stop to this would cause a self destruction to this individual from within. Remarking that sadism is a component of sexuality and brings with it a strong destructive quality to the impulse to love, but masochistic tendencies would be sex and destruction within the self.

Spare begins at sleep and assures us that death is simply another component of eternity: one of many depths of sleep. He suggests that one must be willing to pay towards the give and take without argument, alluding to all of life's pleasures and displeasures, "just be grateful you are alive and that you are here", he implies. Spare references punishment but not a Christian or any other organized religious mythological punishment. Simply that it is a natural thing that occurs if one is immoral or unjust throughout life, and in the end, their Karmic morality will take its due. He brings in the concept of sin, saying that, when one does sin (an immoral act) it is a sin to the self as well as whomever the sin was enacted upon. Surprisingly (or unsurprisingly) Spare ends his thoughts on a mystery. That we have the capability to sin is our "great inferiority" and that because as humans we have morally stepped down to this point psychologically, where to sin against ourselves and others is intrinsically seen as OK, he ominously ends this thought with each of ourselves as prey hiding from an unknown predator, perhaps Death itself. It must be incarnate, but in what or whom? Whatever it so may be "...? – as he deserves". Take from that what you will. With death we all eventually do.

CONCLUSION

Whether the letter from Freud to Spare is still extant or not, and simply cannot be found, and whether or not Freud called The Book of Pleasure "one of the most significant revelations of subconscious mechanisms that had appeared in modern times." (Ibid) or Spare just made it up to impress his friends, the answer to my query as to whether Spare had similar revelations to Freud, is much more nuanced than I had imagined. Although no one may ever know when their various thoughts on these six concepts were conceived in either of their heads, one fact we can automatically give to psychoanalysis is that Freud published his most significant works in the field earlier than Spare, as can be seen above.

As to whether Spare delved deeper than Dr. Freud is where the nuance comes in. Whereas he does find a prognosis for what is now called Dissociative Identity Disorder, within his three separate definitions for types of obsession, Spare also speaks of magic and elementals.

We must remember that Freud was a clinical doctor and everything he published was to be read by his peers, so that they could then test his theories. Anything remotely paranormal was very far out of bounds, whether he had any of those thoughts concerning these concepts or not. Spare, being an occultist did not have this restraint. "Magic" in all caps and all of its branches were welcome for him to philosophize upon. Most of his books were self-published in his lifetime. Using his thoughts and his pen as a kind of conduit for the Kia that flowed through him.

To take each concept in this experiment on a one to one decree of their similarities or disconnects, my own observations would put it at: Love = divergent, Sex = divergent, Obsession = Similar yet different, Unconscious = More similar than they appear, Dreams = Quite different. Spare is perhaps better able to delve deeper into the subject matter, though he had no patients himself to diagnose. And finally Death = quite divergent.

This author believes that Spare did indeed find details within the writings of Freud that he agreed with concerning the human unconscious and other elements of the human condition, but perhaps he let his Ego get to him and would then boast to his peers that he already knew everything that Freud discovered. It is simply the case of one man finding similarities in another's writing and allowing one's mind to find links of chain that connect to the other with a firm belief that he discovered these theories first, but failed to publish in time.

Both Spare and Freud are equally influential in their respective fields: occult art and psychoanalysis. They co-existed in time, and both likely knew of each other's work, whether the letter from one end to the other exists or not. There are endlessly fascinating connective tissue between these two revolutionary thinkers, and I cannot presume to know the mind of one or the other, but to simply search for some clues and see what answers I find. For this question as to who thought what first, it is both more simple and more complex than originally assumed. The threads of similarity are thin in some areas and more taut in others. This is a subject matter that can be dissected and interpreted endlessly.

To end, Spare and Freud were two of the most radical and original thinkers we had in the 20th century. They are immortalized each and every time we contemplate them and their thoughts, their magic and legacy will be forever swimming the seas of eternity as we contemplate their individualistic theories on the nuances of life and its underlying structures. The reason they published their thoughts is for this specific reason: to be endlessly discussed and debated. To that effect, I have done my duty. The reader can speculate and continue the endless process of contemplation.

BIBLIOGRAPHY

—∾— Baker, Phil. *Austin Osman Spare: The Life and Legend of London's Lost Artist.* Strange Attractor Press. London. 2012.
—∾— Freud, Sigmund. *A General Introduction to Psychoanalysis.* 1917. HTML Edition.
—∾— Freud, Sigmund. *Civilization and Its Discontents.* 1929. HTML.

—ᴧ— Freud, Sigmund. *The Interpretation of Dreams*. 1900. HTML.
—ᴧ— Spare, Austin Osman. *The Book of Pleasure (Self – Love): The Psychology of Ecstasy*. 1913. HTML
—ᴧ— Spare, Austin Osman. *The Focus of Life*. 1921. HTML.
—ᴧ— Spare, Austin Osman. *The Zoëtic Grimoire of Zos*. Posthumous. HTML.

Rebis, The Double Being[1]

Júlio Mendes Rodrigo

"Whence comes this androgyne? What is his country, his dress?"
– Aeschylus

The theme of the Androgyne as a universal archetype can be found not only in archaic cosmogonies, but also in Literature and Visual Arts. The woman-man is both a sexual paradox and the main symbol of the juxtaposition of opposites, the first origin and ultimate goal of divine and human beings considered as perfect. This text aims to convey the recurrent way in which this archetype has manifested itself over time, highlighting Androgyny as a form of primordial Totality, using examples gathered from the fields of Arts and Literature.

1. Introduction

The union of opposites and the mystery of totality, designated by Nicholas of Cusa as *coincidentia oppositorum*, amounts to one of the key elements in the History of Ideas, implying that the course of human existence is bounded by pairs of opposites. The awareness of this duality allows us to understand the existence of an archetypal dimension, manifested in a transversal fashion across different periods and cultures. The externalisation of archetypes is clear in the mythological narratives that have been systematised by such diverse areas of Knowledge as, for instance, Ethnography, Compared History of Religions and Psychology. These disciplines have made clear that most divinities of vegetation and fertility are bisexual, or at least contain traces of androgynous characteristics. The alchemical quest, thoroughly studied by Carl Gustav Jung in *Psychology and Alchemy* and *Mysterium Coniunctionis*, is based on the obtaining of the Philosopher's Stone, one of whose epithets is *Rebis*, the "double being" (literally "two things"), or the Hermetic Androgyne.

However, the significance of the Hermaphrodite's figure could not have been grasped without the contribution of anthropological studies that allowed a glimpse of the meaning of Androgyny in its wider scope, its meanders having been further

---

1 This text is the outcome of research carried out for the presentation "O Andrógino Hermético: um Ser Duplo através das Artes e das Letras/The Hermetic Androgyne: a *Double Being* through the Arts and Literature" at the International Lusophone Congress on Western Esotericism, at the Universidade Lusófona for Humanities and Technology, Lisbon – Portugal, May 2016. The original Portuguese text was translated into english by Filipe Silva.

dissected by Psychoanalysis.[2] To psychoanalyse a myth is to disclose the eternal Man, to whom one can return, if necessary, in an attempt at a better understanding, whether through the peculiarities of a certain local cult, an unusual custom or a half-forgotten legend. Androgyny plays an important role in the domain of mythology since it expresses, in its totality, the pairs of opposites at the origin of all things.

Greek traditions already mentioned certain beings that in the course of their earthly existence had experienced both genders; the most widely known story is that of the fortune-teller Tiresias, who, having been born a boy became a woman, only to die a man. This blind soothsayer, endowed with a fabulous longevity, who was a woman for part of his life, stands as an example of successive Androgyny. The legend of Tiresias appears to be a Greek interpretation of the fictitious Androgyny of shamans. These archaic legends are also attested to by Ancient poetry, in which one can credibly verify that the spirit of Hellenic culture was initially geared towards the concept of a double Man or divinity, only to refrain itself in a later period, becoming limited to allusions or symbols. Androgyny would probably imply a strongly elevated state of Nature and the divine, as pointed out in the first theogonies by divinities that conceived themselves, or by the myths designed by philosophers. Androgyny was seen in Classical Antiquity as the symbol of a lost unity, an intuition that has lasted until the present day.

2. VISUAL ARTS

For Marie Delcourt, the subject of the Androgyne is a pure myth, "(…) né dans la pensée de l'homme cherchant à tâtons sa place dans le monde et projetant la représentation la plus capable à la fois de rendre compte de see origines et symboliser quelques-unes de ses aspirations"[3]. The author adds that later cosmogonies, stricken by the dream of Androgyny, attributed that feature to several other divine beings as another symbol of their perfection. Thus, she elaborates, the Hermaphrodite in Literature stands as an ideal, rather than as an individual, bringing into the world of form what should have remained an emanation of spirit. The Hermaphrodite is present in Classical art only from the fourth century onwards[4]. However, still according to Marie Delcourt, the first studies concerning the Hermaphrodite gave a disproportionate importance to iconography, the author adding that literary testimonies of the period are not considerably valuable, and are very scarce in the description of authentic beliefs. On the other hand, statues are numerous, and the paintings found in Pompeii attest to the subject's popularity[5]. Greek art does not convey the myth of the Androgyne; it only carries out the synthesis of the masculine and the feminine.

---

2 C.G. Jung studied its role in the universe of Alchemy, a practice that echoes the guidelines of Dreams, in which the Conscious is combined with the Unconscious; the animus is combined with the anima in re-establishing balance in the psyche.

3 Marie Delcourt, *HERMAPHRODITE, Mythes et rites de la Bisexualité dans l'Antiquité classique,* p.1.

4 Camille Paglia, *PERSONAS SEXUAIS, Arte e Decadência de Nefertiti a Emily Dickinson,* p.135.

5 Marie Delcourt, *HERMAPHRODITE, Mythes et rites de la Bisexualité dans l'Antiquité classique,* p.83.

Still, the subject has endured in Art. The pictorial representation of the *Land of hermaphrodites* can be found in the 14th century *Livre des merveilles*. This myth extends across the Middle Ages, achieving a new splendor during the Renaissance. According to Elémire Zolla, the flowers that represent the Androgyne in Art are the heartsease and the lily[6]. Heartseases can be found in several pictorial works by Leonardo da Vinci and his school. Zolla, elaborating on the subject of lilies, states that along with red or white roses, they stand as symbols of the re-androgynization of the alchemical process's final outcome, whose development slowly and gradually stems from the androgynous primordial *nigredo*[7]. The Renaissance features the Androgyne in the representations of Saint John the Baptist by Leonardo, and by his student Andrea Saiano, to name only two examples.

The Androgyne, or alchemical Rebis, is usually represented as a winged being, at the semblance of Sophia – thereby personifying cosmic wisdom. The organisation of chaos always depends on the establishment of a binary system. The attempt to escape this dual state has been one of the main goals of philosophers, mystics and occultists alike. This quest became particularly evident in an end-of-century context, through the work of the Symbolist artists affiliated to the Salon Rose + Croix in the late 19th century. The Salon, founded by Sar Joséphin Péladan, included artists such as Jean Delville, Georges Minne, Armand Point, Fernand Khnopff and Jean Dampt. By exploring the subject, Péladan proclaimed the Androgyne a plastic ideal. The Salon's artists aspired to the (re)creation of a form of mystical Art, aiming towards a re-establishment of the role of such an Art in the intellectual circles of the time[8].

The early 20th century sees a rapport between Science, Psychology and Sexuality which is a characteristic of the period's cultural activity. The artistic and theoretical practices of Elisàr von Kupfer (1872-1942) and his partner, the philosopher Edward von Mayer (1873-1960), represent an alternative approach to Sexuality and Spirituality at the time, through the metaphysical use of the myth of Androgyny. Supported by an artistic and philosophical programme that they named *Clarismus*[9], von Kupfer and von Mayer aspired to the creation of an utopian ideal geared towards the deactivation of an overly masculine society. This aesthetic system combined the decompartmentalisation of the concepts of masculine and feminine with the use of religious iconography. The aim of this visual utopia was an asexual view of human Sexuality through the use of Androgyny's metaphysical mysticism.

Within the counterculture, the 20th century witnessed the arrival of two seminal characters: Aleister Crowley and William S. Burroughs. The latter has exerted a profound influence on the British artist Genesis P-Orridge, a key figure in the current cultural circuit, through his/her role in the projects Throbbing Gristle and Psychic TV, while also developing a parallel career as a plastic artist. In 1993, P-Orridge met Jacqueline Mary Breyer, and upon marrying they created the Pandrogeny

---

6 Elémire Zolla, *The Androgyne, reconciliation of male and female*, p.53.
7 Ibidem, p.53.
8 Sven Davisson, *The Plastic Ideal: The Androgyne in Fin de Siècle Occulture*, p.34.
9 Damien Delille, *Queer Mysticism: Elisàr von Kupffer and the androgynous reform of art*, p.45.

Project, a radical attempt at uniting the two into a single ("pandrogynous") entity through a series of plastic surgery procedures, with the aim of becoming identical. However, their efforts didn't achieve the success they envisioned due to the premature death of Jacqueline Mary Breyer in 2007. The disavowal of the physical conditioning to which human beings are subjected and the union of a fragmented Self exalted by this couple of artists are documented by two films[10]. "We are but one" was their common motto.

One last example from the field of cinema is *L'Hypothèse du tableau volé*, directed by Raoul Ruiz in 1976. This film is a poetic documentary on the philosophical system created by Pierre Klossovski, and is entirely based on that artist's aesthetic universe. Its central theme is the cult of the Androgyne epitomised by the figure of Baphomet, the name given by 19th century occultists to the androgynous idol supposedly worshipped by the Knights Templar.

3. Literature

The most celebrated narrative about Mankind's primeval unity and the origin of sexual differentiation can be found in Plato's *Symposium*, a dialogue on the subject of Love. In that work, Aristophanes describes the ancient nature of humans and the changes it has gone through, detailing three spherical human types: men, women, and the union of both – androgynes/hermaphrodites. This symbol is present in Ovid's *Metamorphoses*, in polytheistic religions (through the element of androgynous divinities), and also in foundational texts such as the Bible, escorting Mankind in its long march through the centuries.

In *Méphistophélès et l'Androgyne ou le Mystère de la Totalité*, the second chapter of Mircea Eliade's *Méphistophélès et l'Androgyne*[11], the author justifies his impulse for the production of that study with the reading of two seminal works in universal literature: *Faust* and *Séraphîta*. The Romanian historian of religions praises Balzac's work, not only for its systematisation of Emanuel Swedenborg's thinking but, mainly, because it raises the theme of the Androgyne to an unparalleled level. Eliade goes as far as considering it the last great European literary work to approach the subject as a central element[12]. However, the theme was returned to at various times in the late 19th and early 20th century, namely by Sar Joséphin Péladan (previously mentioned in the "Visual Arts" section), in *L'Androgyne* (1891), and also by the English and French Decadent movements[13]. In the literary domain, and in the scope of Decadent aesthetics, the Androgyne comes to be considered merely

---

10 *PANDROGENY MANIFESTO*, Aldo Lee and Dionysos Andronis, Greece / France, 2005, 11 minutes and *The Ballad of Genesis and Lady Jaye*, Marie Loisier, France, 2011, 72 minutes.

11 Originally published in french (Gallimard, 1962); the English translation of this work boasts a more appropriate title for the subject analysed in this article: *The Two and the One*.

12 Mircea Eliade, *Mefistófeles e o Andrógino*, p. 101.

13 Through an approach that Eliade doesn't hesitate to qualify as always being addressed through the angle of a morbid, even satanic hermaphroditism by Aleister Crowley, among others. The Romanian author sees here, as in all other European spiritual crises, a corruption of symbols that renders impossible their metaphysical apprehension.

as a Hermaphrodite being, in which both genders coexist. For Mircea Eliade, this misrepresentation stems from the Decadent writers' ignorance of the fact that, in Classical Antiquity, the Hermaphrodite was meant to represent an ideal situation, in a process of permanent spiritual renewal through the practice of ritual[14]. Only the ritual Androgyne could act as a model, since it did not only encompass the accumulation of anatomical organs, but also symbolized the totality of magical and religious powers associated to both genders[15].

The ideal of a Land of Hermaphrodites was a fantasy born from the metaphysical conception of Man as an Androgyne. The reports of *berdaches*, the androgynous shamans of North American tribes, spread in Europe by the first explorers, probably influenced Thomas Artus's work *Les hermaphrodites* (1605), a satire on the court of Henry III. Also in the 17th century, Gabriel de Foigny, a French monk, anonymously published *La terre australe connue*, a utopian novel based upon an imagined trip to Australia, whose population lived according to a Spinozian ethic, always acting as instructed by reason, thanks to their bisexual nature. The subject has, more recently, been taken up by Science Fiction in the second half of the 20th century. The best example of this is *The Left Hand of Darkness* (1969), by Ursula K. Le Guin. Besides receiving literary accolades in the form of exegeses by authors such as Harold Bloom, this work has inspired the discipline of Gender Studies, especially certain feminist tendencies that are critical of the current social model, putting forth some possible alternatives.

In German Romanticism, the Androgyne was idealized as the perfect Man of the Future. A friend of Novalis, the German scientist Ritter laid out, in his *Fragments From The Estate Of A Young Physicist*, a theory of the Androgyne that described a Mankind he had imagined, using an alchemical term – the Rebis. We should also point out Franz von Baader, who paid particular attention to the subject of the Androgyne, drawing from the works of Johann Grichtel and Jakob Böhme. The theme is inexhaustible and has been constantly addressed until the present time by authors such as Robert Musil, in *The Man Without Qualities*, and Herman Hesse, in *Demian*, among others.

4. CONCLUSION

The rites, cults and cosmogonical speculations of Classical Antiquity convey a common aspiration towards Unity, a dream of regeneration and an ambition for perennity. The Hermaphrodite's figure expresses this yearning and its reflections are mirrored by stoic philosophy, by gnosis, by the revelations of Hermes Trismegistus, by the mystical commentaries and writings of classical philosophers, by magic and by the teachings of Alchemy. The primeval Androgyne is a symbol of the union of complementary elements and of the original unity to which the world may return

---

14 It is important to emphasise that only ritual androgyny was used as a model. Children born with signs of hermaphroditism were slain by their own parents.
15 According to Marie Delcourt, symbolic androgyny should have a positive, beneficial value: "chacun des deux sexes recevant quelque chose des pouvoirs de l'autre."

one day, the dream of a primal unity manifested by this image, strongly rooted in the unconscious and carrying a remarkable cosmological weight. Hermes's *Poimandres* describes the Nous as the archetypal form, the beginning emanating from the infinite beginning. The Nous is androgynous and exists as Life and Light, corresponding to the concept of the Collective Unconscious, also due to the fact that it includes opposites such as the ones found in creation myths. The Unconscious is the primordial, as is stated by Portuguese author Yvette K. Centeno, quoting B.C. Sproul[16].

According to Jung, every archetype is in its essence a specific unknown factor, therefore taking multiple forms that are translated by tales, myths and symbols. In their capacity as structuring elements of the human psyche, archetypes as a whole constitute the Collective Unconscious. Such archetypes are manifested through primordial, archetypal images, found in myths, tales and religions, but also in everyday existence. In this way, a symbol becomes a living reality, a bridge between Conscious and Unconscious that nourishes the Self, in the words of Yvette K. Centeno, who concludes her essay *O Símbolo, Forma «Impura»* by stating that "the Self is enrichened, enlarged, made to participate in another dimension, *the other* dimension, that of pure Otherness in which the Self is on one hand dissolved, and on the other is given substance and roots"[17]. The importance of symbols lies in their collective nature, one of its main characteristics being the spontaneity with which that nature emerges. Jung states that no artist is able to consciously create a symbol. Intention is a sign, not a symbol. The latter, as a spontaneous manifestation, points to the unknown, the realm of the Unconscious. Symbols come from a collective, primordial manifestation, developed in the Unconscious. In this lies their timelessness. In their psychological dimension, symbols are instruments of the imagination, common to all Mankind.

The myth of the Androgyne has accompanied Mankind for millennia. A possible answer to Aeschylus's question stated in this article's epigraph can be: this myth comes from far away and long ago, its origins lying in Pre-History[18].

References

—⁓— Centeno, Yvette K. – *Literatura e Alquimia*. Lisboa: Editorial Presença, 1987.
—⁓— Davisson, Sven – "The Plastic Ideal: The Androgyne in Fin de Siècle Occulture". In *Ashé*, Vol. 4, Number 1. Hulls Cove: Lulu Press, 2005.
—⁓— Delcourt, Marie – *Hermaphrodite: mythes et rites de la Bisexualité dans l'Antiquité classique*. Paris: Presses Universitaires de France, 1958.
—⁓— Delille, Damien – "Queer Mysticism: Elisàr von Kupffer and the androgynous reform of art". In *Between Light and Darkness: New Perspectives in Symbolism Re-*

---

16 Yvette K. Centeno, *Literatura e Alquimia*, p.59.
17 Ibidem, p.61.
18 Mircea Eliade, *Mefistófeles e o Andrógino*, p. 101.

search. Helsinki: The Birch and the Star – Finnish Perspectives on the Long 19th Century, 1958.

–∞– Eliade, Mircea – *Mefistófeles e o Andrógino*. São Paulo: Martins Fontes, 1999.

__________ *Tratado da História das Religiões*. Lisboa: Edições Cosmos, 1977.

–∞– Evola, Julius – *A Metafísica do Sexo*. Lisboa: Editorial Vega, 1993.

- Jung, Carl Gustav – *Mysterium Coniunctionis*. Petrópolis: Editora Vozes, 1997.

__________ *Literatura e Alquimia*. Petrópolis: Editora Vozes, 1994.

–∞– Paglia, Camille – *Personas Sexuais – Arte e Decadência de Nefertiti a Emily Dickinson*. Lisboa: Relógio D'Agua, 2007.

–∞– Plato – *The Symposium*. London: Penguin, 2005.

–∞– Zolla, *Elémire – The Androgyne: Reconciliation of Male and Female*. New York: Crossroad Publishing Co., 1981.

Bowie's Non-Human Effect:
Alien/Alienation in The Man Who Fell
to Earth (1976) and The Hunger (1983)

Eve Watson

Introduction

Psychoanalysis, art and the occult – for this enticing theme it seems fitting to use the work of the sublime space oddity Major Tom himself, recently departed from this mortal coil (Jan 10, 2016). I have long loved the genre of science fiction especially in filmic form, from the early black and white television episodes of *Flash Gordon* to *Star Trek* and its various spin-offs, and *X-Files*, to films such *Solaris, Star Wars, Mad Max, Blade Runner, ET, Close Encounters of the Third Kind, Alien, Gattaca, Event Horizon, The Matrix Trilogy* and more recently the excellent *Elysium, Moon, Gravity* and *The Martian*. Science fiction is about outsiderness and the externalization of what is at once intimate and most alien about us. Some argue that science fiction and horror, which are often co-mingled, replaces the dream as a vehicle for representing the unrepressed and is thus a perfect medium for psychoanalytic interpretation. There is little doubt that science fiction is an excellent medium for representing a range of cultural and popular fantasies, anxieties, paranoias and delusionary systems as the work of Edgar Allan Poe, Tolkien, Jules Verne, H. P. Lovecraft and the wonderful terrors of HG Wells testify. But we can also recognise the deconstructing effect of science fiction in the areas of identity, sexuality, mortality, futurity, morality, law, embodiment and subjectivity. Psychoanalysis is, after all, concerned with articulating the fantastical and the archaic, constructing infantile states of mind that determine later states and conflict. These often take on the form of phantasmagoria, alien forms, ghosts and the undead – a quick recollection of your recent dreams will remind you of that. In terms of its method, the dissecting and revelatory work of psychoanalysis is not done by the dreaded empirical method but by inference, interpretation, construction in dreams, the sifting work of parapraxes, art and other neurotic states that carry the archaic messages and imputations of the unconscious and its archaic stratum.

In its work, psychoanalysis has been viewed by some as science fiction and similar to the occult: a religion, all powder and smoke, hocus-pocus, illusion. In distinguishing itself from science, which bases certainty in the domain of knowledge, psychoanalysis bases its certainty in the domain of truth, the very ground of scientific exclusion. That is not to say that science excludes the idea of truth, but it excludes truth on the ground that it does not provide the certainty proper to science. In psychoanalysis, truth cannot be based on the accumulation of knowledge because truth is what makes a hole in knowledge and it is on the basis of this hole that a different mode of knowledge is possible.[1] Importantly, psychoanalysis takes "fiction" as an exemplary mode of expressing the truth and indeed, Lacan states that truth has the structure of fiction, and even when we lie, we are telling at least a version of the truth. In order to tell the truth, we must lie, invent and construct. The unconscious is, as Lacan puts it, the chapter of my history that is marked by a blank or occupied by a lie," (1953, 215) and the truth is what is refound in hysterical symptoms, childhood memories, family traditions and a layering process of remembering. To reduce this process to some kind of measurable, quantifiably observable process fits with the idea that people tend to prefer pretty neatly wrapped lies over the truth. As Doris Lessing put it, "there is no doubt that fiction makes a better job of the truth" (1994, 314).

In this sense, psychoanalysis, science fiction and the supernatural share a goal – the exposure of the unbridgeable gap at the heart of the scientific enterprise, a gap that is truth-bearing and outside of universal knowledge, an idea that is derided by science, which bases its explorations on the belief that explanations will inevitably be discovered; the answers ultimately sought are those of existence and being. Other approaches take the "unbridgeable," the lacuna at the heart of humanity, as its essential and elemental driving force. Psychoanalysis, by contrast, poses the human subject as inherently divided between consciousness and the unconscious, between drive and desire, between what we think we want and what we actually want. Language, art and even systems of knowledge are motivated by the fundamental gap at the heart of human subjectivity, as well as fundamental dissatisfaction at the not-enough pleasure that life ultimately affords, none the least being our status as beings-for-death. For Lacan, the acquisition of language is what determines us as divided between knowledge that we know and knowledge that cannot be known – the Real – and destines us to an infinite production of words (signifiers) and language to encode and script the Real. The Real, he wrote, is what "doesn't stop not being written" (1999, 94).

Against this, science, especially natural science is a theory of the whole that seeks to ultimately explain everything: psychology (the brain), literature, history, religion, the arts, sociology, health and even happiness (there are now national index tables of happiness in different countries). It is the very dividedness of human beings that the rationality of the universal discourse subsumes in everyday commonsense "colonizing" and simplistic behaviourialist approaches to human frailty and limitation.

Human subjectivity for psychoanalysis, at least in the Lacanian field, is charac-

---

1 Lacan writes, "The true basis of the Freudian discovery of the unconscious... can be formulated in the following terms: The unconscious is that part of concrete discourse qua transindividual, which is not at the subject's disposal in reestablishing the continuity of his conscious discourse" (1953, 214).

terised by its temporality, its effect as sliding away, in the fact that it is omnipresent in speech, and it sometimes lies. And as far as behaviour goes, it is in the very concept of repetition, in that "what cannot be remembered is repeated in behaviour" (Lacan 1964, 129).

Against this, tales of science fiction, the supernatural, fantasy and the uncanny serve an important purpose and often represent a rupturing of the "reality" of our world and its "colonization" by commonsense, rationality and science. Reality, as understood by psychoanalysis, is structured by the ego and is never simply a *sine qua non* element of the "natural" world. The supernatural, the occult and the uncanny can be thought of as events of both drive and desire, the drives being the unreasonable, untamed part of ourselves that are subsumed by the civilizing forces of the ego, conscience and the superego. When the drive breaks through and finds expression, it often takes on horrifying aspects that are deeply distressing. This allows us to circumvent the fantasy of complete mastery and total representation. In desire, the process of repression is often lifted in the appearance or revelation of the uncanny, the strange, the alien. In a return of the repressed, there is an eruption of the failure of naming. This is the event of the queer, of the freaks, of that which does not fit with any system of categories, names, places, or identities. It is the space of desire refusing to identify with the options offered by the Other (socio-symbolic world).

The zombie will mark and mock, for example, the mortification that takes place in in the process of naming, how language has the effect of deadening us from the very Thing that we desire, while also being the very condition in which desire comes into being and is fomented.[2] The vampire will signify the undead, those who are mortified in the universal discourse. The ghost is perhaps the best example of the return of the repressed. The alien represents the real and its Other *jouissance*, so foreign and untamable and un-incorporable. It is not for nothing that so often in science fiction and tales of the supernatural, science is impotently pitted against alien or occult protagonists and usually loses out. Think of *War of the Worlds, The Mummy, Signs, The Day the Earth Stood Still, Mars Attacks, Independence Day.* What usually wins out is human morality or ingenuity or good luck, not science. Similarly, sci-fi challenges the misuse of science when it goes horribly wrong or is incapable of detecting aliens among us as in the stories of H.G. Wells – *The Island of Dr. Moreau, The Invisible Man*; also *The Incredible Shrinking Man, The Fly, Frankenstein, Dr. Jekyll and Mr. Hyde, The Incredible Hulk, Invasion of the Body Snatchers, Men in Black, The X-Files.*

In tales of science fiction, horror and the supernatural it seems our interest continues because something primal in us is satisfied, but what is it exactly that we "enjoy" when it comes to such tales? Freud offers some help here, in his idea of the omnipotence of children's thoughts, which carry over to adulthood. He writes of magic as: "an over-estimation of the influence which our mental (in this case,

---

2 Lacan writes, "Thus the symbol first manifests as the killing of the thing, and this death results in the endless perpetuation of the subject's desire" (1953, 262).

intellectual) can exercise in altering the external world. At bottom, all magic, the precursor of our technology, rests on this premise. All the magic of words too, has its place here, and the conviction of the power which is bound up with the knowledge and pronouncing of a name" (1939, 113).

And we can add in image, so words and images offer the conditions for the emergence of a child's perception of the world as magical and their own sense of omnipotence in relation to it. As cinematic spectators, are we not placed in a position of omnipotence with respect to the unfolding story that is both revealed and contained? Are our most primitive anxieties not picqued, given a mode of expression and then "bound" by the narrative function of the story? Susan Sontag, in her essay "The Imagination of Disaster," argues that while sci-fi fantasies distract us from real and anticipated terrors and lift us out of "the unbearably humdrum," they also serve to "normalize what is psychologically unbearable" (1965, 42). Art, Adorno writes, is opposed to empirical reality and in the age of mass consumerism, "it assumes a parasitic character" (1991, 65). Cultural fantasies and anxieties are given expression in science fiction and the function of films is to allay them, but as Sontag discerns, they also "contain something which is painful and in deadly earnest" (42). Similarly, Adorno, writing about the relationship between mass culture, truth and art in "The Schema of Mass Culture," asserts that "the true source of self-reflection lies in the fact that decisive aspects of reality today elude representation through the aesthetic image" (1981, 65). In this, it may be helpful to approach the scopic drive, our drive to look (and be looked-at) and its object-cause, as cleaved, as permeated with bits of real, imaginary and symbolic excess that film spectatorship solicits and draws out in us. Let's explore these ideas in the two films, *The Man Who Fell to Earth* and *The Hunger* and in the personage of the ultimate starman himself, Mr. David Bowie.

The (Science) Fiction and Alien/Alienation of Bowie

The future rock God, David Bowie made his first public appearance in front of a midwife-cum-clairvoyant who allegedly remarked, "this child has been on earth before" (Buckley 2005, 11). How seemingly perfect an entry to the world for one who would become the self-invented "space oddity" of the seventies, the "heroic heretic" of the eighties, self-invented cultural aesthete of the nineties and for five decades was the biggest cult icon in music, a style guru who ingeniously combined both the vocal and the visual, sound and vision. Bowie was undoubtedly a product of mass culture, which took off in the 1950s, and which left young people intensely alienated by the cultural hegemony of the mass market, consumerism, the rise of surburbanisation and its purpose-built model communities, which was basically the rise of the sterile same, what cultural theorists such as Adorno have coined as "the liquidation of the individual" (1981, 40). Here, a link to science fiction theory can be made in its elaboration of the concept of "estrangement." Borrowed from Russian Formalism and with influences from Surrealism and postmodernism, the concept was devised by Darko Suvin in his *Metamorphoses of Science Fiction* (1979), and has links to the notions of "defamiliarization" and "alienation" (369). It is a kind of making strange that takes many forms in science fiction: creatures (human and non-human), time-travel, new inventions, hideous monsters, collision of worlds, breaking the illusion of realism (374-375).

Bowie's interest in the outlandish, the macabre and the supernatural, started early with *Space Oddity* (1969). Written as a response to Stanley Kubrick's film, *2001: A Space Odyssey*, the song is a beautifully haunting tale of the alienation of Major Tom destined to roam the universe forever. A perfect metaphor of requiem for its time, according to Camille Paglia, who wrote in 2004: "As his psychedelic astronaut, Major Tom, floats helplessly in outer space, we sense that the 60's counterculture has transmuted into a hopelessness about political reform" (quoted in Buckley, 61). Major Tom was Bowie's most constant companion and was re-incarnated in the songs *Starman* (1971), *Ashes to Ashes* (1983) and *Hallo Spaceboy* (1995). The influence of the alienated and the monstrous is everywhere in so many of the albums, *The Rise and Fall of Ziggy Stardust, Aladdin Sane, Scary Monsters, Loving the Alien, Earthling* and of course in this year's *Blackstar*, and in two films, *The Man Who Fell to Earth* (1978) and *The Hunger* (1983) where Bowie plays two deeply alienated beings, an alien from outer space who falls to Earth and a vampire who is suddenly confronted with deadly mortality.

I'd like to suggest that there is a certain logic to Bowie's "alien-ation." Even if I wanted to, which I absolutely don't, a psychobiography of him is not possible. He was in fact largely unknown and is unobtainable. He rarely appeared in public, performed relatively few concerts after the early years, gave very few interviews and was intensively private behind the extreme theatricality and showmanship. No biographer can say much about him and the best biography written leaves the reader intensively dissatisfied as nothing much about the man behind the enormous self-styled self-invention is discernable. This of course adds to the sense of mystique and "mythification" about him. While we might be tempted to say that Bowie lived up well to his birth-prediction, it seems that Bowie the persona in this sense is inseparable from everything he did. There is no other Bowie than the one shown to us. With that in mind, I'd like to try and parse some of the interesting ideas, paradoxes and discontinuities that are provoked in both films in relation to alienation, the uncanny, the gaze, spectatorship and beauty.

First a few words about alienation. In psychoanalysis, it is a cornerstone of human subjectivity that ensues from the acquisition of language and the loss of immediacy with the material world of objects, people and even our own bodies. Our alienation in language or "submission to the signifier" is caused by the Other's desire (Lacan 2004, 235). If we think of the child's encounter with the desire of the (m)Other – the Other as desire – the child's attempts to stitch language onto the enigmatic desire of the Other founder on the rock of the empty place upon which desire itself is founded. This foundering occurs because desire is grounded in loss; not the loss of any particular object but the loss of being itself, and it is what Lacan refers to as *manqué-a-être* or lack-in-being. This is why Lacan says, "you are yourself betrayed in that your desire has slept with the signifier" (1957-58: 8 Jan '58, 105). So recognizing that we can never be at one and perfectly synchronised with what we say, with our bodies and with the world, is important. There will always be a gap.

This gap is also another name for the foreclosure of our proximity to the Thing, an originary, anterior Other before the separation into subject and object. The Thing is a site of traumatic Otherness, a site of real violence, the traces of which confer uncanny monstrous effects on the subject. Lacan describes the Thing in his seminar on the ethics of psychoanalysis as "that which is most in myself, that which is at the heart of myself, and beyond me... I don't know if it belongs to me or nobody" (1999[1959-60], 186). So our acquisition of language subjectifies us while also destining us to be alienated from our very essence, our being. "Your money or your life," Lacan described this stacked choice (2004, 212), a choice against a choice already made insofar as we are born into the auspices of the big Other; no choice there, and the choice left is that of losing ourselves (life) or losing less (money) (Fink 2004, 181). The idea of an "alien," a being from another world, plays with the fantasy of one who is not subject to the alienating effects of the signifier, who has not undergone "castration," which, as Lacan puts it in "The Subversion of the Subject," means that "jouissance must be refused, so that it can be reached on the inverted ladder (or inverse scale) of the Law of desire" (2006, 700). When we enter into language and the signifier, we give up absolute or full enjoyment (*jouissance*) for a partial one delimited by the castrating effects of the symbolic field.

Both the alien and the vampire embody a subject not split by the castrating effects of language, who has refused to give up jouissance "on the inverted ladder of the Law of desire." What do these tropic figures do to the spectator? It depends. Do they manage to momentarily wedge open the gaps and failures in representation and thus effect, shall we say, angst in the spectator? The gaps are moments when the symbolic and the imaginary are permeated by the *Real* – that is, the domain of the extra-discursive – which Lacan variously understands as the brute materiality of bodily or traumatic experience beyond the symbolic. Usually the masterful power of the image, or rather image-making, covers over these gaps – hence the success and popularity of cinema. Any intimation of these gaps is anxiety, which in psychoanalysis we refer to as castration anxiety, the sense of the loss of "being," and anxiety also accompanies the appearance of something that shouldn't be there: a presence of an object when there should be an absence. Anxiety, in this sense, "is not without an object," it is a "lack of lack" (Lacan 1962-63). Death is one such point in which representation fails and anxiety is a point in which both the gap appears and simultaneously the missing object, and it is too close.

The object I'm referring to here is a psychic elaboration or entity that falls out from the archaic splitting of the subject and is linked to certain corporeal, sensory or perceptual zones – the oral, anal, aural and phallic mainly. These o-objects, as they are called, are inaccessible and imageless and are caused by cuts from bodily events cleaved onto the real by the signifier/language. Desire circulates around these o-objects, constantly finding new fantasy objects/partners that enflame the subject. While we may move from object to object, we in fact are circulating monotonously around the same unreachable object. With the vampire, the monotonous repetition of the object is shown, the vampire also returns to the same object. When we "see" things, when things suddenly appear and frighten or disturb us, it can be because what is typically occluded from the field of vision appears momentarily with devastating effect. The gaze is the point at which the scopic object is absent, it is the gap between the eye and image, the vanishing point in the image that looks at the subject. It is a dimension that has nothing to do with vision as such; it is as if the image is looking at us, rather than the other way around and this surprises us and can even reduce us to shame (Lacan 2004, 84, 88-89). It is disturbing because for us, while the world is "all-seeing" and we mostly like the idea of being looked at, it generally does not provoke our gaze and when it does (like when we suddenly "realize" that the internet is watching us, not the other way around), we experience a feeling of strangeness (75).

As an object of fascination, Bowie enthralls, and my question is directed to what he provokes in his audience. While principally a singer, and his trade being his voice, he always used the device of spectatorship as his musical co-conspirator, from *Ziggy Stardust* to *Blackstar*. To fascinate is to lure and draw in and synonyms include magic, enchantment, magnetism, witchcraft, charisma, sorcery, spell and trance. A cultural chameleon with multiple personas, he was obsessed by the idea of creating and then hiding behind a series of diaphanous disguises that were designed to both reveal and throw people off the scent. The most inventive rock star of his generation, he lived in a fog of mystique, constantly changing his looks, and wrote in a strange and secret code that nobody, least of all himself really understood, with his cut-up technique of song writing (*Life on Mars*): "It's a god-awful small affair, to the girl with the mousy hair," and then "it's on America's tortured brow, That Mickey Mouse has grown up a cow, Now the workers have struck for fame, 'Cause Lennon's on sale again, See the mice in their million hordes, From Ibiza to the Norfolk Broads, Rule Britannia is out of bounds, To my mother, my dog, and clowns." I'd like to suggest that in the guises of alien and the vampire in the two films, Bowie proffers both a reflection on the big Other and its signifying hold over the subject as well as points in which the Other's hold teeters and is weak and its authority and existence is called into question. *The Man Who Fell to Earth* tells us there will be no revolution while people are fucking, "jouir-ing," slavishly watching television and making money. Here, arguably what is revealed is the ideological thrust of the social order, that is, the rise to dominance by culture of the individual's excessive drive to enjoy, perfectly facilitated by consumerist capitalism, in which people work to slavishly buy mass produced objects that are ultimately worthless, if sometimes utilitarian, and then they must "enjoy" at all costs to make up for it.

This is reminiscent of Adorno's instantiation of mass culture as a great leveler of the individual, and its ideology hides the monstrousness of the system that supports it (1991, 66-68). Isn't Bowie in *The Man Who Who Fell to Earth* foreshadowing the entropic and ultimately self- and planetarily-destructive effects of the individual "consumer" and new technologies? It is worth pausing to think through one of his strongest sentiments in this respect, written in the 70's and in this he is already speaking to the effect of technology:

> If indeed the advances in technology largely determine the fate of society, then the technized forms of modern consciousness are also heralds of that fate. They transform culture into a total lie, but this untruth confesses the truth about the socio-economic base with which it has now become identical. The neon signs which hang over our cities and outshine the natural light of the night with their own are comets presaging the natural disaster of society, its frozen death. Yet they do not come from the sky. They come from earth. It depends upon human beings themselves whether they will extinguish these lights and awake from a nightmare which only threatens to become actual as long as men believe it (1991, 96).

In *The Man Who Fell to Earth*, Bowie falls into this dystopian nightmare and cannot wake up from it.

What interests me especially is whether there are points of rupture or discontinuity in the two films where the gaze emerges. Let's not forget that Bowie's incarnations include his mismatching eyes, his beauty, his obvious and self-conscious accumulations of personae, the strange sonority of his voice and experimentation with sound, all perfect for representing the uncanny, the alien, the un-integrable. There is already an excess about him, as a "star," that overflows, as a real-life junkie, and the death-bearing aspects of the alien and vampire, with their obscene and very Other enjoyment, adds a sense of alterity and strangeness to this "star's" mélange of characters.

In *The Man Who Fell to Earth*, the scene in which Bowie reveals his alien body and strange eyes beneath his human form is, I suggest, an instance of the simultaneous appearance of the gap in the visual field and an accompanying "lack of lack." The image is horrifying because it exposes the hidden enjoyment of the Other and it confronts spectators with their own obscene Other enjoyment. In other words, it threatens the illusion of neutral social reality and as a result exposes the non-neutrality in the spectator's subjective position. The horror of the alien is a moment of non-recognition, when the Other, through which we recognise ourselves, doesn't recognise us and doesn't want anything from us. Phantasy stages desire and allows for a phantasmatic trace of the real at the same time that it attempts to disguise the frailty they imply for the subject. Cinema, good cinema, can provide the possibility of going beyond the illusory mastery of the image and both immerse and propel the spectator out of phantasy, the binding by image of the trace of the real. In *The Hunger*, in the guise of the vampire – a vampire who suddenly ages and becomes mortal in the absence of the Other's desire – a mortal excess is revealed and it brokers the seeing of what should most remain unseen: the death-drive. Bowie's incarnations, with their Other enjoyment, and non-adherence to the dictates of the social order, confront the spectator with a distortion, a stain if you will, that in these two films discomfits easy or neutral spectatorship.

Ambient throughout Bowie's characterological presences is the lure of beauty, which we understand as bearing a death drive. Beauty is a mask covering over the skeletal. Lacan writes, "it being precisely the function of the beautiful to reveal to us the site of man's relationship to his own death, and to reveal it to us only in a blinding flash." (1999, 295) This is why cosmetic surgery often ends up literally being corpse-like – a frozen look. Bowie is supremely beautiful. In both films, our fascination of the horror behind the screen of beauty is revealed, saturated with the death drive and we are inescapably drawn in to what we want to turn away from yet most desperately want to see. While the horror of death is transmogrified and tamed into the alien's becoming ineffably and pathetically human in The Man Who Fell to Earth, in The Hunger Bowie's vampiric incarnation, who eventually crumbles away into dust, "ashes to ashes, dust to dust," is a crumbling away of the economy of looking which seeks to bind death and provides instead a veritable haunting; a spectre of the real of the fragmented, disintegrated, disinterred body that we would do almost anything to avoid. In this instance, the aesthetic aspect of Bowie takes on revelatory desublimation and the ideal he embodies transforms alien and vampire morphology into the mortally limited human but with an edge – a luminous deathly Other excess.

CONCLUSION

Both of Bowie's beautiful non-human characters, the alien and vampire, in their deathly excess, show that the image alone isn't capable of binding trauma; a surplus remains, in other words; something exceeds the image. Vampires, ghosts and zombies are the unburied, the disinterred, the excess that we cannot get rid of. In this, Bowie's provides an uncanny paradox in that he seems to exceed the effect of the camera and the screening proffered by the frame of the film, providing a vanishing point of the beautiful self-image. Bowie's alien and vampire beauty reflect a trace of the "no-Thing" behind the image, the limit point of reflection, the non-alignment of the identification of the reflected image of the self with the body: a dead point to the spectator. This is traced in the path of the subject from primary narcissism to the disruption of the self-image in the separating function of the symbolic breaking up of the mother-child dyad. The fantasy of unity and wholeness must be given up but often returns in adult life to mitigate the narcissistic wound of giving up the maternal body. Love is a powerful mitigation and provides pleasurable illusory integrity and unity. Love is problematized in both films. It is left out and not provided as a solution to *The Man Who Fell to Earth*, while in *The Hunger*, love is the vampire's problem and it has to be killed off, in order for the vampire to rest in peace. You promised it would be forever, Bowie's vampire complains to Miriam, played by the inimitable Catherine Deneuve. There is no forever, not even in love, and as there is no forever, there is the symbolic route of inscription. That is why there is and always will be, the engraved tombstone. But as we know, even that can tell a lie. He will be missed, Mr. Bowie: "Planet Earth is blue, and there's nothing I can do."

Blackstar (2016)

I can't answer why (I'm a blackstar)
Just go with me (I'm not a filmstar)
I'm a take you home (I'm a blackstar)
Take your passport and shoes (I'm not a popstar)
And your sedatives, boo (I'm a blackstar)
You're the flash in the pan (I'm not a marvelstar)
I'm the great I am (I'm a blackstar)

I'm a blackstar, way up, on money, I've got game
I see right, so wide, so open-hearted pain
I want eagles in my daydreams, diamonds in my eyes
(I'm a blackstar, I'm a blackstar)

Something happened on the day he died
Spirit rose a metre and stepped aside
Somebody else took his place, and bravely cried:
(I'm a blackstar, I'm a starstar, I'm a blackstar)

I can't answer why (I'm not a gangster)
But I can tell you how (I'm not a flamstar)
We were born upside-down (I'm a starstar)
Born the wrong way 'round (I'm not a white star, I'm a blackstar)
Oo-oo-oo (I'm not a gangster, I'm a blackstar, I'm a blackstar)
Oo-oo-oo (I'm not a pornstar, I'm not a wandering star)
Oo-oo-oo (I'm a blackstar, I'm a blackstar)

BOOK LIST

–∾– Adorno, Theodor. *The Culture Industry*. London: Routledge, 1981.
–∾– Bowie, David. *Blackstar*, lyrics by David Bowie's. On the album, *Blackstar*, released 8 January 2016.
–∾– Buckley, David. *Strange Fascination. David Bowie: The Definitive Story*. London, Virgin, 2005[1999].
–∾– Eisenstein, Paul. "Visions and Numbers: Aronofsky's π and the Primordial Number," in *Lacan and Contemporary Film*, ed. by Todd McGowan and Sheila

Kunkle, 1-28. New York: Other Press, 2004.

—⁓— Fink, Bruce. *Lacan to the Letter.* University of Minneapolis and London: Minnesota Press, 2004.

—⁓— Freud, Sigmund. "Moses and Monotheism: Three Essays" (1939[1934-38]). *The Standard Edition of the Complete Psychological Works of Sigmund Freud,* Vol. XXIII, 3-137. London: Vintage, 2001.

—⁓— Lacan, Jacques. *Book XX: Encore, On Feminine Sexuality, The Limits of Love and Knowledge* (1972-73), ed. by J.-A. Miller. London: W.W. Norton and Co., 1999.

______. *Book XI: The Four Fundamental Concepts of Psycho-Analysis,* (1963-64). London: Karnac Books, 2004.

______. "The Subversion of the Subject and Dialectic of Desire in the Freudian Unconscious" (1960). In *Ecrits,* trans. by Bruce Fink, 671-701. London: W.W. Norton and Co., 2006.

______. *Book VII: The Ethics of Psychoanalysis,* (1959-60), ed. by Jacques-Alain Miller, trans. by Denis Porter. London: Routledge, 1999.

______. *Book V: The Formations of the Unconscious,* (1957-58), private translation Cormac Gallagher. See http://www.lacaninireland.com/web/wp-content/uploads/2010/06/Book-05-the-formations-of-the-unconscious.pdf. Accessed September 1, 2016.

______. "The Function and Field of Speech and Language in Psychoanalysis" (1953). In *Ecrits*, trans. by Bruce Fink, 197-268. London: W.W. Norton and Co., 2006.

—⁓— Lessing, Doris. *Under My Skin: Vol. 1 of My Autobiography to 1949.* New York: Harper Perennial, 1994.

—⁓— Sontag, Susan. "The Imagination of Disaster." See https://americanfuturesiup.files.wordpress.com/2013/01/sontag-the-imagination-of-disaster.pdf. Accessed September 1, 2016.

—⁓— Spiegel, Simon. "Things Made Strange: On the Concept of 'Estrangement in Science Fiction Theory." *Science Fiction Studies,* Vol. 33 (2008): 369-385.

Formulating the Desired:
Some Similarities between Ritual Magic and the Psychoanalytic Process

Carl Abrahamsson

> ... It seems to me that one is displaying no great trust in science if one cannot rely on it to accept and deal with any occult hypothesis that may turn out to be correct. – Sigmund Freud[1]

In a specifically western mind-frame, we can see many similarities between ritual magic and the psychoanalytic process. A lot of it has to do with formulation, lack of formulation or, possibly, misapplied or misdirected formulation. We are creators of our own words, and they in turn create their own, on their own. Usually, for balanced individuals, the interaction between the formulating strata of the psyche and the formulated expressions is well adjusted. There are also many grey areas in which there is a discrepancy between the two. One such area is lying, or should we say "white lying", which could be seen as a minor offense of desired manipulation. Another more pathological area would be a phenomenon like Tourette's syndrome, in which there is a distinct lack of control of expression of key strata terms.

No matter from which perspective we choose to regard this interaction, there are analogies within the fascinating spheres of occultism and magic. I'd like to narrow that down to a specifically western mind-frame, meaning: fairly rational, decidedly intellectual and to a great extent ego-based. Different systems could be looked at here: western ceremonial, chaos, witchcraft etc. I'd also like to narrow it down to the individual perspective. What does the individual magician do or express? With this in mind, the equivalent of a white lie could for instance be a misdirected expression of "will", meaning one that's not rooted in thought-through, individuated reasoning but perhaps more immediate, ephemeral or reactive. And the Tourette's angle could be the equivalent of magic as a lifestyle attribute rather than an essential, transforming tool that's perfectly valuable even though it's not visible and frequent on social media platforms.

Human language is both a blessing and a curse. Nowhere is this so apparent as when one is talking about oneself or expressing what one wants in ritual. Well, it's apparent in politics too, and in device instruction manuals. The formulation seems

---

1 Sigmund Freud: "Dreams and the Occult", in Devereux (ed.): *Psychoanalysis and the Occult*, International Universities Press, New York 1953, p. 108.

to take place right after the need to express has encountered the comfort zone filter, and substantial things are usually lost in this translation. It becomes a compromise that makes perfect sense to the ego: a signal filtered out with safe noise.

The destinations in terms of psychoanalysis and magical practice are basically one and the same: in order to change negative behavioural loops and hindrances, we gradually work on small steps and changes, very much through formulation, and hopefully learn more about ourselves while doing that. But in both cases, the road to insight is paved with eloquent defense mechanisms and delusions of grandeur. In both, the underlying problematic emotional or psychic cluster is protected by expressions of what seems to be will (that is, a desired direction). But usually it is not ingrained existential will based on a 100% genuine honesty (if there is such a thing) but rather momentary bursts of what appears to be it.

I am not a psychoanalyst but was in Freudian analysis for four and half years, five days a week. So, if you're tired of my voice already now, try to imagine what it was like for me back then! Endless verbiage, swinging from low self-esteem to perfected hubris. But what gradually dawned, as it does, was the insight about the verbal mind's capacity to cheat in order to be safe, to be escapist in order to stay put and to be intellectually alluring to stay emotionally remote. This insight was of great help in many ways. Not least in the magical work. Because I eventually realised that formulation is truly the key to development and success in this field too.

If I say something like, "It is my will to resolve this current problematic issue by changing these related things", which is what one often does early on in the magical career, as well as in psychoanalysis, this presupposes that I know A) exactly what the issue consists of, and B) how the inter-related things are actually connected. But is this usually the case? I can only answer for myself and say that initially, I was very quick in both definition and formulation. Meaning: I assumed that my formulations were based on insight and genuine will. Thereby I was very intellectual, specific and causal in my approach. But I'd say that two thirds of the time, in both ritual work and analysis, what was formulated was mere regurgitation of current affairs, frustrations and haphazard attempts at solution rather than honest expressions of a deeper will to change myself, which would incorporate various causal changes in daily life. I wanted the world to spin around me, but that can only happen when I'm perfectly still and balanced.

An example from both spheres: Magic: I wanted to boost a creative project to manifestation in a climactic ritual state of mind, and focussed on that in a distinct mental-verbal expression, with high causal hopes. In analysis: I wanted to counteract then current topics of low self esteem in relationships by "becoming" more extroverted and socially active in a quite forced way.

A wiser approach would have been, in the case of magic, to express this little specific need through a filter of much deeper resonance: "I want this project to be successfully manifested because that would give me a greater visibility in a field in which I honestly feel I belong on emotional levels." And in the case of analysis a better approach would of course be to not counteract but instead try to constantly get to a deeper insight into why the low self esteem was there in the first place. And resolve the issue. Basically, you can always go deeper and further and when you do that in an honest way, the perfect solutions for minor issues will become evident.

In the western sphere of occultism there is a concept called the Holy Guardian Angel. It's integrated into many systems but often called by different names. This relates to a principle that is either a more elevated level of your own consciousness that guides you, or an external principle that guides you, depending on which cosmology you ascribe to, or subscribe to. Regardless of which main field we look at, it's an intelligent principle of externalisation, not necessarily as a kind of mirror (as in the case of friends in a conversation which can evoke a "third mind" of creative epiphanies) but rather as an ideal that nudges you in intuitive, personal ways. Like someone with a bigger picture not only of where you come from and where you are, but also of where you should be going based on who you truly are.

Does that ring a bell? In analysis, this would be the analyst who remains hidden, out of sight, and who, after an initial period of bonding, passive aggressiveness and transference, subtly hints or suggests where to go based on the level of sincerity of the horizontally positioned vertical aspirant.

This leads on to the question if it's at all possible to be alone in the process of self-knowledge? Do we all need a Holy Guardian Angel and/or a therapist? Of course we're all social animals with needs of different kinds of interaction. But what I mean is that if it's at all possible to develop alone in spiritual, magical or therapeutic contexts? Very likely not. Even the sternest gnostics and shamans need to contextualise, share information and insights, and compare the personal findings with those of others to refine a process that is potentially endless.

One area that's usually at the attractive center of modern magical life, or the appreciation of modern magical life, is that of dreams. Magicians have tended to see dreams as prophetic or as a similar kind of interactive sphere as that of an inner core, or active imagination/day dreaming, visions during scrying or astral travel. That is, a considerably more active phase than the standard Freudian approach to dreams: as reminders in symbol of unresolved issues. But the emphasis is there in both environments; a validation of a psychic sphere that demands a third of our lives, and which contains valuable information or fodder for development. We usually refer to the dream sphere as a magical one, meaning, I suspect, that it's devoid of mental, intellectual and verbal shenanigans. Other, deeper forces are at play.

The complex symbolic language of ritual magic and occultism may be filtered down pictograms from dreams, passed down throughout the millennia. If we accept the interior interpretation of the Holy Guardian Angel concept, including gradual accessibility to Gnostic wisdom, then all of the stuff comes from the psyches of our ancestors. Before the book form, and before formulated written language, it was easier to contain a lot within fewer symbols. Perhaps that's when the corruption and self-deceit began, i.e. when we left the inherent meaning of pictograms or symbols in favour of abstracted letters? And that that's the reason why many of them linger on in specifically magical spheres: as a needed counterforce to the more recent mental particles of formulation?

From an analytic perspective this would make sense too. As we develop as individuals through anal and oral phases and close ties to the mother, formulation is actually what sets us free and makes us able to interact with more people than the mother. Spoken and then written language is what we use to construct identities apart from the merely biological ones. But it's a two-edged sword. Because if we have the power to define through formulation, we also have to power to cosmetically adjust and redefine ourselves in different contexts, like playing out daddy against mommy to please your immediate ego. Or vice versa if that's what matters just then. The symbols of dreamland here become non-verbal soothsayers and truth-sayers, and the pain of confrontation with certain dreams stands in parity with the degree of actual validity.

Freud's sexualisation of human behaviour, as compared to the more cosmic interpretation variant of Jung, also finds its expression in traditional ritual magic in the western sense. We usually see ritualised behaviour based in a dramaturgy that mimics male sexual expression: intellectual outset, transcendence into an encompassing energy, increasing frenzy, ecstatic upheaval with exclamation of more or less formulated desire, and a meditative aftermath in which the wand is laid to well-needed rest. Much of traditional ritual contains symbolic recreations of the original creation. Almost like play-acting a Genesis or Big Bang for personal purposes. This can be expressed in inner preparations through invocations or evocations of third party helpers, or in outer mapping of complex yet conducive symbologies (astrological, elemental, planetary etc) where the magician becomes a seed sower for a specific goal.

One problem with this dramaturgy as well as with western systems and traditions is that they're all alluring, complicated, challenging and mentally strenuous. Which means "perfect" to the western psyche. This goes for both ritual magic and psychoanalysis. Where there's a system that requires method, devotion, knowledge and a lot of time (and in the case of analysis, a lot of money), you go to master it, with the causal hope of receiving a degree, a funny hat or a declaration of good mental health at the end of the process tunnel. But still, the system in itself is not the refining or magical matrix. The gradual waking up to self-deceit is.

Freud's schematic model of the psyche stems from a hierarchical cultural tradition, in which the motivating desires and drives are "sub" conscious and that which guides us is "above" us. This is a prevalent model for most of human life and not even specifically based in a western sphere. It's thereby no surprise that causal, hierarchical models appear in ritual magic contexts too. Whether in group settings in elaborate temples or solitary workings in the mind, there is the magician at the top, commanding the sub-forces via the centred consciousness of formulation. Even angelic beings within a romanticised pseudo-religious context are commanded by words of power and elaborate symbolic structures of correspondences in time and space. The more complex it becomes, the more complex it becomes. If the formulation of the will isn't founded in genuine self-knowledge, things can easily get topsy-turvy. Because a human drive is always stronger than a human intellectual concept or structure. Externalised dualistic concepts with projected or invested moral qualities can absolutely bite back if what you exclaim doesn't resonate with your own genuine morals.

In a more analytical language, you could say that striking out in compensation or projection may not resolve the issues at all. Very likely not. What's needed is self-reflection and soul-stripping in a chamber with different kinds of reflective surfaces; many of them will be symbolic. If you're diligent and honest, all mirrors will crack and there will be no more self-images to see because you have become the sole soul-seer. That's also the result of the magical process. You may have wallowed through endless systems and initiations (and related power trips) but when push comes to shove comes to compensatory quaquaversalism comes to final stillness – hopefully! – there is only one unique and noise-free mind that is resonant with all other minds. On that level, a brand new magic is available, with no hocus pocus needed whatsoever.

My advice both in terms of ritual magic and analysis is to dig deeper before something is eventually expressed in an intellectual decompression chamber that allows for things to manifest. The causal manifestation of something desired is totally fine as the cherry on top, but the cake as such is usually baked with considerably more complex and not seldom painful ingredients. That goes for both these areas. If you strive for the cherry but can't properly make a great chocolate cake first, you may instead end up with steak- and kidney pie, and ensuing disappointment.

Contributors

VANESSA SINCLAIR, Psy.D. is a psychoanalyst based in Sweden, who sees analysands internationally. Dr. Sinclair is a Senior Research Fellow at Global Centre for Advanced Studies (GCAS), as well as the host of Rendering Unconscious Podcast. Her books include *The Pathways of the Heart* (Trapart Books, 2021), *Scansion in Psychoanalysis and Art: the Cut in Creation* (Routledge, 2020), *Rendering Unconscious: Psychoanalytic Perspectives, Politics & Poetry* (Trapart Books, 2019), *Outsider Inpatient: Reflections on Art as Therapy* (Trapart Books, 2021) with Elisabeth Punzi, *On Psychoanalysis and Violence: Contemporary Lacanian Perspectives* (Routledge, 2018) with Manya Steinkoler and *The Fenris Wolf, vol 9* (Trapart Books, 2017) with Carl Abrahamsson. www.drvanessasinclair.net

CARL ABRAHAMSSON (b. 1966) is the editor of *The Fenris Wolf* and the founder of The Institute of Comparative Magico-anthropology. He likes to write and read, take an occasional photograph and at times converse with the audio structure spirits. He is also a filmmaker, predominantly with the documentary series *An Art Apart*. www.carlabrahamsson.com

KATELAN FOISY is a multimedia artist and writer. Her fine art pieces have been displayed at The Worcester Art Museum, Ohio History Museum, MODA, WEAM, A&D Gallery, and Last Rights. She has graced the pages of the Grammy Award programs and the stage of Cynthia von Buhler's immersive historical plays Speakeasy Dollhouse and The Brothers Booth. Katelan has been featured in *NY Times, Elle magazine, Paper magazine, GQ Italy, Time Out NY*, and many others—for her work both as an artist and curator. She has written for *Motherboard/VICE, Electric Literature, Luna Luna, ERIS magazine*, and *COILHOUSE*. She was called a "Female Jack Kerouac" by Taylor Mead and a "Modern Day Francesca Woodman" by Cynthia von Buhler.

SHARRON KRAUS is a folk musician and composer inspired by traditional music, psychedelia, horror soundtracks, surrealism, mythology, and gothic and magical literature. She has released five solo albums, the first of which, *Beautiful Twisted*, was named by *Rolling Stone Magazine* in their Critics' Top Albums of 2002. She is one of the musicians focused on in Jeanette Leech's *Seasons They Change: The Story of Acid, Psych and Experimental Folk*. She has a doctorate in Philosophy from the University of Oxford and has written on many themes, including creating music in response to landscape; Harry Smith and the weirdness of folk music; magic as portrayed in chidren's literature and *The Wicker Man*.

DEMETRIUS LACROIX has dedicated his life to the study of the occult, spirituality and religion of Traditional societies in the ancient and modern world, having studied many forms of traditional belief. From his own upbringing, and later initiation into Haitian Vodou, Lacroix comes from a multicultural background, offering a worldview shaped by his immersion into misunderstood and vilified cultures. Lacroix seeks to present the underrepresented "occult" in an understandable and edifying way. Lacroix is a professional Psychic, spiritual counselor and advisor in Salem, MA.

GRAHAM DUFF is a prolific screenwriter, producer and show runner. He created and wrote the Sky Arts anthology horror series *The Nightmare Worlds of H.G. Wells* starring Michael Gambon. He also created and wrote all 53 episodes of BBC3's dark comedy drama *Ideal* starring Johnny Vegas, three series of Radio 4's sci-fi sit-com *Nebulous* starring Mark Gatiss and BBC2's *Dr. Terrible's House of Horrible* starring Steve Coogan. He script edited the movie *Alan Partridge: Alpha Papa* as well as seven series of Radio 4's Sony award winning *Count Arthur Strong's Radio Show*. As an actor his appearances include *Doctor Who* and the Harry Potter films. He also writes about art, music and underground culture and owns a modest collection of contemporary and surrealist art.

KEN HENSON blends magic and mysticism with art processes. He is an Associate Professor and the Head of Illustration at the Art Academy of Cincinnati in Ohio, where he teaches studio courses and Art and the Occult. Ken has been named a Curtis G. Lloyd Fellow twice by the Lloyd Library and Museum, and is the author/illustrator of *Alchemy and Astral Projection: Ecstatic Trance in the Hermetic Tradition* (LLM, 2014), the channeler of *HIGH GRAVITY: Werewolves, Ghosts, and Magick Most Black*, and the illustrator of *Blue Jay Slayer* (Aurore Press, 2016), which is a collaboration with poet Matt Hart.

GARY LACHMAN is the author of more than a dozen books charting the meeting ground between esotericism and culture, including the highly praised *Secret Teachers of the Western World* (Tarcher/Penguin 2015). Other titles include *Aleister Crowley: Magick, Rock and Roll, and the Wickedest Man in the World* (Tarcher/Penguin 2014), *Turn Off Your Mind: The Mystic Sixties and the Dark Side of the Age of Aquarius* (Disinformation 2003), *The Secret History of Consciousness* (Lindisfarne 2003), and *Politics and the Occult* (Quest 2008). He is a regular contributor to *Fortean Times, Independent on Sunday, Guardian, LA Review of Books* and other journals in the UK and US. He lectures frequently in the UK and Europe. In a previous life, he was a founding member of the rock group Blondie, and in 2006 was inducted into the Rock and Roll Hall of Fame. www.garylachman.co.uk

PETER GREY is a writer and co-founder of occult publisher Scarlet Imprint. He is the author of three books, *The Red Goddess, Apocalyptic Witchcraft* and *Lucifer: Princeps*. His essays have been disseminated widely in print and online, and he has lectured internationally. An exponent of low witchcraft and high ritual; he is particularly noted for his work on eschatology, ecology and Babalon.

VAL DENHAM, born 14.11.1957 in Yorkshire is the kind of artist you'd normally expect to learn about only after their passing, when crates of wonderful obsessively detailed artworks and diaries would be revealed Darger-like to an unsuspecting public. Formally trained at Bradford College and the Royal College of Art in London, she has been originally associated with that true counter-cultural revolution of the late 1970s and early 80s which came to be known as "industrial culture". Apart from creating richly detailed works which deal with personal themes like her OCD, gender dysphoria and transgender issues, she is also an accomplished portrait artist. Two volumes of her art and thoughts have been published by Timeless Editions out of Toulouse in 2012 and 2015 respectively and met with wide approval.

CLAIRE-MADELINE CULKIN is an MFA candidate at Sarah Lawrence College in their Non-Fiction program. Her work – equal parts personal narrative, theoretical analysis, and criticism – aims to reconcile the artifice of theory with the reality of lived experience by using her subjectivity means of approaching her subject matter. "Beds, Bodies, and Other Books of Common Prayer" was previously presented at the Das Unbehagen sponsored conference, "Psychoanalysis on Ice" in Iceland. A detailed description of her creative and professional work can be found on her website www.clairemadelineculkin.squarespace.com.

STEVEN REISNER, PhD, is a Psychological Ethics Advisor to PHR and was a co-author on *Experiments in Torture*. A founding member of the Coalition for an Ethical Psychology, Dr. Reisner is also on the primary faculty of the International Trauma Studies program at New York University and is an Adjunct Professor in the Program in Clinical Psychology at the Columbia University Teachers College and at the New York University School of Medicine.

KATY BOHINC was born November 19, 1983 at 6:04 PM in Cleveland, OH. June 5, 2012 in the Western Roman calendar the planet Venus traveled directly between the sun and earth, an event referred to as the Transit of Venus. Occurring every 100 years or so in eight year pairs, the Transit of Venus is of unknown and extreme astrological significance. Bohinc's *Dear Alain* is a poetic epistolary, a psycho-sexual thriller, a metaphor for the relationship between poetry and Western philosophy, a personal address to Alain Badiou. Slavoj Zizek said, "This book should be banished!" She collaborates as Star Arkestress on Tender Buttons Press with Lee Ann Brown in the TornPage House in New York City.

DR. OLGA COX CAMERON is a psychoanalyst in private practice in Dublin for the past 27 years. She lectured in Psychoanalytic Theory and also in Psychoanalysis and Literature at St. Vincent's University Hospital and Trinity College from 1991 to 2013 and has published numerous articles on these topics in national and international journals. She is the founder of the annual Psychoanalysis and Cinema Festival.

INGO LAMBRECHT, Ph.D., is a clinical psychologist and psychoanalytic therapist for over twenty years, and has practiced in South Africa and New Zealand. He works in the public sector and has a private practice. Besides his PhD in psychology and MA in Comparative Literature, he has been the clinical leader of the Child and Adolescent Mental Health Service in Hawke's Bay (HBDHB) in New Zealand. Currently he is providing clinical leadership at Manawanui Maori Mental Health Service (ADHB). As a clinical advisor to He Kamaka Oranga (Maori Health Service, ADHB), he is a consultant and project leader on the integration of various Maori mental health services. He has also published various book chapters, and is the author of *Sangoma Trance States: Exploring Indigenous Consciousness Disciplines in South Africa* (2014) that weaves personal experiences of being trained as a sangoma, a South African shaman, together with the complex relations of clinical psychology, anthropology, and indigenous knowledges.

ELIOTT EDGE is a multidisciplinary artist, writer, philosopher, humorist, and netizen who operates under the online handle OddEdges. Edge describes Odd as "A prolific noösphere squatter spreading Awareness Awareness." Edge's primary occupations include cyborg anthropology, universal free education, simulism and digital mechanics, virtual reality and media literacy, psychedelics and psychology, ethical transhumanism, culture jamming, liminality, esoterica, meditation, and consciousness. His artwork has appeared at the Museum of Computer Arts, Stevens Institute of Technology, Anthology Film Archives, and other galleries. He is on the advisory board of The Lifeboat Foundation, a member of Das Ubehagen, the founder of EducatingEarth, and published in The Institute of Ethics and Emerging Technologies. He is also a poet, blogger, and YouTuber.

CHARLOTTE RODGERS is an animist and magickian. She is also a writer, artist, performer and public speaker. Charlotte has contributed to many magazines and anthologies and wrote the books *The Bloody Sacrifice* and *P is for Prostitution: A Modern Primer.* She conceived, introduced and co edited *A Contemporary Western Book of the Dead* (all published by Mandrake of Oxford). *The Sky is a Gateway not a Ceiling* (illustrated by Roberto Migliussi) published in Italy, is a recently published collection of her work. She has exhibited her totemic, talismanic art work which incorporates bones, road kill and elements of death, in numerous galleries including London's Chelsea Gallery and the Bath Royal Institute and has given presentations at Edinburgh and Leicester University.

ALKISTIS DIMECH is a dancer/choreographer, artist, writer and magician, whose practice is principally grounded in the ankoku butoh of Hijikata Tatsumi, a discipline/philosophy of dance that she has trained in and performed since 2002. The sabbatic dance is her personal progression of this "dance of darkness," a project exploring the intersection of the dancing, affective body, consciousness and practices associated with magic, witchcraft and shamanism. Her dance work is documented at sabbaticdance.com. With Peter Grey she co-founded the esoteric publishing house Scarlet Imprint in 2007. Her essays will be gathered in *The Brazen Vessel.*

FRED YEE is a NYC based meditation instructor. He focuses on direct felt experience. Influenced by his Taoist heritage and a D.I.Y. approach to magic.

ROBERT ANSELL (b.1965) is a publisher, art dealer, curator and scholar. His field of expertise is esoteric art of the 20th century with a specific focus on Austin Osman Spare. Through his company Fulgur Esoterica he has represented esoteric artists in book form since 1992. In recent years he has also gained note as an independent art curator specializing in the esoteric. Robert is also the publisher and art editor of *Abraxas Journal,* which has been described as 'today's pre-eminent voice for the serious study of occult and esoteric expression.' He has been interviewed for the *BBC Culture Show,* the blog *Boing Boing,* and *Dazed and Confused.*

DR. RAY O NEILL, MA, MSc, MPhil is an Irish writer and psychoanalytic psychotherapist working in private practice in Dublin, Ireland. As Ireland's only resident male Agony Aunt, Ray works significantly (and sometimes with significance) with the media in discoursing love, relationships, and desire in the twenty-first century. Current research includes explorations of the interrelations between contemporary desire and technology; and that transmission of trauma across generations, with particular emphasis on the Irish experience.

DEREK MATHEW ELMORE is an artist and art conservator living and working in New York. He has studied Studio Art in London and Italy and received a Masters for Conservation of Works of Art on Paper in London. As an artist his work attempts to expand the "periphery of consciousness". He cites his fundamental influences as sequential art, the Italian Renaissance and Surrealism. In the field of art conservation Derek has always sought to work with visionary art or objects with sacred qualities. He has worked as a conservator or archivist at

St. Paul's Cathedral, John Latham's Flat Time House, The 9/11 Memorial and the Nicholas Roerich Museum. He is currently completing work for a solo exhibition.

Júlio Mendes Rodrigo, writer, independent researcher and broadcaster, is a votary of Fragmentary Wisdom and a devout of the Knowledge transmitted through the interacting shards that make up the art of quotation. ANDRÓMEDA – Management & Production, the entity he currently administers, usurps its name from the shackled-up princess of pagan Antiquity, with the intent of embodying a creative device for mythical epiphanies. The author is willing to admit that the "science of legend" is the "science" of circular motion, always at the same distance, around an inaccessible centre: Myth. Education: degree in History (1998) and high degree in Museology (2004), both at Faculdade de Letras da Universidade do Porto, Portugal.

Eve Watson, Ph.D. is is a psychoanalytic practitioner working in a city centre practice in Dublin, Ireland. She also works at American College Dublin in the delivery of academic and clinical programmes in Freudian-Lacanian psychoanalysis. She is affiliated with APW and is a registered practitioner member of APPI and is organisationally on the APPI Executive Committee and the editorial board of *Lacunae*, the Irish Journal of Psychoanalysis. Published in the areas of psychoanalysis, critical psychology, sexuality studies, poetics and social/critical theory, she has co-edited a book with Noreen Giffney entitled *Clinical Encounters: Psychoanalytic Practice and Queer Theory.*

Also Available from Trapart Books

The Fenris Wolf 10 (2020)

Carl Abrahamsson – *Editor's Introduction*, Carl Abrahamsson – *Onwards to the Source!*, Ludwig Klages – *On the Essence of Ecstasy*, David Beth – *Katabasis and Erotognosis*, Henrik Dahl – *An Introduction to Eroto-Psychedelic Art*, Peter Sjöstedt-H – *Antichrist Psychonaut: Nietzsche's Psychoactive Drugs*, Carl Abrahamsson – *Lux Per Nox – The Fenris Wolf As Libidinal Liberator*, Jesse Bransford & Max Razdow – *Revisiting the Veil of Dreams*, Christopher Webster – *Beyond the North Wind*, Kendell Geers – *A Long Boundless Systematized...*, Kadmus – *Seeking the Three-Headed Saint*, Billie Steigerwald – *The Chthonic Seed: Reflections of an Ancient Death Gnosis*, Fred Andersson – *The Gospel According to the Tomb Man*, Zaheer Gulamhusein – *Sunflower*, Charlotte Rodgers – *The Riderless Horse...*, Craig Slee – *The Occult Nature of Cripkult*, Damien Patrick Williams – *Daoism, Buddhism and Machine Consciousness*, Philip H. Farber – *Thoughts on the Creation of Memetic Entities*, Thomas Bey William Bailey – *Memetic Magick*, Mitch Horowitz – *Is Your Mind a Technology for Utopia?*, Ramsey Dukes – *I'm Gonna Blow Your Mind*, Carl Abrahamsson – *Grasping Reality with Gary Lachman*, Anders Lundgren – *Mike Mignola and the Lovecraft Circle*, Peggy Nadramia – *So It Was Written*, Peggy Nadramia – *Addendum to So It Was Written*, Nina Antonia – *Maya*, Jack Stevenson – *Häxan/Witchcraft Through the Ages*, Andrea Kundry – *The Demonic Cultural Legacy of Antonin Artaud*, Joan Pope – *The Birth of Ideas*, Genesis Breyer P-Orridge – *Idiosyncratic Use Ov Language...*, Vanessa Sinclair – *Try To Altar Everything*, Claire-Madeline Corso – *Cutting Up a New Conversation*

The Fenris Wolf 8 (2016)

Carl Abrahamsson – *Editor's Introduction*, Vanessa Sinclair – *Polymorphous Perversity and Pandrogeny*, Charles Stansfield Jones (Frater Achad) – *Alchymia*, Tim O'Neill: *Black Lodge/White Lodge*, Nina Antonia – *Bosie & The Beast*, Aki Cederberg – *Festivals of Spring*, Michael Moynihan – *Friedrich Hielscher's Vision of the Real Powers*, Friedrich Hielscher – *The Real Powers*, Orryelle Defenestrate Bascule – *Ear Horn: Shamanic Perspectives and Multi-Sensory Inversion*, Zbigniew Lagos – *The Figure of the Polish Magician: Czesław Czynski (1858-1932)*, Gary Lachman – *Rejected Knowledge: A Look At Our Other Way of Knowing*, Carl Abrahamsson – *Intuition as a State of Grace*, Bishop T Omphalos – *The Golden Thread: Soteriological Aspects of the Gnostic Catholicism in E.G.C.*, Kendell Geers – *iMagus*, Johan Nilsson – *Defending Paper Gods: Aleister Crowley and the Reception of Daoism in Early 20th*

Century Esotericism, Gordan Djurdjevic – *The Birth of the New Aeon: Magick and Mysticism of Thelema from the Perspective of Postmodern A/Theology*, Tim O'Neill – *The Derleth Error*, Antti P Balk – *Greek Mysteries*, Carl Abrahamsson – *The Economy of Magic*, Stephen Sennitt – *The Book of the Sentient Night: 23 Nails*, Henrik Dahl – *We Ate the Acid: A Note on Psychedelic Imagery*, Jason Louv – *Robert Anton Wilson's Cosmic Trigger and the Psychedelic Interstellar Future we need*, Carey Hodges & Chad Hensley – *New Orleans Voodoo: An Oddity Unto Itself*, Alexander Nym – *Kabbalah references in contemporary culture*, Zaheer Gulamhusein – *Standing in Line*, Carl Abrahamsson – *As the Wolf Lies Down to Rest*, Vanessa Sinclair & Ingo Lambrecht – *Ritual and Psychoanalytical Spaces as Transitional, featuring Sangoma Trance States*, Hagen von Julien – *Listening to the Voice of Silence: A Contemporary Perspective on the Fraternities Saturni*, Erik Davis – *Infectious Hoax: Robert Anton Wilson reads H.P. Lovecraft*, N – II. *Land*, Cadmus – *Neo-Chthonia*, Kadmus – *A Fragment of Heart: A contribution to the Mega-Golem*, Stojan Nikolic – *The One True Church of the Dark Age of Scientism*, Miguel Marques – *The Labors of Seeing: A Journey Through the Works of Peter Whitehead*, Renata Wieczorek – *The Conception of Number According to Aleister Crowley*, Orryelle Defenestrate Bascule – *Fragments of Fact*, Derek Seagrief – *Conscious ExIt*, Kasper Opstrup – *By This, That: A spin on Lea Porsager's Spin*, and Genesis Breyer P-Orridge – *Greyhounds of the future*.

THE FENRIS WOLF 7 (2014)

Carl Abrahamsson – *Editor's Introduction*, Sara George & Carl Abrahamsson – *Fernand Khnopff, Symbolist*, Sasha Chaitow – *Making the Invisible Visible*, Vanessa Sinclair – *Psychoanalysis and Dada*, Kendell Geers – *Tu Marcellus Eris*, Stephen Sennitt – *Fallen Worlds, Without Shadows*, Antony Hequet – *Slam Poetry: The Warrior Poet*, Antony Hequet – *Slam Poetry: The Rebel Poet*, Genesis Breyer P-Orridge – *Alien Lightning Meat Machine*, Genesis Breyer P-Orridge – *This Is A Nice Planet*, Patrick Lundborg – *Psychedelic Philosophy*, Henrik Dahl – *Visionary Design*, Philip Farber – *Higher Magick*, Kendell Geers – *Painting My Will*, Carl Abrahamsson – *The Imaginative Libido*, Angela Edwards – *The Sacred Whore*, Vera Nikolich – *The Women of the Aeon*, Jason Louv – *Wilhelm Reich*, Kasper Opstrup – *To Make It Happen*, Peter Grey – *A Manifesto of Apocalyptic Witchcraft*, Timothy O'Neill – *The Gospel of Cosmic Terror*, Stephen Sennitt – *Sentient Absence*, Carl Abrahamsson – *Anton LaVey, Magical Innovator*, Alexander Nym – *Magicians: Evolutionary Agents or Regressive Twats?*, Antti P Balk – *Thelema*, Kjetil Fjell – *The Vindication of Thelema*, Derek Seagrief – *Exploring Past Lives*, Sandy Robertson – *The Fictional Aleister Crowley*, Adam Rostoker – *Whence Came the Stranger?*, Emory Cranston – *A Preface to the Scented Garden*, Manon Hedenborg-White – *Erotic Submission to the Divine*, Carl Abrahamsson – *What Remains for the Future?*, Frater Achad – *Living In the Sunlight*, Genesis Breyer P-Orridge – *Magick Squares and Future Beats*

226

Also Available from Trapart Books

THE FENRIS WOLF 6 (2013)

Carl Abrahamsson – *Editor's Introduction*, Frater Achad – *A Litany of Ra*, Kendell Geers – *Tripping over Darwin's Hangover*, Vera Nikolich – *Eastern Connections*, Carl Abrahamsson – *Babalon*, Freya Aswynn – *On the Influence of Odin*, Marita – *Runic Magic through the Odinic Dialectic*, Aki Cederberg – *Afterword: The River of Story*, Shri Gurudev Mahendranath – *The Londinium Temple Strain*, Gary Dickinson – *An Orient Pearl*, Derek Seagrief – *Aleister Crowley's Birth & Death Horoscopes*, Tim O'Neill – *Shades of Void*, Nema – *Magickal Healing*, Nema – *A Greater Feast*, Philip Farber – *Sacred Smoke*, Robert Taylor – *Death & the Psychedelic Experience*, Michael Horowitz – *LSD: the Antidote to Everything*, Alexander Nym – *Transcendence as an Operative Category...*, Carl Abrahamsson – *Approaching the Approaching*, Renata Wieczorek – *The Secret Book of the Tatra Mountains*, Sasha Chaitow – *Legends of the Fall Retold*, Sara George & Carl Abrahamsson – *Sulamith Wülfing*, Robert C Morgan – *Hans Bellmer*, Genesis Breyer P-Orridge – *Tagged for Life*, Carl Abrahamsson – *Go Forth and Let Your Brain-halves Procreate*, Anders Lundgren – *Satanic Cinema is Alive and Well*, Anton LaVey – *Appendices*

THE FENRIS WOLF 5 (2012)

Carl Abrahamsson – *Editor's Introduction*, Jason Louv – *The Freedom of Imagination Act*, Patrick Lundborg – *Such Stuff as Dreams are Made of*, Gary Lachman – *Secret Societies and the Modern World*, Tim O'Neill – *The War of the Owl and the Pelican*, Dianus del Bosco Sacro – *The Great Rite*, Philip H Farber – *Entities in the Brain*, Aki Cederberg – *At the Well of Initiation*, Renata, Wieczorek – *The Magical Life of Derek Jarman*, Genesis Breyer P-Orridge – *A Dark Room of Desire*, Genesis Breyer P-Orridge – *Kreeme Horne*, Ezra Pound – *Translator's Postscript*, Stephen Ellis – *Poems for The Fenris Wolf*, Hiram Corso – *Mel Lyman*, Mel Lyman – *Plea for Courage*, Gary Dickinson – *The Daughter of Astrology*, Robert Podgurski – *Sigils and Extra Dimensionality*, Frater Nigris – *Liber Al As-if*, Peter Grey – *The Abbey Must be Built*, Vera Mladenovska Nikolich – *A Different Perspective of the Undead*, Kevin Slaughter – *The Great Satan*, Lionel Snell – *The Art of Evil*, Phenex Apollonius – *The Quintessence of Daimonic Ipseity*, Phanes Apollonius – *Infernal Diabolism in Theory and Practice*, Anonymous – *Falling with Love: Embracing the Infernal Host*, Lana Krieg – *Sympathy with the Devil: Faust's Infernal Formula*, Carl Abrahamsson – *State of the Art: Birthpangs of a Mega-Golem*, Carl Abrahamsson – *Hounded by the Dogs of Reason*

THE FENRIS WOLF 4 (2011)

Carl Abrahamsson – *The whys of yesterday are the why-nots of today*, Hermann Hesse – *The Execution*, Fredrik Söderberg – *Black and White Meditations 1-23*, Peter Gilmore – *Every Man and Woman Is a Star*, Peter Grey – *Barbarians at the Gates*,

John Duncan – *Hallelujah*, Ramsey Dukes – *Democracy Is Dying of AIDS*, Tim O'Neill – *The Technology of Civilization X*, Thomas Karlsson – *Religion and Science*, David Beth – *Bloodsongs*, Payam Nabarz – *Liber Astrum*, Hiram Corso – *Unveiling the Mysteries of the Process Church*, Jean-Pierre Turmel – *The Pantheon of Genesis Breyer P-Orridge*, Kendell Geers – *The Penis Might Ier Than Thes Word*, Z'EV – *The Calls*, Robert Taylor – *Dreamachine: The Alchemy of Light*, Phil Farber – *An Interview with Terence McKenna*, Phil Farber – *McKenna, Ramachandran and the Orgy*, Thomas Bey William Bailey – *The Twilight of Psychedelic America?*, Ernst Jünger – *LSD Again/Nochmals LSD*, Baba Rampuri – *The Edge of Indian Spirituality*, Aki Cederberg – *In Search of Magic Mirrors*, Carl Abrahamsson – *Thelema and Politics*, Carl Abrahamsson – *Someone's Messing with the Big Picture*, Carl Abrahamsson – *An Art of High Intent?*, Carl Abrahamsson – *A Conversation with Kenneth Anger*

THE FENRIS WOLF 1-3 (1989-1993-2011)

Carl Abrahamsson – *Editor's Introduction*
Carl Abrahamsson – *'Zine und Zeit (2011)*

THE FENRIS WOLF 1 (1989)
John Alexander – *The Strange Phenomena of the Dream*, Helgi Pjeturss – *The Nature of Sleep and Dreams*, Tim O'Neill – *A Dark Storm Rising*, Carl Abrahamsson – *Inauguration of Kenneth Anger*, Carl Abrahamsson – *An Interview with Genesis P-Orridge*, William S Burroughs – *Points of Distinction between Sedative and Consciousness-Expanding Drugs*, Carl Abrahamsson – *Jayne Mansfield: Satanist*, TOPYUS – *Television Magick*, Anton LaVey – *Evangelists vs The New God*

THE FENRIS WOLF 2 (1990)
Lionel Snell – *The Satan Game*, Carl Abrahamsson – *In Defence of Satanism*, Anton LaVey – *The Horns of Dilemma*, Genesis P-Orridge – *Beyond thee Valley ov Acid*, Phauss – *Photographs*, Jack Stevenson – *15 Voices from God*, Jack Stevenson – *18 Fatal Arguments*, Tim O'Neill – *Art On the Edge of Life*, Terence Sellers – *To Achieve Death*, Stein Jarving – *Choice and Process*, Tim O'Neill – *Under the Sign of Gemini*, 93/696 – *The Forgotten Ones In Magick*, Tim O'Neill – *The Mechanics of Maya*, Coyote 12 – *The Thin Line*, Genesis P-Orridge – *Thee Only Language Is Light*, Jack Stevenson – *Porno on Film*, Carl Abrahamsson – *An Interview with Kenneth Anger*

THE FENRIS WOLF 3 (1993)
Jack Stevenson – *Vandals, Vikings and Nazis*, von Hausswolff & Elggren – *Inauguration of two new Kingdoms*, Tim O'Neill – *A Flame in the Holy Mountain*, Frater Tigris – *A Preliminary Vision*, Carl Abrahamsson – *The Demonic Glamour of Cinema*, William Heidrick – *Some Crowley Sources*, Peter H Gilmore – *The Rite of Ragnarök*, ONA – *The Left-Handed Path*, Zbigniew Karkowski – *The Method Is Science...*, Fetish 23 – *Demonic Poetry*, Ben Kadosh – *Lucifer-Hiram*, Freya Aswynn

– *The Northern Magical Tradition*, Anton LaVey – *Tests*, Austin Osman Spare – *Anathema of Zos*, Rodney Orpheus – *Thelemic Morality*, Nemo – *Recognizing Pseudo-Satanism*, Philip Marsh – *Pythagoras, Plato and the Hellenes*, Terence Sellers – *A Few Acid Writings*, Hymenæus Beta – *Harry Smith 1923-1991*, Andrew M McKenzie – *Outofinto*, Beatrice Eggers – *Nature: Now, Then and Never*

Carl Abrahamsson (Ed): The Trapartisan Review, Issue No 1

The Trapartisan Review welcomes you to enjoy unique works of art created by a number of highly talented contemporary and international painters, writers, photographers, poets, performance- and collage artists, etc, jointly assembling a strong and elegant bouquet of timeless expressions for your pleasure and inspiration. This first issue contains contributions by Jason Atomic, Hector Domiane, Val Denham, Johan Hamrin, Billy Chainsaw, Andreas Kalliaridis, Jordi Valls, Peter Köhler, Nicolas Ballet, Carl Michael von Hausswolff, Carl Abrahamsson, Anna Sebastian, Gabriella Eriksson, Karl Max Fredriksson, Vanessa Sinclair, Susana Vico Valero, Jake Kobrin, Tom Banger, Tim Pewe, Gunner Wright, Sean Bonner, Charlotte Rodgers, Annsofie Jonsson, Jason Haaf, Hazel Cline, Ruby Ray, Lars Sundestrand, Åsa Ersmark, Nestor Povarnin, Hannah Haddix, Sergey Martyn, Gustaf Broms, MV Carbon, Steven Cline, Paul Bee Hampshire, Christopher Mealie, Gabriela Herstik, and Tom Benson.

Genesis Breyer P-Orridge: Sacred Intent
– Conversations with Carl Abrahamsson 1986-2019

Sacred Intent gathers conversations between artist Genesis Breyer P-Orridge and longtime friend and collaborator, the Swedish author Carl Abrahamsson. From the first 1986 fanzine interview about current projects, over philosophical insights, magical workings, international travels, art theory and gender revolutions, to 2019's thoughts on life and death in the the shadow of battling leukaemia, *Sacred Intent* is a unique journey in which the art of conversation blooms.

With (in)famous projects like C.O.U.M. Transmissions, Throbbing Gristle, Psychic TV, Thee Temple Ov Psychick Youth (TOPY) and Pandrogeny, Breyer P-Orridge has consistently thwarted preconceived ideas and transformed disciplines such as performance art, music, collage, poetry and social criticism; always cutting up the building blocks to dismantle control structures and authority. But underneath the socially conscious and pathologically rebellious spirit, there has always been a devout respect for a holistic, spiritual, magical worldview – one of "sacred intent."

Sacred Intent is a must read for anyone interested in contemporary art, deconstructed identity, gender evolution, and magical philosophy. The book not only celebrates an intimate friendship, but also the work and ideas of an artist who has never ceased to amaze and provoke. Also included are photographic portraits of Breyer P-Orridge taken by Carl Abrahamsson, transcripts of key lectures, and an interview with Jacqueline "Lady Jaye" Breyer P-Orridge from 2004.

GENESIS BREYER P-ORRIDGE: BRION GYSIN – HIS NAME WAS MASTER

Brion Gysin (1916–86) has been an incredibly influential artist and iconoclast: his development of the "cut-up" technique with William S. Burroughs has inspired generations of writers, artists and musicians. Gysin was also a skilled networker and revered expat: together with his friend Paul Bowles, he more or less constructed the post-beatnik romanticism for life and magic in Morocco, and was also a protagonist in an international gay culture with inspirational reaches in both America and Europe. Not surprisingly, Gysin has become something of a cult figure.

One of the artists he inspired is Genesis Breyer P-Orridge, who collaborated with both Gysin and Burroughs in the 1970s, during his work with Throbbing Gristle and C.O.U.M. Transmissions. The interviews made by P-Orridge have since become part of a New Wave/Industrial mythos. This volume presents them in their entirety alongside three texts on Gysin by P-Orridge, plus an introduction. This book is an exclusive insight into the mind of a man P-Orridge describes as "a kind of Leonardo da Vinci of the last century," and a fantastic complement to existing biographies and monographs.

CARL ABRAHAMSSON: TEMPORARILY ETERNAL
– PHOTOGRAPHS OF GENESIS P-ORRIDGE 1986-2018

A photobook with snapshots as well as structured portraits of artist Genesis P-Orridge from 1986 to 2018. A great visual companion to P-Orridge's and Abrahamsson's highly lauded anthology of interviews, *Sacred Intent*, this book is an inspiring journey through the mind and life of someone who never stopped exploring and changing. Also contains an essay by Abrahamsson on P-Orridge's "psychic anarcho-sartorialism."

CARL ABRAHAMSSON: DIFFERENT PEOPLE

Different People is an anthology of interviews by Swedish author Carl Abrahamsson, focusing on art, life and the creative process. Included are in-depth conversations with Conrad Rooks, Malcolm McLaren, Stelarc, John Duncan, Charles Gatewood, Mark McCloud, Ralph Metzner, Peter Beard, Bill Landis, Ralph Gibson, Maja Elliott, Michael Bowen, Bob Colacello, Dian Hanson, Anton Corbijn, June Newton, Kendell Geers, Simeon Coxe III (Silver Apples), Vicki Bennett (People Like Us), and Brian Williams (Lustmord). These groundbreaking artists, writers, musicians, photographers, filmmakers, editors and psychedelic researchers have all helped shape the culture we live in. But what makes them do what they do? Which are their driving forces and their inspirations; their joys and fears?

Also Available from Trapart Books

CARL ABRAHAMSSON: FANZINERA EXPANDED – PHOTOGRAPHS 1985-1988

Swedish writer Carl Abrahamsson started taking photos to go along with the interviews he made for the fanzines *Lollipop* and *Acts Of Interstellar Torture* (1985-1988). From this vast and snap-happy collection comes *FanzinEra...* A selection which includes portraits and live shots of underground superstars like: Iggy Pop, Sonic Youth, Lydia Lunch, Richard Kern, Nick Zedd, Joe Coleman, The Gun Club, The Cramps, Union Carbide Productions, The Leather Nun, Screamin' Jay Hawkins, Alex Chilton, The Church, The Go-Betweens, Long Ryders, Died Pretty, The Scientists, The Saints, Sort Sol, Sator, John Lydon, Legendary Stardust Cowboy, New Order, The Godfathers, Genesis P-Orridge, Henry Rollins, Pere Ubu, Hüsker Dü, The Shamen, The Jesus and Mary Chain, Zodiac Mindwarp and the Love Reaction, Dom Dummaste, The Stomachmouths, The Nomads, The Creeps, Pushtwangers, Livingstones, Wylde Mammoths, Blue For Two and Cortex... To mention but a few! Also included are textual flashbacks and quotes from the interviews, full color reproductions of the fanzine covers, and an introduction by American photographer Richard Kern.

CARL ABRAHAMSSON: THE DEVIL'S FOOTPRINT

God proposes the challenge of the millennium: if Satan sorts out the ever growing human mess on Earth, God will lovingly take him back to Heaven as his favorite Archangel. Satan accepts, and sets out on a massive operation to balance out over-population, pollution, corruption, and other severely Satanic headaches – many of which he originally helped create... Easier said than done! Satan's love of the ambitiously mischievous humans is challenged as his own "Team Apocalypse" fervently sets to work. But as the world begins to change quickly and dramatically for the better, a new question arises: can God and his suspicious Archangels really be trusted in this cataclysmic, cosmic undertaking?

CARL ABRAHAMSSON: MOTHER, HAVE A SAFE TRIP

Unearthed plans and designs stemming from radical inventor Nikola Tesla could solve the world's energy problems. These plans suddenly generate a vortex of interest from various powers. Thrown into this maelstrom of international intrigue is Victor Ritterstadt – a soul searching magician with a mysterious and troubled past. From Berlin, over Macedonia, and all the way to Nepal, Ritterstadt sets out on an outer as well as inner quest. Espionage, love, UFOs, magic, telepathy, conspiracies, LSD, and more in this shocking story of a world about to be changed forever...

"*Mother, Have A Safe Trip* is a highly entertaining and thought-provoking novel. Chock-full of psychedelia, the book is also a much welcome addition to the far too few fictional works published dealing with psychedelic culture."
– Henrik Dahl, Psychedelic Press

"It's a thrilling roller coaster ride through psychedelic adventures, juicy romantic interludes, metaphoric dreamscapes, high Himalayan yoga enclaves, telepathic portals, 60's flashbacks, magical constructs, secret government pursuits and many more twists that kept all three of my eyes open. It's a story that you'll definitely want to keep non-stop reading, which I enthusiastically recommend."
　　　　　　　　　　　　　　– George Douvris, Links by George

"The dialogues are great. But it's too short. I wanted more."
　　　　　　　　　　　　　　– Genesis Breyer P-Orridge, Artist

"It's a wonderful read. A lovely book."
　　　　　　　　　　　　　　– June Newton/Alice Springs, Photographer

CARL ABRAHAMSSON (ED.): THE MEGA GOLEM:
A WOMANUAL FOR ALL TIMES AND SPACES

An anthology of texts and images constituting the current Corpus of the Mega Golem – the talismanic being/sentience created by Carl Abrahamsson in 2009. With contributions by Carl Abrahamsson, Vanessa Sinclair, Kadmus, Gabriel McCaughry, and others.

VANESSA SINCLAIR: THE PATHWAYS OF THE HEART

Vanessa Sinclair's new collection of poems and collages is rooted in the dark earth of death, but to an equal degree it also celebrates the vibrant life-force that grows inside this eternal darkness, and the transformation, love and magic we all need to live. The constant interplay of motion and emotion filters fragments of questions we try so hard to avoid but always fail to. The Pathways to the Heart are many but they need to be trodden lightly, with love and deep appreciation. Once there, you can assemble the fragments of your life and see what they say – the poetry of an existence that is inevitable until it is not.

VANESSA SINCLAIR: SWITCHING MIRRORS

Switching Mirrors is an amazing collection of cut-ups and mind-expanding poetry by Vanessa Sinclair. Delving into the unconscious and actively utilising the "third mind" as developed by William S Burroughs and Brion Gysin, Sinclair roams through suggestive vistas of magic, witchcraft, dreams, psychoanalysis, sex and sexuality (and more). Causal apprehensions are disrupted by a flow of impressions that open up the mind of the reader. What's behind language and our use of it? What happens when random factors and the unconscious are given free reign in poetic form? *Switching Mirrors* is what happens.

Also Available from Trapart Books

Vanessa Sinclair (ed.): Rendering Unconscious
– Psychoanalytic Perspectives, Politics & Poetry

In times of crisis, one needs to stop and ask, "How did we get here?" Our contemporary chaos is the result of a society built upon pervasive systems of oppression, discrimination and violence that run deeper and reach further than most understand or care to realize. These draconian systems have been fundamental to many aspects of our lives, and we seem to have gradually allowed them more power. However, our foundation is not solid; it is fractured and collapsing – if we allow that. We need to start applying new models of interpretation and analysis to the deep-rooted problems at hand.

Rendering Unconscious brings together international scholars, psychoanalysts, psychologists, philosophers, researchers, writers and poets; reflecting on current events, politics, the state of mental health care, the arts, literature, mythology, and the cultural climate; thoughtfully evaluating this moment of crisis, its implications, wide-ranging effects, and the social structures that have brought us to this point of urgency.

Hate speech, Internet stalking, virtual violence, the horde mentality of the alt-right, systematic racism, the psychology of rioting, the theater of violence, fake news, the power of disability, erotic transference and counter-transference, the economics of libido, Eros and the death drive, fascist narratives, psychoanalytic formation as resistance, surrealism and sexuality, traversing genders, and colonial counterviolence are but a few of the topics addressed in this thought-provoking and inspiring volume.

Contributions by Vanessa Sinclair, Gavriel Reisner, Alison Annunziata, Kendalle Aubra, Gerald Sand, Tanya White-Davis & Anu Kotay, Luce deLire, Jason Haaf, Simon Critchley & Brad Evans, Marc Strauss, Chiara Bottici, Manya Steinkoler, Emma Lieber, Damien Patrick Williams, Shara Hardeson, Jill Gentile, Angelo Villa, Gabriela Costardi, Jamieson Webster, Sergio Benvenuto, Craig Slee, Álvaro D. Moreira, David Lichtenstein, Julie Fotheringham, John Dall'aglio, Matthew Oyer, Jessica Datema, Olga Cox Cameron, Katie Ebbitt, Juliana Portilho, Trevor Pederson, Elisabeth Punzi & Per-Magnus Johansson, Meredith Friedson, Steven Reisner, Léa Silveira, Patrick Scanlon, Júlio Mendes Rodrigo, Daniel Deweese, Julie Futrell, Gregory J. Stevens, Benjamin Y. Fong, Katy Bohinc, Wayne Wapeemukwa, Patricia Gherovici & Cassandra Seltman, Marie Brown, Buffy Cain, Claire-Madeline Culkin, Andrew Daul, Germ Lynn, Adel Souto, and paul aster stone-tsao.

Ruby Ray: Kalifornia Kool (Photographs 1976-1982)

Spanning music, art and literature, the industrial and punk scenes of San Francisco in the late 1970s and early 1980s were diverse but united by a DIY, anti-authoritarian attitude. Photographer Ruby Ray was there to capture it all in the same spirit. With her work appearing in the legendary punk zine *Search & Destroy* and its successor *RE/Search*, Ray was at the epicenter of, and a key participant in, a vital cultural moment vibrant with provocation and creativity. A local experimental music and art scene supported artists like Bruce Conner and William S. Burroughs, and attracted groundbreaking bands like Devo, the Mutants, Boyd Rice and the Dead Kennedys, as well as established international bands like Throbbing Gristle, the Clash and the Sex Pistols. *Ruby Ray: Kalifornia Kool* collects the photographer's images from this time: live shots, backstage parties, apartments overflowing with youthful exuberance, elegant portraits of key people and photographic experiments. Her work captures a time and a place where West Coast open-mindedness, youth, art, music and electricity merged.

Sir Edward Bulwer Lytton: Vril – The Power of the Coming Race

Sir Edward Bulwer Lytton's cautionary tale of occult super-powers and advanced subterranean cultures have fascinated readers since 1871. Part early science-fiction, part educational tract, part occult romance, Vril keeps spellbinding readers thanks to its wide range of themes and emotions, as well as its thrilling sense of adventure.

A curious man descends into a mountain through a mine and experiences far more than he bargained for. Deep inside the mountain lies a completely different world. Its inhabitants, the Vril-ya, are human-like but physically superior and philosophically more advanced. They live in harmony made possible by their wisdom but also by the powerful and potentially destructive magical energy they call "Vril."

The impressed yet terrified visitor is allowed to stay and learn more about their ancient and advanced culture, something very few visitors have – it seems that all the previous adventurers have been mercilessly disposed of by the Vril-ya...

This edition includes an introductory essay by Swedish author Carl Abrahamsson.

More information can be found at our web site: www.trapart.net

www.ingramcontent.com/pod-product-compliance
Lightning Source LLC
LaVergne TN
LVHW091451170726
843492LV00001B/133